OTHER BOOKS BY THE AUTHOR

British Paternalism and Africa 1920–1940, Frank Cass, London, 1978

The Making of a Labor Politician: family and politics in South Australia, 1900–1980, Perth, 1982 (winner of the South Australian prize for Biography, 1983)

The Third Ear: explorations in poetic form, 1984–1996, Perth, 1996

Settlers, Servants and Slaves: Aboriginal and European children in nineteenth-century Western Australia, UWA Press, Perth, 2002

Twentieth Century Woman: an autobiography, Access Press, Perth, 2007

Paupers, Poor Relief and Poor Houses in Western Australia 1829–1910, UWA Publishing, Perth, 2009 (winner of the History prize in the Western Australian Premier's Book Awards, 2009)

The publication of this book has been assisted by a grant from the Western Australian History Foundation.

THE MARRIAGE KNOT

Marriage & divorce in colonial Western Australia 1829–1900

Penelope Hetherington

U W
A P
UWA PUBLISHING

First published in 2013 by
UWA Publishing
Crawley, Western Australia 6009
www.uwap.uwa.edu.au

THE UNIVERSITY OF
WESTERN AUSTRALIA

National Library of Australia
Cataloguing-in-Publication entry:

Hetherington, Penelope, 1928–   .
The Marriage Knot: Marriage and divorce in colonial Western Australia, 1829–1900/
Penelope Hetherington
ISBN: 9781742585215 (pbk.)

Includes bibliographical references.
Marriage—Australia—History—19th century.
Western Australia—History.
Australia—Social life and customs.
306.810994

Typeset in Bembo by Lasertype
Printed by Lightning Source

CONTENTS

FOREWORD

This is a history of marriage and divorce law in colonial Western Australia. The colonial governments of Australia all followed English marriage laws after first settlement, then gradually introduced their own laws. In doing so, they were influenced by advice and instructions from the British Secretary of State for the Colonies, by the religious beliefs of the dominant clergy, and by the experience of other colonies. The colonial laws, and then those of the states, varied from one another in various ways.

After the establishment of the Commonwealth of Australia in 1901, Section 51 of the Federal Constitution gave the government power to legislate on 'marriage, divorce and matrimonial causes, and in relation thereto, parental rights and custody and guardianship of children'. However, the Commonwealth Government did not act in this field until it passed the Matrimonial Causes Act of 1959 and the Marriage Act of 1961.

In this history of early marriage and divorce laws in nineteenth-century Western Australia, I make no attempt to compare the laws of the several colonies, but concentrate on Western Australia. This study begins with a brief consideration of the English laws. I then consider the position of the Church of England in the new colony, and the question of whether or not it was the 'established church', an issue of considerable importance in the debates about marriage law. The following chapter describes the marriage practices in the colony from 1829 until 1841, when the first colonial marriage law was introduced.

After an account of the building of early churches, several chapters focus on the events leading to the passage of changes to the marriage law in the Colony of Western Australia. These changes were the subject of intense debate and disagreement. Governor Hutt introduced the first two colonial laws for the solemnisation and registration of marriage in 1841. Acting Governor Irwin changed these laws in 1847, after strong protests by spokesmen for the Church of England. Governor Fitzgerald made further changes in 1849, but these failed to satisfy the Catholic minority. Finally, in 1856, Governor Kennedy passed two new acts, which remained in place until 1894. I discuss these new 1894 acts on the registration and celebration of marriage in the final chapter.

The story of changes to the marriage laws up to 1856 is followed by a discussion on the introduction of the divorce law in 1863, and its subsequent amendments. In the three following chapters, divided according to time, I discuss the operations of the Magistrate's Courts in matters concerning the breakdown of marriage, as well as the activities of the Divorce Court. The passage of the Married Women's Property Act in 1892 is discussed at length, as well as the result of its introduction on the nature of women's Divorce Court petitions. These later chapters therefore deal with the ending of a husband's control of women's property, the obligation of husbands to support their families, and questions concerning the custody of children.

Various legal changes, both in the nineteenth and early twentieth century, although not central to the main chapters, complete the record by referring to related issues. In this final section I ask why many people had no easy access to the Divorce Court.

There is a brief survey of the fate of many children, known at that time as 'paupers, bastards, delinquents and larrikins', who were either illegitimate or the product of failed marriages. Some of these children were placed in institutions by their parents, some were abandoned and ended up in the Rottnest Reformatory or one of the orphanages. These issues raise unanswered questions about the nature of many nineteenth-century marriages and the operations of the Magistrate's Courts and Divorce Court. I have written detailed histories of these children in other publications.

The Legislative Council records, the Colonial Secretary's records and the correspondence in local newspapers were all essential sources for following the gradual processes of change, as English laws came under critical analysis and were either amended or re-enacted by the Western Australian legislature. The analysis of divorce law also involved a consideration of related legislation and a careful analysis of the detailed records of the Divorce Court.

I discuss the role of various governors and members of parliament in making the law, and try to show the influences at work in the final decisions, with special emphasis on local religious differences in Western Australia.

The generalisations in some existing literature, which describe Australian practices in the fields of marriage and divorce, not only obscure the early differences between the colonies, but also ignore the crucial importance of these practices in people's daily lives. I hope this account will provide a clear picture of the experience of marriage and divorce for many people in colonial Western Australia.

ACKNOWLEDGEMENTS

I want to thank the librarians of the Western Australian State Records Office and the Battye Library for their assistance over many years. I have also had advice and help from Sister Stibi at the Roman Catholic Archives, from Lara Lynch at the Archives of the Anglican Church, and from Sheena Hesse at the Uniting Church Archives. I thank each of them for their friendly response to my inquiries.

My friends Lenore Layman, Catherine May, Catherine Macdonald and Jeremy Martens have encouraged me and made valuable comments on my manuscript. My husband, Robert, has always supported my projects and offered editorial advice. In this way, many mistakes have been avoided. Those remaining are my responsibility.

1

The English background

From the middle of the twelfth century, marriage in English law 'belonged to the spiritual forum' and was controlled by canon law.[1] This ecclesiastical law, as it was also called, was the canon law of Rome brought into England with the introduction of Christianity. The break from Rome occurred after the passage of three important acts in the 1530s, including the Act for the Submission of the Clergy in 1533; the Act of Supremacy in 1534, making Henry VIII the supreme head of the Church of England; and the Act to Extinguish the Authority of the Bishop of Rome in 1536.[2] These changes were responsible for the severance of canon law from the Roman Catholic Church and, as the ecclesiastical courts were no longer connected with the Catholic Church, this meant the end of appeals to the Pope.

The subsequent tensions between the Roman Church and the Church of England in the seventeenth century contributed to the outbreak of the English Civil War. The Toleration Act of 1689 defined the position of the churches, and became the basis of the present relationship between the state and the Church of England, with its status as the 'established church' involving special legal privileges and responsibilities.

The power of the Church of England has remained dominant in England until the present day. The 'establishment' of the Church of England derived from the fact that the reigning monarch was the Supreme Governor of the Church. It was the monarch's prerogative to approve the appointment of archbishops, bishops and deans, on the recommendation of the Prime Minister; formally to open each new five-yearly session of the Church Synod; and, in the Coronation oath, promise to maintain the Church of England. There are still twenty-six bishops sitting in the House of Lords, participating in the law-making process, while Church of England bishops and priests have a variety of civic responsibilities connected with acts of remembrance, state weddings and funerals, and memorial services.[3]

From the time of the Reformation, the Church of England made the rules about marriage services. Most marriages took place after the calling of banns, a process whereby, for three Sundays, the clergyman announced the details of the forthcoming marriage. In this way, objections could be raised by members of the congregation, some of whom knew the personal history of the persons involved. A marriage could only be held in a building consecrated by the Church of England.

The only alternative to banns was the costly process of obtaining a 'special license'[4] from a bishop, which allowed the participants to avoid the publication of banns, and to choose a particular church for their marriage, practices originally introduced and followed by the Catholic Church. Church of England parish priests were required to keep records with signatures in the parish register of all marriages, although this was often done poorly and the records were sometimes lost. Until 1836, there was no government administrative system for recording marriages in England.

It was in the middle of the eighteenth century that the British Government enacted its first secular law respecting marriage. This law was aimed primarily at preventing clandestine marriage. An apparently increasing anxiety about illegitimate children underpinned the 1753 law. The introduction of 'spurious offspring' was considered a very serious matter for those who controlled large estates, which were normally inherited through the male line.

This 1753 law, called Lord Hardwicke's Marriage Act, set out the requirements for a valid marriage.[5] As previously under canon law, ecclesiastical authorities, now the members of the Church of England, carried out the service after the calling of banns or the purchase of a special bishop's license.[6] However, after the passage of the 1753 act, state authorities could intervene to enforce the law, which had not been possible under canon law.[7] It is worth noting that, at this time, it was still possible to arrange a marriage at the Scottish border. The law did not apply in Scotland, and such marriages continued to be carried out in townships on the border, including at Gretna Green. This was sometimes the solution for eloping couples when neither partner had made any of the usual preparations for marriage.

Most of the statutory requirements under this 1753 act simply endorsed existing Anglican practice. Banns had to be read in the Church of England, or a special license had to be obtained from a Church of England bishop. This costly special license could help secure speed and privacy for the wealthier members of the community. The license also allowed people to be married in a distant and therefore more private, or more fashionable, church.[8]

To the chagrin of Catholics and dissenters, only the Church of England clergy could conduct marriage ceremonies after the calling of banns or by obtaining a special bishop's license. After the passage of this act, if the participants were under twenty-one years of age, consent to a marriage had to be obtained from both sets of parents. This limited the not uncommon practice of arranging child marriages in order to secure future property rights and inheritance. Only the royal family, Quakers and Jews were exempt from this law.

In 1823, a new English Marriage Act repealed some of the provisions of the act of 1753, although it was still preoccupied with preventing clandestine marriage. There were rules in these acts about the registration of marriages by the Church of England but still no system of government registration.[9] The age for marriage was still twenty-one years, except with the consent of parents or guardian, while the act contained details about the punishment for fraud in connection with marriage. Further amendments after 1823 covered particular issues as they arose, but none of them detracted from the power of the Church of England. This power remained in England until the passage of the Marriage Act of 1836.

The history of divorce law in England is one way of exploring the deep gender divisions, as well as those of class and religion, before the revolutionary changes of the nineteenth century. One of the earliest and most influential critics of these laws was Mary Wollstonecraft, who lived between 1759 and 1797. In her biography of Wollstonecraft, Claire Tomalin claims that 'Wollstonecraft attempted something new: to see life through the eyes of the poorest sorts of women, without caricaturing them'.

Wollstonecraft's book *Maria*, published after her death,

is full of servant girls turned away by their mistresses when found to be pregnant, girls who try to abort their babies or kill themselves, girls bullied by employers, women ill-treated and insulted by landladies, working wives whose husbands take all their earnings, and hospital patients whose treatment is experimental and dictated by the convenience of the doctors and students rather than their own well-being.[10]

Wollstonecraft's most important work was undoubtedly *A Vindication of the Rights of Women, with Strictures on Political and Moral Subjects*, first published in London in 1792. She scandalised her readers with her claims that marriage was 'legal prostitution' and that married women were 'convenient slaves'.

In the nineteenth century, the greatest advocate of individual liberty, John Stuart Mill, also took up the question of women's rights, including those within marriage, which he saw as 'the principal site of women's subjection and an institution which oppressed wives, disfigured the character of men and provided a daily lesson in despotism to children'.[11] By the time the book from which this quote is taken, *The Subjection of Women*, was published in 1869, great changes were occurring in English society. The book was an instant success and is sometimes called the bible of the first English feminists.

In order to understand the background to the introduction of the divorce law in Western Australia, which would begin a process of momentous consequences for women, we need to consider the background to divorce law in England. Until the middle of the nineteenth century in England, the term 'divorce' usually referred to the right of two spouses to separate but without the right to remarry, a practice originating in ecclesiastical law. This was divorce *a mensa et thoro*, translated as 'from table and marriage bed' or, more colloquially, as 'from bed and board'.

There was another form of divorce called *a vinculo matrimonii*, translated as 'from the bond of marriage', available by a private act of parliament from 1670. This was allowable only under exceptional circumstances, including the resolution of problems concerning the legitimacy of a particular marriage.[12]

A man could file for divorce *a mensa et thoro* from his wife if he believed that she had compromised herself in a relationship with another man or if she had committed adultery. The proceedings were complicated when the paternity of a child was under question, since this involved matters of future inheritance.[13] Women could seldom apply for this kind of divorce because their husbands controlled all the financial resources and also because, whereas a man could obtain a divorce by proving his wife had been unfaithful, a woman had to prove adultery and either incest, bigamy, cruelty or desertion. This pattern continued in the English divorce law passed in 1857, which maintained these deliberate discriminatory practices against women.[14]

According to English common law,[15] most of a woman's property after she married was in the hands of her husband to dispose of as he wished. After marriage, a woman had no separate legal existence from her husband who, under the law of coverture, could claim her property, her money and her valuable private possessions. This included any money she earned and any gifts she received, as well as inherited property.

In practice, this law could be qualified by an appeal to the English Court of Equity, something only available to those who could afford the legal fees. This court could vary the common law practice in a particular case, so that a woman could retain her money, or so that she could inherit property and retain it as her own. Considerate fathers and husbands, who had sufficient wealth, occasionally protected the future inheritance of their daughters or wives in this way. While many marriage and inheritance arrangements were undoubtedly arrived at after joint and amicable discussion, most women remained powerless in legal terms under common law.

The English laws governing the custody of children also discriminated against women. Under common law, a woman could not leave her husband if he was violent to her, and she had no right to remove her children from his control. However, a new law passed in 1839, known as Serjeant Talfourd's Act, gave power to the courts to grant the mother access to her children and custody of those below seven years of age.[16]

Until the middle of the nineteenth century, the law about divorce was still a combination of civil law, canon law (or ecclesiastical law), common law and statute law. However, a Royal Commission on Divorce in England, set up in 1850, produced a three-volume report in 1853, that recommended a major reconstruction of the courts. The changes would effectively destroy the fifty local ecclesiastical courts by removing their power to deal with probate and matrimonial affairs, which were soon transferred to two new secular courts.

English Ecclesiastical law came to an end as a living body of civil law at the beginning of 1858, when the Matrimonial and Probate Jurisdictions of the

Ecclesiastical Courts passed to two new Courts of Common law, namely the Court for Divorce and Matrimonial Causes and the Court of Probate.[17]

The 1857 Divorce Act in England, finally passed after months of dispute in parliament, did make considerable changes. As well as taking all control away from the church, the new law made divorce cheaper. However, these changes did not give women any greater access to divorce, although a few men wanted to see the introduction of more equal rights. These 'modest changes', as they are called by historian Lawrence Stone, were accompanied by endless debate both inside and outside parliament, and therefore 'set the precedents for the changing attitudes towards divorce for the next century'.[18]

In 1857, the Matrimonial Causes Court was empowered to allocate the custody of children in divorce cases. This law was changed again in 1873,[19] when Chancery was enabled to award custody as it saw fit. By 1886, it had become morally acceptable that it was only right to grant custody of young children to their mother[20] but, even then, the mother could still be excluded from guardianship of her children in favour of someone appointed by her husband.[21]

In late eighteenth- and early nineteenth-century England, the controls surrounding the institution of marriage, and the implications of marriage for women, demonstrated male dominance in all areas of public life. The rules were laid out in laws made by men, while the administrative services that recorded marriages employed only men. The clergy of the Church of England, who performed marriage ceremonies, were all men. The laws were designed to keep marriage under the control of the dominant males in the community, who wanted to establish the legitimacy of every child born into a respectable family through the male line.

By the end of the third decade of the nineteenth century, the dominance of the Church of England was no longer so absolute. Catholics were gradually being granted religious and civil rights. In 1828, the repeal of the Test and Corporation acts allowed Catholics to hold public office; the Catholic Emancipation Act of 1829 allowed Catholics to sit in parliament; while the Reform Act of 1832 extended the franchise beyond the gentry and aristocracy to include many more citizens of various religious persuasions.

As these great debates and legislative changes were occurring in England, the first settlers were preparing to set sail for the coast of Western Australia.

However, in spite of great political changes in England at this time, the Church of England continued to control all marriages, subject only to the introduction after 1753 of the secular requirements mentioned above. These practices were also followed in the new colony from the time of settlement in 1829.

Most of the dominant figures among the new settlers of Swan River colony, permanently occupied in 1829, were from estates in Ireland or Scotland, all of them active worshippers in the Church of England. Although they may have had little detailed knowledge of the nature and origins of marriage laws and customs in England, they understood that the solemnisation of marriage was a process controlled by the Church of England, according to certain longstanding customs. These English laws and practices had taken shape over a long period, after great political conflict caused by deeply held religious beliefs.

But not everyone in the new Swan River colony in Western Australia was aware that by 1829 there were also secular laws in place to limit certain aspects of these marriage practices. These secular marriage laws embodied prevailing English assumptions about the importance of maintaining male dominance in society. Several years passed before the important changes to English marriage law in 1836, 1837 and 1840, allowing civil marriage and requiring marriage registration, were introduced in the colony. These new rules were enshrined in the two new colonial marriage acts introduced by Governor Hutt in 1841.

But there are two issues to be explored before discussing these new acts of 1841. The first concerns the dominance of the Church of England and whether or not it was the 'established church' in the new colony; the second explores marriage practices from 1829 until 1841. These questions are considered in the next two chapters.

2

Church of England dominance

In 1829, the first British settlement was made at Swan River in Western Australia in order to establish a new British colony.[22] During the previous ten years, a growing number of free settlers had left England, Ireland and Scotland to establish new lives for themselves in New South Wales. By the end of Lachlan Macquarie's period as Governor in 1821, vast new tracts of land had been explored and the colony was no longer regarded as simply a dumping ground for convicts.[23] The idea of settling in a new land had taken hold among some people in England as they struggled with economic problems, largely due to the growing industrialisation of the economy.

Captain James Stirling was responsible for the first proposal that a new colony should be developed on the west coast of Australia. He was the fifth son, in a family of fifteen children, of Andrew Stirling of Lanarkshire, Scotland. The number of sons in these upper-class families presented a major problem, solved in the case of James Stirling by his enrolment in the Royal Navy in 1803, when he was twelve years old. In 1823, during a period of leave from his wide experiences in the navy, he married Ellen Mangles, the daughter of a wealthy family in Surrey.[24]

In 1827, Governor Ralph Darling of New South Wales encouraged James Stirling, captain of the ship *Success*, to examine the coast of Western Australia to see whether it provided a suitable site for a garrison or settlement. The authorities in the Colonial Office in London were initially sceptical about arguments in favour of a new settlement in the west of the continent but were finally persuaded to agree.[25] The initial planning for the settlement depended on Lieutenant-Governor Stirling's limited knowledge of the land and his careful consideration of the practical problems likely to be faced.[26]

He was influenced in his advocacy of settlement by a conviction that the colony would provide large landholdings for himself and others who, as younger sons, had no access to large holdings in England. In English society, the possession of a large private estate was still the dominant symbol of wealth and status.

It is apparent that there was a strong religious bond between those occupying key positions in the early Swan River colony, many of whom knew one another before departing for the new settlement. The many servants brought with their masters included a few Protestants of other persuasions, and some Catholics, but the number of settlers before 1850 who were not members of the Church of England remained very small.

Stirling, whose original title was Lieutenant-Governor, would make all the important early decisions with the help of Peter Brown, who was appointed Colonial Secretary in 1828. Originally called 'Broun', he always used the name 'Brown' in his official correspondence. Brown was born in Guernsey, Channel Islands, and spent his early years in Scotland. Like Stirling, who had grown up in Lanarkshire, he was a member of the Church of England. These two men were the key figures on the first ship of settlers to arrive in Western Australia, the *Parmelia*, which contained seventy people and considerable stock and food supplies.

Five ships left England with similar cargoes in January 1829 and began to arrive in the new colony in June. Many of these early settlers came with sufficient capital in money or servants to acquire large landholdings, since land was partly allocated at first according to the number of servants accompanying their master. These Church of England landholders exercised considerable power in the first two decades of political life in the colony.

Two important figures on board the *Parmelia* were the surveyors John Septimus Roe and H. C. Sutherland, whose work would be essential for the allocation of land. John Septimus Roe, the first Surveyor-General of Western Australia, was born at Newbury in Berkshire, England, the son of a Church of England clergyman. He was in office in the colony for fifty-seven years, carrying out government surveys and training other surveyors. Apart from his long career as a surveyor, he is remembered for his promotion of many early cultural activities in Perth.[27]

Henry Willey Reveley, another passenger on the *Parmelia*, was also a member of the Church of England, the son of an architect. He had graduated as a civil engineer at the University of Pisa and taken up an appointment at Cape Town in South Africa, which he held for a year. He then accepted the position of civil engineer for the new Colony of Western Australia, offered to him when the *Parmelia* called at Cape Town. He was responsible for the design and construction of government buildings, including the first Government House, the Round House at Fremantle and the old Courthouse in Perth. He returned to England in 1838.[28]

John Morgan, a Church of England member from Petersfield, England, was to act as storekeeper, while George Mangles, the cousin of Ellen, James Stirling's wife, was to be the superintendent of stock. Another figure of importance on board was Commander M. Currie, born into a large Church of England family of Scottish ancestry and educated at Charterhouse School. He was appointed Harbour Master at Fremantle and, in 1831, the colony's first Auditor-General. Other passengers included two surgeons, a superintendent of gardens and a group of men required for quite specific skilled tasks. They included a cooper, an artificer, a blacksmith and a boatbuilder.

Before Stirling left England, the British Government appointed Captain Frederick Irwin as officer-in-charge of a detachment of the 63rd Regiment of troops. He and his men arrived on the escort vessel the *Sulphur* in June 1829, just six days after the *Parmelia*. On board, were the wives and children of the soldiers, some of them Catholics.[29] Irwin was born in Enniskillen in Ireland and was active in promoting the interests of the Church of England in the colony, where he served as commander of the British troops until 1854. He was instrumental in the formation in Dublin of a society called the Swan River Mission, which planned to send Church of England missionaries to minister to the settlers and the Aboriginal population.[30]

Irwin's optimism and his personal energy are revealed in his account of the situation in the new colony, which was published in 1835.[31] He conducted church services soon after his arrival, and he and his troops erected the so-called 'Rush' Church using wood, mud and rushes, probably with the help of the visiting clergyman Thomas Hobbes Scott.[32] Scott had recently resigned his position as archdeacon in New South Wales and was on his voyage home in the *Success* when it struck a reef and was wrecked off Fremantle in November 1830.[33]

Two other early settlers would become important figures in the legal fraternity in the colony. William Mackie, a cousin of Frederick Irwin, who was born in India, was the son of a surgeon in the East India Company and had spent part of his childhood in Londonderry in Ireland. At fifteen, he entered Trinity College, Cambridge, where he studied law. He arrived in Western Australia on the *Caroline* in 1829 as a private settler but was immediately appointed a justice of the peace. He was then appointed Chairman of the Courts of Petty and Quarter Sessions. Mackie was a strong and active supporter of the Church of England. His power in the colony grew as he was appointed Advocate-General in 1832 and also became one of the foundation members of the Legislative Council. In 1834, he became the Commissioner of the Civil Court, a post previously held by George Fletcher Moore.[34]

Also an Irishman, George Fletcher Moore was born in County Tyrone and educated at Trinity College, Dublin. Originally founded by Queen Elizabeth in 1592, Trinity College was seen then as the college of the Protestant ascendancy in Ireland. Moore spent six years at the Irish Bar before he emigrated in the *Cleopatra* in 1830 as a free settler, but hoping for an official appointment. He was made Commissioner of the Civil Court in 1832, and in 1834 became the Advocate-General, which gave him a seat in the Legislative Council.[35]

George Leake also became one of the independent members of the Legislative Council in 1839. An Englishman of Anglican faith and a merchant, Leake arrived at the Swan River in the *Calista* in August 1829. He is remembered for his business success and his advice to Governor Stirling on financial matters. He held various positions in the colony and became the first director of the Bank of Western Australia in 1837.[36]

The Irish connection continued with the arrival in 1839 of Richard West Nash, who served briefly as Advocate-General of Western Australia in 1841. He was the son of a Church of England rector in Londonderry and was admitted to the Irish bar after an education at Trinity College, Dublin. He edited the newspaper *The Inquirer* between 1846 and 1852. In 1847, he was made Secretary of the General Board of Education set up to create government-funded schools in Western Australia. He was an active participant in various disputes between members of the Church of England and the Roman Catholic Church.[37]

The settlement plans were clearly much more straightforward than for many earlier imperial adventures.[38] The Colonial Office no doubt considered the advisability of preventing the intrusion of the French in the west of Australia. But the main impetus for this new agricultural settlement seems to have come from landholders, and from a wide range of other people, who were suffering from the effects of the post-1815 depression in England, Ireland and Scotland. There was no intention at first that convicts should be brought to the colony and, while it was understood that Aboriginal people occupied the land, their presence was not considered an impediment to white settlement.[39] The land would be defined as Crown land, and granted or sold to settlers in accordance with policies determined by the Colonial Office.[40]

Before leaving England, Captain James Stirling was instructed that, upon arriving in the new colony, he was to use his own 'firmness and discretion' to overcome all the difficulties that would arise due to 'the absence of all Civil Institutions'. He was advised

> to bear in mind that, in allocations of Territory, a due proportion must be reserved for the Crown, as well as for the maintenance of the Clergy, support of Establishments for the purposes of Religion and the Education of youth, concerning which objects, more particulars will be transmitted to you hereafter.[41]

There was, however, no explicit statement at this time concerning the status of the Church of England. Nor were there any particular instructions about marriage practice. But it is apparent that the Anglican Church was embedded in the English political hierarchy and was regarded as essential to the functioning of society.

But further instructions to Lieutenant-Governor Stirling early in 1830, about the rules to be followed in the new colony, stated that, until the appropriate institutions were established for law-making, 'the British Law, in so far as it is applicable to the conditions of the New Settlement...will... be the Code of the Community under your Government'.[42] This was taken to include the conduct of marriage by the Church of England.

These sentiments were underlined in March and April of the following year, when the Secretary of State for the Colonies, Lord Goderich, issued further instructions to

> our trusty and well beloved James Stirling, stating that the King's subjects residing there, are, by a general principle of Law, entitled to all the Rights and

Privileges of British subjects, and carry with them the Law of their Native Country, so far as it is applicable to their new situation and circumstances.

Stirling was officially appointed the Governor of Western Australia in 1831 and was instructed to establish an Executive Council, as well as a Legislative Council, to assist him in making the law. After 1832, members of both councils included the Commandant of the Armed Forces, Frederick Irwin; the Colonial Secretary, Peter Brown; the Surveyor-General, John Septimus Roe; and the Advocate-General, at first William Mackie, then George Fletcher Moore. After 1839, when some unofficial members of the Legislative Council were appointed by the Governor, William Mackie again became a member.

The first laws made by the Governor with the support of the Legislative Council concerned very practical questions arising in the process of establishing a stable society. For example, they included acts to establish courts of law, to control the use of weights and measures and to restrict the sale of alcohol. They established the size of ferry tolls, the rules concerning the trespass of stock and the necessity for the fencing of private property, and set up a system of postage. In this early stage, discussion began about what taxes might be collected, and how much revenue would be needed to provide various services, including roads and public buildings.

But the 1831 instructions specifically forbade the passage of certain laws. Clause 14 instructed that 'you do not upon any pretence whatever propose the enactment of any Law or Ordinance for the Naturalization of Aliens nor for the Divorce of Persons joined together in Holy Matrimony'.[43]

All colonial legislation had to be sent to the Colonial Office in London for scrutiny by the Secretary of State for the Colonies. Occasionally, an act was disallowed and was either entirely withdrawn or reworded, a process that often took many months. People were to be provided with notification of the government's intention to apply each new law for three Sundays in several churches, an echo of the practice of publishing marriage banns.[44]

The directions to Governor Stirling about law-making were much more specific after 1836. The Colonial Office informed him that, in 1835, the British Government had passed an act requiring the colony to adopt certain English acts. Stirling was instructed to introduce a bill giving the Legislative Council the power to adopt English acts, and he was provided with a list of these acts to be adopted immediately.[45]

As a result of these instructions, Governor Stirling addressed the Legislative Council in March 1836, reminding the members of the general principles underlying the operations of the council and the obligations of people with official positions. He listed his earliest instructions about English law and then introduced the recent English act of 1835, which obliged the legislature to adopt the list of English acts. All this information was laid on the table in the Legislative Council in 1836.[46]

This meant that there were now three categories of law in Western Australia. The first were those acts already made in the colony to meet particular local problems and approved by the Colonial Office. The second consisted of the laws introduced in 1836, which were copies of laws already made in England. Some of them would give greater legitimacy to practices already followed in the colony. There were eighteen of these English laws listed for adoption on this occasion, all amendments to earlier English acts. Once each English law was adopted, it officially became colonial law.

The third category consisted of those English laws being used in the colony without having been either passed or officially adopted by the Legislative Council. For example, the list of English acts adopted in 1836 did not include any act concerning the solemnisation of marriage, possibly because changes to the English marriage acts were being prepared. These changes were introduced in England in 1836, 1837 and 1840. Instructions for change in all the Australian colonies would follow.[47]

The obvious dominance of the Church of England in Swan River colony was bolstered from the beginning by the appointment of an Anglican chaplain to service the population. In July 1829, as the *Parmelia* and *Sulphur* were arriving at the Swan River, the government appointed John Burdett Wittenoom as Colonial Chaplain. After an education at Winchester and Brasenose College, Oxford, Wittenoom had been headmaster of Newstead Grammar School. Soon after the death of his first wife, he accepted the offer of a chaplaincy in the new colony. He arrived in January 1830 on the ship *Wanstead* with his mother, sister and four sons. He soon began conducting Church of England services in Perth, Guildford and Fremantle. Reverend Wittenoom took up a grant of 5,000 acres of land, while retaining his position of 'chaplain to the Civil Establishment of the Colony of Western Australia' until his death in 1855.[48]

For nearly thirty years after settlement, there was no Church of England bishop solely responsible for the Swan River colony. However, in February

1848, the *Perth Gazette* reported the appointment of the Right Reverend Augustus Short as the new bishop of both South Australia and Western Australia, the seat of the bishopric to be in Adelaide. The paper reported that Her Majesty's patent was read out in Trinity Church in Adelaide.[49]

Some eight months later, the *Government Gazette* published a despatch sent to the Colonial Secretary of Western Australia, Richard Madden, stating that Queen Victoria

> has been pleased to erect as a separate See and Diocese so much of the Bishopric of Australia as is included within the limits of the Provinces of South Australia and Western Australia, and to appoint Reverend Augustus Short, DD, under the style and title of the Bishop of Adelaide.[50]

Not until July 1857 was the See of Perth established, when Matthew Blagden Hale was appointed the Anglican bishop at a ceremony in Lambeth by the Archbishop of Canterbury. Hale arrived in Perth on New Year's Day 1858 on the convict ship the *Nile*.[51]

The failure to appoint a Church of England bishop solely for Western Australia may be explained by the contemporary uncertainty about the survival of the colony. The absence of a bishop was frequently regretted by the local Church of England clergy in their correspondence. However, the situation changed with the appointment of Reverend Augustus Short as Bishop of South Australia and Western Australia in 1848.[52]

Governor Fitzgerald, in office from 1848, was very supportive of this move, and sent the steamer the *Champion* to South Australia to bring Bishop Short on the first of his three visits. On this occasion, Bishop Short was accompanied by Archdeacon Matthew Hale of South Australia, who would be consecrated Bishop of Western Australia in 1858.[53] On this first occasion, Short met Sabina, the eldest daughter of Colonel Molloy, and she became his second wife.[54]

In spite of Governor Fitzgerald's initial welcoming behaviour, it proved difficult for Bishop Short to exercise any real influence in Church of England politics in Western Australia. At first all went well. Bishop Short corresponded with Governor Fitzgerald about the possibility of appointing an archdeacon for the Colony of Western Australia, signing his name as 'Augustus Adelaide'. The Governor replied that such a position was 'much wanted' and that he would support an appointment from among the colonial chaplains.[55] The new bishop proceeded to appoint Reverend J. R. Wollaston to this position.[56]

However, a few months later, Bishop Short indicated that he believed he should have considerable power over the colony's ecclesiastical affairs when he wrote to Governor Fitzgerald concerning Reverend Mears of York, who had relinquished his post 'without asking...my permission'. He claimed that Mears was 'guilty of an Ecclesiastical offence' and that he must forfeit his stipend. He hoped that the Governor would agree that the stipend should be transferred to Reverend Charles Harper, who would take up the position in York.[57]

Governor Fitzgerald replied that Reverend Mears had informed him that he intended to stay at York until he was replaced, implying that there was no need for the Bishop of Adelaide to concern himself over any offence Mears might have committed. He told Bishop Short that he had consulted the Advocate-General and that he had been informed that the government could not appoint Charles Harper to the York position until he was an ordained minister.[58]

Bishop Short also indicated that he wished to play some part in local Church of England politics when he corresponded with Governor Fitzgerald in 1848 and 1849 concerning a proposal emanating from the Church of England of Western Australia for the allocation of 1,300 acres of land in order to provide a home and land for a future Western Australian bishop. He wanted to be the official custodian of any such property

> as Lord Bishop of Adelaide, ordinary of the Diocese comprising Western and Southern Australia, and required to visit and perform Ecclesiastical and Episcopal duties in both, until such time as the provinces shall be erected into separate sees...[59]

Several people had offered grants of land for a future bishop, and Governor Fitzgerald informed Bishop Short that he would be provided with more information in due course.[60]

He was subsequently informed that the Governor had consulted the Secretary of the Trustees of Church Property, and that they had told him that it was not possible for them to give the bishop the control of church property. Perhaps Governor Fitzgerald intended to placate Bishop Short by concluding this letter with a request that he visit the colony more often, 'with consequent advantage to the community'.[61] While it is clear that, because of the great distance between the two colonies, Short would find it difficult to exercise his special authority in Western Australia, his appointment seems to have resolved a problem for those who believed that the 'establishment' of the church depended on the appointment of a bishop.

However, the real dominance of the Church of England rested largely on the preponderance of Church of England supporters in the local population. Quite apart from the identity of the most important political figures, the number of worshippers in the Church of England was approximately ten times that of any other religious group. The first colonial census did not list religious affiliation but, in 1848, the census claimed that the total population numbered 4,622. At least four-fifths of the population were believed to be members of the Anglican Church. The other two largest denominations represented in the colony were each estimated to have less than 500 followers.[62]

These smaller religious groups in the colony included the Wesleyan Methodists, who were among some of the first settlers to arrive in February 1830.[63] Methodism had its origins in the religious activities of a group of students at Oxford in 1729, who believed that the practices of the Church of England were not only corrupt, but lacked moral purpose. The early Methodists at Oxford, following the example of John and Charles Wesley, spent 'several evenings a week reading the New Testament to each other'. They supported charitable work, and a fixed pattern of Bible reading and religious observances, hence the name, 'Methodism'.[64]

The ship the *Tranby*, which arrived in the colony in February 1830, was hired by the committed Methodist Joseph Hardey, along with Michael and James Clarkson and Hardey's brother, John Wall Hardey. They brought their indentured workers with them and began successful farming ventures, first on 512 acres at Peninsula Farm at Maylands, and then on a selection of 16,000 acres at York.[65] The first Wesleyan Church services were held in the open air near Hardey's house on the banks of the Swan River, with Hardey acting as the local preacher. Then they built 'a neat brick chapel capable of seating about 130 people, which is the private property of about 20 subscribers' on a small block of land in Murray Street belonging to James Inkpen.[66] However, there was no Wesleyan minister until the Reverend John Smithies arrived in 1840[67] and immediately began planning the building of what he called the Centenary Chapel in remembrance of the conversion of John Wesley. This building in William Street could seat almost 400 and was opened in 1841.[68] The number of people in Western Australia who claimed to be Wesleyans was estimated to be 456 in 1848.[69]

The number of Catholics in the community was very small until the coming of convicts and free immigrants after 1850, many of them of Irish origin. According to the 1848 census, there were slightly fewer Catholics than Wesleyans, their number estimated to be 406. The Roman Catholics among the settlers had no leadership and no church before 1843, when Father John Brady arrived.[70] Before coming to Western Australia, Brady had worked in New South Wales, mainly among Irish Catholic convicts assigned to landholders, a responsibility involving constant travel on horseback over long distances.

John Brady was appointed Vicar-General of the Catholic population in Western Australia in 1843, and arrived in Perth at the end of that year, accompanied by the Belgian priest Father Joostens. In 1844, he set out for Europe to seek permission from Rome to bring priests and missionaries to the colony. His appointment as Roman Catholic Bishop of Western Australia occurred in May 1845. He returned in January 1846 with twenty-seven priests and missionaries, most of whom were soon transferred to Mauritius because there were no established mission settlements in the colony.

However, Dom Rosendo Salvado and Dom Joseph Serra began work as missionaries, founding the settlement at New Norcia. Serra became Coadjutor of the Western Australian diocese in 1850, but he and Bishop Brady disagreed over many issues, leading eventually to Brady's permanent withdrawal from the colony in 1852. Brady retained the title of Bishop until he died in December 1871. Joseph Serra remained the Coadjutor-Bishop and Temporal Administrator of Perth from 1849 to 1862, except for three years from 1853, when Salvado took over his position while Serra was in Europe.[71]

The Wesleyan Methodists were the only well-recognised group of Protestant non-conformist Christians in the early settlement. However, there were references to 'Independents' in the debates about religion and marriage in the 1840s, suggesting the presence of at least a few people of other persuasions. The Independents separated themselves from the Church of England by advocating congregational control of religious and church affairs, and the complete separation of church and state. They were the forerunners of the Congregational Church, many members of which many years later united with the Methodists or the Presbyterians to make up the modern Uniting Church.

One of the early founders of the Congregationalists in Perth was Henry Trigg, who arrived in the colony in 1829. He was an expert builder and also owned a large landholding. He was appointed Superintendent of Public Works in 1838, but resigned in 1851 to become a full-time pastor of the Congregational Church.[72] He worshipped with the Wesleyans at first, but in 1843 he began meetings to develop a Congregational Church. He was responsible for the building of the first Congregational Chapel in Perth in 1846.[73]

There were also a few Presbyterians present in the colony from the time of first settlement, although they were not so conspicuous in their religious activities. The Presbyterians were generally of Scottish origin, influenced in their religious beliefs by the teachings of John Calvin and rejecting the idea of a permanent church hierarchy. They emphasised reliance on the teachings of the Bible and had a system for electing the elders of their churches for fixed periods.[74]

Both in terms of numbers and political power, the members of the Church of England took precedence over these Protestant groups and the few members of the Catholic Church. Given the general edict that the laws of England applied in the colony, it is not surprising that members of the Church of England believed that theirs was the 'established church'.

While the debate about whether the Church of England was 'established' continues to the present day, the idea of 'establishment' was kept alive in the local population of the Swan River colony for several reasons. It seemed to be supported by the fact that the Anglican Reverend Wittenoom, officially appointed Colonial Chaplain in 1829, received a government salary of £250 per year with an extra £50 for his living expenses. Over the next few years, other Church of England chaplains received lesser amounts, their incomes supplemented by donations from their congregations.

The special status of the Church of England from the time of first settlement was also demonstrated by the attempts of other religious bodies to achieve equal recognition. In November 1837, these groups were optimistic about impending change. A group of ministers of the Church of Scotland and the Synod of Ulster in the north of Ireland called at King George's Sound on the ship *Portland* on their way to New South Wales. They sent a letter on 13 November from their leader, Reverend J. Dunmore-Lang, DD, Senior Minister of the Presbyterian Church in New South Wales, offering assistance to the Scottish and other Presbyterian inhabitants of the colony of Swan River.

> That Church [Presbyterian] we are most happy to inform you, has been already placed by Her Majesty's Government on precisely the same footing as the Church of England in the Colonies of New South Wales and Van Diemen's land; and we are virtually authorized to inform you, on the express declaration of Her Majesty's Under Secretary of State for the Colonies, made to one of our number, that this important arrangement, in virtue of which this most desirable and salutary change has been effected in the whole Ecclesiastical System of the Empire, will be extended also to this Colony, in the event of the Presbyterian inhabitants being desirous of availing themselves of it.

The letter explained that 'when one hundred adult persons shall subscribe to a declaration of their adherence to the Minister of their communion', a salary of £100 would be provided for the minister. This amount would rise by £50 when the number of worshippers reached 200 and by another £50 when the number reached 400 adults.[75]

Clearly, Colonial Office policy had shifted in favour of treating the churches equally, foreshadowing certain future changes in the payment of salaries to ministers other than those of the Church of England. However, stipends would not be granted until a certain number of people attended the church regularly and the financial support was sufficient to suggest its likely survival. This helps explain the difficulties faced by early governors in satisfying local demands for such salary payment.[76]

Although this letter from Dunmore-Lang was not published in the *Government Gazette* until 27 January 1838, Governor Stirling may have known of its existence. It was on 18 November 1837, five days after Dunmore-Lang's letter was sent to the Presbyterians, that Governor Stirling's 'Table of Precedency' was published in the *Government Gazette*, implying the continuing 'establishment' of the Anglican Church.[77] This was essentially a statement about where individuals came in a hierarchy of people with official positions. The Church of England interest was strongly represented in that the Anglican Bishop, still not appointed, was the third in line, after the Governor and the Lieutenant-Governor or Senior Officer Commanding Troops. Lower in the scale was the Anglican Archdeacon at number sixteen in a list ending with the Clerk of the House of Assembly at number twenty-five.[78]

It is also possible to see the application of the English marriage law in the colony between 1829 and 1841 as promoting the belief that the 'established church' had been brought unchanged to the colony. Because Reverend Wittenoom and several other Church of England clergymen were the only ministers of religion conducting marriage services, it was apparently assumed by some of the early settlers that this special status of the Church of England continued to apply in the colonial situation.[79]

The early historian of the colony J. S. Battye assumed the Anglican Church was 'established' in Western Australia because he stated that it was 'dis-established' in 1872 under Governor Weld, 'when the Anglican clergy were placed in the same category as other religious bodies'.[80] The appointment of the first Catholic Governor, Frederick Weld, suggests that the Colonial Office desperately wanted to see the settlement of disputes between the Roman Catholics and the members of Church of England. More skilled in the use of diplomatic language than the Roman Catholic protestors of earlier times, Weld said that his perusal of official documents convinced him that no legislative action was necessary to attain the principle of religious equality, which had long been recognised in the Australian colonies. 'Though the position of the Church of England in the Colony is to some extent that of the State Church', he could not find 'any valid legal superiority derivable from any local enactment'. He therefore advised that the Church of England be placed on a footing of equality with others.[81] It seems that Governor Weld was declaring that the Church of England had never been the 'established church' and was putting the issue to rest.

This question of whether or not the Church of England was 'established' was to become an important issue in the colonial debates surrounding later changes to the marriage laws. Whatever the answer to this difficult question, it is clear that the Church of England was given priority, at least until the middle of the 1850s. This history of early settlement and the making of marriage laws will reveal how the Anglicans, both those in political power and the clergy, attempted to maintain their position of dominance.

From the time of first settlement, questions arose about how marriages were to be conducted. The newly settled population knew that they should follow English law for the solemnisation of marriage and that they had a specially appointed clergyman in Reverend Wittenoom. The usual procedures could be followed in the Guildford area among the wealthier settlers because there were three Anglican chapels. The chapel at Guilford, connected to the Colonial Church Society, could accommodate 150 people, while the two other chapels, at Middle Swan and Ellens Brook, both had room for seventy worshippers.[82] There was the 'Rush' Church in Perth for Church of England marriages and the small chapel built for the Wesleyans in Murray Street.

But, in the absence of church buildings in the rest of the colony, where would marriages be solemnised? How could banns be called for three Sundays before the solemnisation ceremony where there were no churches? How could people apply for a special bishop's license when there was no bishop? Who would perform the ceremonies in places of settlement where there were no clergymen? Would couples have to travel long distances to contract a marriage?

3

Marriage practice, 1829–41

The difficulties of early settlement in Western Australia were such that very little was done at first to promote the building of substantial churches, although there were some attempts to provide places of worship. Probably the first site for Church of England worship was the 'Rush' Church in Perth, consisting of a framework of timber, the sides filled with rushes from the shores of the Swan River. In the absence of any public buildings, this was apparently used for church services, and as a courthouse and a school until 1837.[83]

There is little evidence of debate or discussion about marriage practices during the period of Stirling's governorship. The official correspondence passed on to the Secretary of State for the Colonies reveals understandable preoccupation with administrative matters, the development of basic infrastructure, and disputes over the allocation of land. The building of houses to replace the first bark and rush huts took priority over the establishment of churches.

Many of the wealthiest settlers lived on land at the Upper Swan, and three Anglican churches were established there – one at Woodbridge, one at Middle Swan and one at Upper Swan – before any churches were built in Perth or Fremantle.[84] These churches in the Swan Valley were the obvious buildings where marriages were conducted, after banns had been posted for three Sundays. But other buildings, and the private homes of colonial officials, also referred to as offices, were sometimes used as places to conduct a marriage ceremony. After 1837, some marriages were solemnised in the newly built Perth Courthouse, one of the only official government buildings in the colony.[85] Captain Frederick Irwin acted as the first lay preacher, although there was no official authorisation of his activity.[86]

Because of the absence of churches, various sites and early buildings in Western Australia were defined as having been set apart for sacred use. Many of the earliest marriages in the colony were solemnised in one of these consecrated buildings, perhaps half of them after the publication of banns for three Sundays. The cost of banns was three guineas. The other alternative – to obtain a special license – was followed by the other half, apparently without any charge.[87]

Marriages were conducted at Fremantle, for example, on board the ship the *Marquis of Anglesea*, which had run aground at Fremantle and was being used as the Harbour Master's Office. In the more distant settlements, they were solemnised in the office, usually also the home, of the Resident Magistrate. In some cases, it was he who performed the ceremony.

Marriage by special license from the Lieutenant-Governor or the Governor was probably much more common in Western Australia than in England, where those marrying in this way had to obtain a special license from the local bishop. This power had passed in colonial circumstances to the Governor of the colony because there was no bishop. Governor Stirling agreed 'to stand in place of a Bishop' in order to grant special marriage licenses because of his earliest instructions to use 'firmness and discretion' to overcome all the difficulties that would arise, due to 'the absence of all Civil Institutions'. However, it was not the case that the Governor of the colony was recognised as the temporal head of the church.

These special licenses were issued by Governor Stirling and then, from 1839, by Governor Hutt, until the new Marriage Act of 1841 made them illegal. Those about to marry had to request that their local clergyman send a letter to the Governor stating that there was no legal impediment to the marriage. The Governor then provided the necessary permission in the form of a reply. These replies were sent regularly to the officiating clergymen by the Colonial Secretary, as instructed by the Governor. These notices informed Reverend Wittenoom, or other Church of England ministers, that a marriage was allowed to proceed. On 6 October 1840, for example, the Colonial Secretary sent the following message to Reverend Wittenoom: 'Enclosing License for the marriage of George Leake and Georgiana Mary Kingford'.[88]

The Church of England marriage records before 1841 are divided according to regions and do not always indicate whether the marriage was by banns or special license. This makes it difficult to establish the exact number of marriages by special license between 1830 and 1841, but it is certainly the case that marriage without banns was very common. In the early years, this was perhaps because of the absence of churches where banns might be declared. In fact, the evidence suggests that, towards the end of this period, it was more common to marry by license than by banns. For example, there were fourteen marriages in Perth in 1840, only three of them by banns.[89]

The nature of the marriage service had been defined in 1662 in England. After the long preliminary statement beginning 'Dearly beloved, we are gathered here in the sight of God...', the service outlines the three causes for which matrimony was ordained:

> First, It was ordained for the procreation of children, to be brought up in the fear and nurture of the Lord, and to the praise of his holy name. Secondly, It was ordained for a remedy against sin, and to avoid fornication... Thirdly, It was ordained for the mutual society, help and comfort, that the one ought to have of the other, both in prosperity and adversity.[90]

The first recorded marriage in the new colony was that of James Knight and Mary Ann Smith on 8 January 1830. It was conducted by T. H. Scott, who signed himself 'Rector of Whitfield in the Diocese of Durham'. One of the witnesses to this marriage by banns was Peter Brown, the Colonial Secretary. Thomas Hobbes Scott, previously the Archdeacon of New South Wales, was waiting in Perth for the departure of a ship that could take him home.

Reverend Wittenoom had not yet arrived in Perth and, for two months, Scott was the only ordained minister in the settlement. He was warmly welcomed by the struggling settlers, who were still trying to establish safe shelters for themselves. It was Scott who held the colony's first Christmas service and first Holy Communion. He welcomed and advised Reverend Wittenoom about his new role as Colonial Chaplain before leaving for England on the ship *William*.[91]

By early 1830, the marriage records show that the person officiating at marriages was usually the Colonial Chaplain, the Reverend J. B. Wittenoom. He documented the third marriage in the colony, for example, in the Church of England records, as follows:

James Cockman, late of the Parish of South Mims in the County of Middlesex, England, and Mary Ann Ropper, of the Parish of Plymouth, England, were married by Banns at Fremantle, Swan River, this 15th day of March 1830 by me. Signed: J.B. Wittenoom, Chaplain.

The actual building is not designated here nor, in this case, did Reverend Wittenoom remember that he was supposed to record the signatures of the couple being married and of those who were witnesses. However, this required information began to appear almost immediately on all the entries in the Church of England records. This marriage was by banns, but three days later Wittenoom officiated at a marriage by special license.

Daniel Scott, now residing at Fremantle, and Frances Davis, now residing at Fremantle, were married by Special License on board the ship, Marquis of Anglesea, the Harbour Master's Office, this eighteenth day of March 1830 by me, J.B. Wittenoom, Chaplain of the Swan River.
This marriage was solemnized between us: signed Daniel Scott and Frances Davis.
In the presence of us: signed Mary Ann Lamb and John Okey Davis.

The option of a special license was still popular in the late 1830s. Reverend Wittenoom married 'by license' an American sailor, John Henry Huckpole, and Laura Thomson from Fremantle on 25 September 1838. In the following year, Reverend John Burdett Wittenoom, a widower, was himself married by special license to Mary Watson Helms, spinster.[92]

However, Reverend Wittenoom was not the only Church of England marriage celebrant before the passage of the new marriage law in 1841. The missionary clergyman Dr Louis Giustiniani, who was in the colony from 1836 to 1838, married several couples at Guildford. An Italian by birth, Dr Giustiniani, originally a Catholic, came to the Colony of Western Australia largely as a result of Frederick Irwin's desire to set up a mission to the Aborigines. The Western Australian Colonial Church Society employed Giustiniani for two years until he left in disgust at the way the Aboriginal people were being treated, and because he had aroused the anger of many settlers by trying to defend Aborigines in court.[93] Dr Louis Giustiniani recorded the marriages in somewhat different language from that used by Wittenoom.

This day the twenty fourth of June (one thousand and eight hundred and thirty seven), Edward Gallop, bachelor, is married to Ellen Kelly, widow, according to the forms and institutions of the Established Church of England, by myself, Louis Giustiniani, Missionary.

The names of the married couple have crosses alongside them and Alexander Ferguson and Abraham Jones are recorded as the witnesses.

There were also several marriages conducted at Middle Swan by William Mitchell, who signed himself either 'Minister' or 'Clerk'. One example is the marriage on 19 December 1840 of Henry Camfield of 'Burrswood [sic]', well known in the Church of England community, and Anne Breeze, who were married by special license by W. Mitchell in the presence of M. MacDermott and Frederick Irwin. In another marriage in December of that year, the record identifies W. Mitchell as the Minister of the Church at Guildford.[94]

William Mitchell arrived in Perth on the *Shepherd* on 4 August 1838, sent out to the colony by the English missionary body the Colonial Church Society following the earlier appointment of Dr Guistiniani. According to Mitchell's wife, the title of 'missionary' was really a misnomer, since he was the second rector of the Swan parish.[95] He was appointed in 1841 as the first minister in the small church at Henley Brook.[96] It was William Mitchell who travelled to Perth from the Swan Valley to solemnise the second marriage of Reverend Wittenoom.

Finally, some marriages were conducted by a resident magistrate or justice of the peace in a local district acting as a surrogate for an ordained member of the Church of England. Sir Richard Spencer,[97] Government Resident at Albany, performed the marriage service for a local couple in May 1839: 'Married: At Albany on the 23rd of May, by Sir R. Spencer, J. McKail to Henrietta, eldest daughter of Mr. Jenkins, Ship-Builder'.[98]

The *Perth Gazette* published this entry rather belatedly in September 1839. Sir Richard Spencer had died in July 1839 and George Grey had taken over as Government Resident in Albany. He was also married in 1839, and the service was conducted by Patrick Taylor, Justice of the Peace, 'in the absence of any clergyman'.[99]

Since there was no requirement to register the marriages with a government agency, these examples come either from the Church of England records of that time, or from the *Perth Gazette*, which recorded some of these marriages. While most marriages were conducted by the clergy of the Church of England, it is apparent that the great distances between individual settlements allowed for considerable dilution of the ecclesiastical rules. Secular influences intruded, first of all, in that the Governor acted for a bishop in granting special marriage licenses in place of banns, while, secondly, some marriages were conducted in unlikely places, including the office of the Harbour Master. Probably the most doubtful practice was that some marriages were solemnised by a local government resident or a justice of the peace.

Reverend Wittenoom had no doubt that such marriages were invalid. He expressed his disapproval when he heard of the marriage of two young people, James McDermott and Nancy Turner, who met on a boat travelling to the south in 1832. The Government Resident at Augusta married them. When they returned to Perth, they were remarried by Reverend Wittenoom.[100] A family account of this remarriage was later published by J. Munro McDermott, one of the couple's descendants.

> James McDermott, captain of the Emily Tayler, which took the settlers to Augusta, fell in love with Turner's eldest daughter. They were married in 1832 at Augusta in Turner's drawing room, the Government Resident (Captain John Molloy) officiating. On McDermott's return to Perth with his bride, the Colonial Chaplain (Reverend J.B. Wittenoom) declared that Molloy had exceeded his duties in officiating at the wedding. To satisfy all hands, McDermott and his wife knelt down on a box of boots on the open beach at Fremantle, in front of the store, and the Chaplain tied the knot to his satisfaction.[101]

The practice of marrying without the presence of a clergyman was also questioned when Richard Wells, whose marriage to Susanna Fortescue was recorded in the Church of England register at Leschenault, wrote to the Colonial Secretary requesting information about the validity of marriages taking place before a magistrate. In this case, Magistrate George Eliot had conducted the ceremony and signed the marriage certificate.[102]

The Colonial Secretary, on behalf of Governor Hutt, replied that

> the question as to the validity and legality of marriages which have taken place in the Colony before magistrates, without the intervention of the

Colonial Chaplain, or any other Minister of the Established Church, is one
of law which his Excellency does not consider himself required to enter
or to decide upon in any way, as no instructions have ever been issued by
the Government to any of their officers or magistrates on the subject.[103]

This inconclusive response did not satisfy Richard Wells. One year later,
he and Susanna Fortescue were remarried by Reverend Wittenoom in
Perth.[104]

The difficulties outlined above are best understood by an examination
of the geography of early Western Australia. The small colonial settlement
is always represented with Perth as its capital, but there were really three
settled areas of comparable size: Fremantle, Perth and Guildford. These
settlements were separated from one another by miles of uncleared bush,
with few available means of travel. The wealthier members of society
could travel from one area to the next by horse or by boat, but most people
walked for long distances. Apart from these three settlements, there were a
few small rural centres much further from the most highly populated areas.
There were no churches except in Guildford until the 1840s and, therefore,
the clergymen had to conduct marriage ceremonies in the courthouse or
in a private home.

Most people would have been reluctant to query the legitimacy of their
marriages. The obvious difficulty faced by those in outlying regions was that,
even if the cost of some travel could be afforded, there were no clergymen
or churches anywhere in the outlying areas. The Governor clearly had no
intention of pursuing the matter of the legitimacy of marriages performed
by government servants, perhaps because he had received instructions from
England to introduce a new Colonial Marriage Act.

The records do not indicate the religious affiliation of any of the
marriage participants, but it can be assumed that those who were not
members of the Church of England chose marriage by special license to
avoid the publication of banns. There were no dissenting clergymen in the
colony before 1840 but, in any case, the Wesleyans and Independents had
to be married by a Church of England clergyman.

At first sight, it seems that the very few Roman Catholics in the
colony were at the greatest disadvantage because their ecclesiastical law
stated that Catholics were bound to marry in a Catholic Church, or seek
a dispensation from a Catholic bishop, otherwise the marriage might be

considered invalid.[105] Couples had to be married according to the rules of the Church of England, but they had no way of seeking a dispensation, since there was no Catholic bishop in the colony before 1843.

However, the global spread of Catholic Church followers had resulted in exceptional tolerance towards marriage rituals.[106] Some Catholics may not have known the church law, but any marriages of people of the Catholic faith were recorded in the Anglican records, and no attempt was made to obtain dispensations.

It is clear, then, that for the first twelve years after European settlement in Western Australia, there were no marriage laws made in the colony. The Church of England, in solemnising all marriages, followed English law. At first, in terms of legal requirements, this meant observing the rules set out in the English Marriage Act of 1823, which had largely copied and superseded the 1753 Marriage Act.

However, in 1836, 1837 and 1840, three new acts concerning solemnisation and registration of marriage were introduced in England, triggering major changes to long-established marriage patterns. The new acts allowed for civil marriages, and required the appointment of a registrar and the establishment of a system of registration.

It is apparent from the marriage records that these new English acts made no immediate change to the situation in the colony, where marriages continued to follow the earlier English law.[107] But the passage of the legislation in England from 1836 meant that there would eventually be some doubt about the legitimacy of some colonial marriages conducted between 1836 and 1841 according to a law no longer in operation in England.

There is some evidence of local knowledge about the changes made to English law. For example, towards the end of the 1830s, in the newly settled areas near Busselton, the local marriage records were set out according to the pattern introduced in the new marriage-registration law in England. The minister keeping these records used a printed form provided for the registration of baptisms, presumably brought from England, with the word 'Marriage' inserted in place of 'Baptism'.

The marriage of Henry Mortlock Ommanney and Elizabeth Capel Bussell on 12 March 1839, for example, was recorded with details about the ages of the participants, their places of dwelling, their occupations, and details about their fathers, including their rank and profession. The

Government Resident, Captain J. M. Molloy, responsible for performing the ceremony, may have hoped to establish the legitimacy of the marriage by recording it in the way required by the recently passed English law on marriage registration.[108]

According to the new English laws, marriages were henceforth to be registered by the state, and Church of England buildings were to be registered as places where marriages might be solemnised. The Superintendent Registrar had to be provided on a quarterly basis with records of all marriages, including those of Quakers and Jews.[109]

These new marriage laws in England were designed not only to provide an alternative to marriage in the Church of England. They were also part of the gradual move by the British Government to accumulate a vast collection of statistical information. Since the colonies were also expected to collect such information, these radical changes in England were introduced in Western Australia in 1841.

Under the English Marriage Registration Act of 1836, the basis for all subsequent English marriage records, information of all impending marriages had to be provided to the District Registrar, who would issue a license that the marriage could proceed. After the marriage ceremony, a registration form had to be filled in by the participants, and by the clergyman who had conducted the ceremony.

The most radical change introduced by the 1836 English act was that people could now marry without any religious ceremony. This also offered an alternative form of marriage to all those who, although they were members of the Church of England, did not wish to pay the fee for the publication of banns.

In England, these freedoms were extended by another English Solemnization of Marriage Act in 1840, which referred specifically to those who were not members of the Church of England.[110] Clause 2 stated that

> it shall be lawful for any party intending marriage under the 1836 Act, in addition to the notice required to be given by that Act, to declare at the time of giving such notice, by endorsement thereon, the religious appellation of the body of Christians to which the party professeth to belong, and the form, rite, or ceremony which the parties desire to adopt in solemnizing their marriage, and that to the best of his or her knowledge or belief, there is no church building of the persuasion in the district.

These people should let the Registrar know and choose a registered building. The Registrar would then issue a notice saying that the marriage might proceed.

These three acts at the end of the 1830s represented a radical move by the British Government towards greater religious tolerance, even towards an understanding that the state, although it now issued licenses, was no longer necessarily active in the essentially religious aspects of marriage. However, the requirements of the state about notice of marriage and about registration, which involved the provision of considerable personal detail about age and relatives, and about religious affiliation, had to be recorded when the marriage was registered. If the participants wished to contract a civil marriage, this registration was the only legal requirement.

As we have seen, Governor Hutt, who arrived in January 1839, was soon made aware of marriage problems in the colony. The first had arisen because the change to marriage legislation in England could not be introduced without the establishment of a system of registration. But, before the introduction of the new Marriage Act in the colony in April 1841, a Wesleyan clergyman, Reverend John Smithies, who had arrived from England in June 1840, presented Hutt with another problem.

Smithies raised the issue of the 1836 and 1837 changes to the English marriage law, claiming that he was entitled to perform marriages. Reverend Smithies may have been unaware of the 1840 act in England since he was on his way to Australia before it was signed. However, he was apparently familiar with the changes that allowed marriage ceremonies in all churches, as well as civil marriage.

He went further than this and actually sent a letter to the Governor, similar to those used by the clergymen of the Church of England, requesting a license to marry two of his followers.

Sir, I hereby certify that Charles Lawson of Perth, Batchelor [sic], personally appeared before me this day, and was examined touching the legality of his intended marriage with Maria Lockyer of Perth, Spinster, and there is no legal impediment why a license should not be granted for a due solemnization of the same.[111]

The governor replied that it

is not in his power to issue a license for the marriage of persons who are not to be married by a clergyman of the Church of England, as it is only in the absence of a Bishop that Governors of Colonies are empowered to issue such licenses.

But Governor Hutt did not wish to deny that Reverend Smithies was entitled under this new English law to solemnise marriages.

I am, however, to add that such a license is not required, at all events, not indispensable, and that any clergyman of any denomination can solemnise marriages within the Colonies, as in England, without such a document and these marriages are perfectly valid and irrecoverable [sic].[112]

This must have seemed a remarkable statement to many people in the colony, when all marriages had previously been conducted by the clergy of the Church of England (or by surrogate government officials) according to the act of 1823. Although Governor Hutt was about to introduce marriage legislation in the colony, similar to that passed in England in 1836 and 1837, he had not yet publicly raised the issue of marriage law.

Reverend Smithies' claim that he had the right to conduct marriages also inspired a firm response in 1840 from Francis Lochee, the editor of the colonial paper *The Inquirer*, who indicated considerable ignorance about marriage law.[113] Lochee stated incorrectly that English laws did not extend to any parts 'beyond the seas', and that therefore the only law prevailing in the colony concerning marriage was common law. This considered marriage as a natural right and viewed it simply 'as a contract or agreement between the parties'. It followed from this argument that a clergyman of the Wesleyan Church or a magistrate had the same right as everyone else to solemnise marriage. However, the various instructions to Governor Stirling, discussed already, indicate that English laws most definitely did extend to Western Australia.

Governor Hutt, concerned about the confusion over the English law, instructed Peter Brown, the Colonial Secretary, to attempt to clarify the issue raised by Reverend Smithies. This response, which indicated that both William Mackie and Reverend Wittenoom had been consulted, was prepared for *The Inquirer* in late November 1840 and appeared one month later.

The Colonial Secretary asked the editor whether he might be allowed the space in the paper

> to settle a somewhat important question.
>
> It is a subject of enquiry in this community 'can a Wesleyan Missionary celebrate the rites of Marriage? or in case he does perform that ceremony, is it valid in point of law?'
>
> To which question I reply, first, that all Wesleyan Missionaries come out from home (especially under the New Marriage Act) with full legal and ecclesiastical right to celebrate the rite of marriage as well as to Baptise, bury the dead, or preach the gospel.
>
> Secondly, The legal and clerical authorities of this place, as W. H. Mackie Esq. and the Rev. Mr Wittenoom both allow and declare that Ministers of all denominations, Wesleyans, and Dissenters have full right and authority to celebrate marriages.
>
> Thirdly, His Excellency the Governor has instructed that a letter should be issued from the Colonial office fully sanctioning the above right...[114]

Part of this letter, signed by Peter Brown, the Colonial Secretary, was an exact copy of the Governor's earlier letter to Reverend Smithies, to the effect that it was not 'in his power to issue a license for the marriage of persons who are not to be married by a clergyman of the Church of England', but that marriages without a governor's license could be conducted in the colony by clergymen of any denomination.

At the end of this correspondence, John Smithies is quoted as saying that this information was in every way satisfactory 'to every candid and unprejudiced mind'. In other words, he believed he had established his right to conduct marriages in the Wesleyan Church following recent changes to English law. But this information in the local newspaper did not mention that, according to this new English law, the government Registrar had to provide a marriage license, and all marriages had to be recorded in a government registration book. In retrospect, the government reply to Reverend Smithies was misleading. If Smithies conducted a marriage service, would it be legal under the 1836 marriage law when there was no system of registration in the colony?

During the 1830s, the Colony of Western Australia made only slow progress, largely because of the absence of sufficient capital to develop farming land or establish industry, and the absence of an adequate supply of labour. By the time Governor Stirling left the small colony in 1838, there was some semblance of order and an administrative system established, but growing conflict between Aborigines and European settlers. During Stirling's period as governor, the few Church of England clergymen present in the colony followed the 1823 marriage law of England and the long-accepted practices of the Church of England, even though the marriage law had been changed in 1836, 1837 and 1840.

When Governor Hutt introduced new marriage laws in 1841, he seriously upset those who believed in the importance of maintaining the dominance of the Church of England, assumed by many to be the 'established church', implying that it had special rights and obligations over all other churches. The early instructions to Governor Stirling that the colonists carried with them 'the Law of their Native Country' offered some support to those settlers who still believed that they brought the 'established church' with them to Western Australia.

Although he gave considerable support to the Wesleyan interests, Governor Hutt occasionally referred in his correspondence to the 'established church', suggesting that he, too, shared this conviction. However, he had instructions to introduce new legislation to change the marriage law in near conformity with the new laws in England. But before doing that, he decided to introduce legislation to assist in building churches for all denominations and to provide stipends for clergymen. Growing conflict after 1840 between the supporters of the Church of England and the Wesleyans arose first of all over the provision of financial support for church buildings.

4

The Church Buildings Act, 1840

Governor John Hutt, who was born in London and educated at Christ's Hospital, worked in the Indian Civil Service between 1813 and 1826. For some of that time, he was Governor of North Arcot, in the Presidency of Madras. Unusually for colonial governors, John Hutt, a member of the Church of England, was unmarried. During his earlier period in colonial administration, he developed an interest in land laws, and became a supporter of Edward Gibbon Wakefield, who advocated the careful disposal of colonial land according to people's capacity to develop their holdings.

Hutt was familiar with criticisms being made about the allocation of huge areas of land to the first settlers in the Swan River colony. According to the supporters of Wakefield, the colony was slow to develop because these landowners had neither the capital nor the labour to develop their newly acquired property.

Hutt took an active interest in the plans for the first settlement in 1836 of South Australia and was appointed Superintendent of Emigration for the South Australian Colonisation Commission. In 1838, he applied for the position of Governor in South Australia but, instead, was appointed Governor of Western Australia. He arrived at the Swan River on the ship *The Brothers* on 1 January 1839, with his private secretary, Walkinshaw Cowan.[115] Governor Stirling was still waiting for his ship to leave the colony and, for a few days, the first and second governors were able to consult one another.

In an account of a journey they took together, Hutt's secretary, Walkinshaw Cowan, concluded with these carefully balanced remarks about Hutt's personal characteristics:

I cannot but admire the Governor's unwearied attention to every department of the Colony from the most minute to the highest, and I may say the strict impartiality of his conduct looking to the well being of the community and disregarding individual interest. At the same time he is too austere a turn of mind, wanting the kindlier feelings, sympathies of our nature and, as he himself has stated, without generosity, he is too much inclined to stretch the law to the utmost.[116]

Governor Hutt was a member of the English Clapham Sect, a group of evangelical Christians who campaigned for many important causes, including the abolition of slavery and prison reform. However, the members of this group were conservative followers of the Church of England who uncritically accepted its dominance in religious affairs.[117]

When he arrived as the second Governor in late 1839, Hutt was surprised to find that there were no substantial churches in Perth or Fremantle. Most of those with government appointments and large landholdings lived in the Swan Valley, where the three small Church of England chapels had been built. Hutt was a committed Christian and regarded the provision of churches as particularly important, not only because they were places of Christian worship, but also because they were sacred sites for the solemnisation of marriage.

As we have seen, early marriages in a church in Western Australia were often solemnised in the Swan Valley. The wealthier members of the Perth community could have a church wedding by arranging to travel in a boat or in a carriage to one of the Church of England chapels. The poorer members of the community, and those who lived far from Perth, were married in the 'Rush' Church, in government offices or in private homes.

During the period from the 1840s to the 1870s, the Colonial Office gave instructions to the new governors of the colony to treat the religious groups impartially, a change that had already been foreshadowed by Reverend Dunmore-Lang in his 1836 letter to the Presbyterians.

In spite of many serious issues needing his urgent attention, one of Governor Hutt's first decisions was to pass an act 'to promote the building of churches and chapels and to contribute towards the maintenance of Ministers of Religion in Western Australia'.[118] This act considered the questions of government assistance for church buildings, for stipends and for the houses of clergymen.[119]

However, Governor Hutt had trouble persuading the Wesleyans and Roman Catholics that they were receiving equal treatment, and that he was following the rules set out in his Church Building Act. Problems with government funds, promised both for the building of churches and for stipends, fuelled the tensions growing between the more conservative members of the Church of England, especially some of its clergymen, and the leaders of the Wesleyans. The Catholics played little part in these early public disputes during the period of Hutt's governorship, because there were very few Catholics and no priests before Father Brady arrived in 1843, staying for only a short period. He did not return from Europe until 1846, a few days before Governor Hutt's term of office expired.

According to his newly introduced act, the Governor could use government revenue to support church buildings by making a pound-for-pound contribution equal to any funds raised privately, as long as the contribution did not exceed £500. A clause in the act claimed that this support would go equally to the Church of England, the Roman Catholics, the Wesleyans and the so-called Independents. This act about the building of churches was qualified to some extent by another act in passed in 1841, about the necessity for churches other than the Church of England to establish trustees for church buildings before they could be assisted.[120]

The provision of this building subsidy made it possible for Reverend John Smithies, with the help of several other Wesleyan settlers, including Joseph Hardey, to complete the building of chapels at Perth and Fremantle before those of the Church of England. In September 1840, Governor Hutt agreed to provide an allotment at Fremantle for the building of a Wesleyan Chapel and schoolhouse and, in the following month, he instructed the Government Resident at Fremantle to provide the details about this allotment to the Wesleyans as soon as possible.[121] A little later, on 30 December 1840, the cornerstone was laid for another Wesleyan Church, on the corner of Murray and William streets in Perth.[122]

Apart from the government promise of a subsidy, the Wesleyans also raised comparatively large sums from their small community under the leadership of Joseph Hardey, who was successful in his farming ventures and had sufficient capital to assist in the Wesleyan Church's building programs. Their chapels were built at Fremantle and Perth by the end of 1841. They were the first to conduct marriages in a church building in Perth.

The foundation stone was laid on 6 January 1841 for the first Church of England on part of the site now occupied by St George's Cathedral. The original plan to build the church in Victoria Avenue, in a spot later occupied by the Catholic Cathedral, was rejected on the grounds that it was too distant from the centre of the city.[123] Governor Hutt made a speech on the occasion of the laying of the foundation stone, although the editor of *The Inquirer* noted rather critically that he was not dressed in his full gubernatorial regalia.

Governor Hutt seemed to be endorsing the important role of the Church of England as the 'established church' when he stated that

> it was his duty, and the duty of all of us, to do all in the support of the Church in this country; the proceedings of the day had been such, that now they might not only sit every man under his own vine, and his own fig-tree, but they would have the pleasing reflection that they had been instrumental in the planting of that better tree, whose leaves 'were for the healing of the nations,' and which bears 'the peaceable fruits of righteousness;'...[124]

Between the passage of the Church Building Act and the completion of the first church, Governor Hutt must have realised that he had been overambitious in his promises to the clergy. Whether or not particular contemporary criticisms were justified, it is apparent that the problems Governor Hutt faced lay in certain unforeseen circumstances rather than in any personal religious bias or incompetence. The most difficult problem he faced concerned the dramatic drop in colonial government revenue beginning in early 1842.

In 1841, the total revenue was £18,466 and the year's expenditure was £17,019, leaving a small surplus. By 1845, government expenditure was £14,830 and revenue had declined below that sum to £14,795.[125] It was this situation that led Governor Hutt to reconsider the promises made in the Church Building Act.

Because the quarterly figures for revenue and expenditure were published regularly in the *Government Gazette*, the church bodies requesting assistance must have recognised the growing problem. Between 14 January 1841 and 5 November 1841, for example, the Wesleyans asked for government financial assistance for the building of their Fremantle church, on which they had spent just over £486, but for which they had received a government donation of only £300. According to the act, this donation was supposed to be on a pound-for-pound basis to a maximum of £500.[126] When they received another £100 in July 1841, the Wesleyan committee asked when they might expect the rest. Governor Hutt found himself obliged to reply that this must wait until the Legislative Council could consider the estimates.[127]

In an address to the Legislative Council in May 1841, the Governor, still apparently untroubled about government revenue, claimed that the act to establish churches appeared to be working well and that

> churches and chapels are rising in the different located districts, and through the kindness of our friends, and the applications that have been made to those most competent to aid us in England, there will, I hope, be little or no delay in providing the places of worship with zealous, active and pious ministers.[128]

However, the Church of England in Perth took a long time to complete. It was opened on 22 January 1845 and consecrated in 1848 by Bishop Short, who found it 'still unfinished in many respects'.[129] By the end of the 1840s, the leading Anglican clergyman in Western Australia, Reverend John Wittenoom, was still worshipping in an unfinished church.[130] It was renamed a cathedral when Bishop Hale took up his position in 1858. On 7 August 1843, the new Church of England in the centre of King's Square at Fremantle was opened, in the presence of many supporters who arrived by boat from Perth.[131]

The Catholic community, which had no priests, made no progress in buildings until Father John Brady was appointed Vicar-General of Western Australia and arrived in Perth from Sydney in December 1843 with the Belgian priest Father John Joostens. Before Brady left for Rome to recruit Catholic priests and missionaries, he was granted the land previously offered to the Church of England on Church Hill, now called Victoria Avenue.[132] A meeting of Catholics celebrated the laying of the foundation stone for St John's Church on 16 January 1844, and this small Roman Catholic chapel, now known as the pro-cathedral, was opened in 1845.[133]

The second issue of contention at this time concerned the provision of stipends for clergymen. The second part of the 1840 act providing assistance for church-building dealt with other forms of support, including stipends and houses for clergymen, but with the proviso that such support would depend on the number of worshippers and the amount of financial support they provided for their church. There was a special form for making claims under this act, requiring information about the number of people attending the church, and the amount of financial assistance the church authorities were receiving from their followers.

Support did not go automatically to churches with less than one hundred active members. However, according to Clause 3 of the act, those churches could still make a claim, 'accompanied by an explanatory letter setting forth the particular circumstances of the case for the consideration of the Governor and Council'. In other words, the Governor and Legislative Council might consider waiving the rules under certain circumstances.[134]

This part of the 1840 act raised the hopes of the Wesleyans, but the conditions for assistance provided the means whereby some of their hopes would be dashed. While Reverend Wittenoom was supported, and some other Church of England clergymen received the sum of £100 a year after 1844, it was not until 1851 that small stipends were granted to the Wesleyans and the Roman Catholics.[135]

By 1848, the Church of England had over 4,000 supporters in the whole Colony of Western Australia while the Wesleyans and Catholics each had between 400 and 500 followers. Apart from the few members of other persuasions, there were some who made no claim to any religious affiliation. In his introduction to the census of 1848, the Registrar General, George Frederick Stone, commented that several returns 'exhibit the number of Protestants, without particularizing the denominations, and whether from carelessness, recklessness, or temerity, some ventured to profess no religion'. He also observed that 'the various denominations are not placed according to numerical influence, though it should be the regulation point for determining their relative claim to aid from the public purse'. This was a reference to the fact that the new laws to assist churches required information about numbers and local financial support.

In November 1840, the Wesleyans began a correspondence with the Colonial Secretary, asking for the Governor to provide them with assistance in the form of a stipend for Reverend Smithies under Clause 5 of the 1840 act. According to this clause, in areas where there was no church or chapel, if ten heads of families or 25 individuals of 12 years and older, would sign a declaration to provide fifty pounds per annum, the Governor with the advice of the Executive Council, could provide a stipend of any sum not exceeding £100.[136]

However, the rules about the provision of financial assistance from Colonial revenue for a stipend were applied very stringently.[137] From November 1840, in spite of considerable correspondence and protest, the Governor regularly refused the Wesleyan applications for a stipend. In late December, the explanation was that the matter had to be discussed carefully in the Executive Council, because the final decision would establish a precedent by which 'all similar applications would have to be governed'. On this occasion, it was refused because the names of supporters listed according to the requirements of Clause 5 were apparently not all of the Wesleyan denomination.[138]

The Wesleyans claimed that they had given evidence that they had over 200 adults providing them with financial support. The application continued to be rejected. The Colonial Secretary, on behalf of the Governor, wrote to the manager of Wesleyan affairs, George Johnson, explaining that

> the 5th clause of the Act of Council does not apply to the conditions of the members of the Wesleyan body in Perth. [It] is confined in its operation to places where there is neither church nor chapel and where there shall also appear seasonable cause for delaying the erection of a permanent church or chapel.[139]

He suggested that their application might be more successful if they applied under Clause 3 of the act.

Clause 3 offered the possibility of special consideration being given to an appeal for a stipend if all the relevant detail was provided. In January 1841, the Wesleyans wrote asking for a stipend according to Clause 3 of the act, again without success. The Governor replied that before the application could be considered again, the government would have to be satisfied of three things. First was the question of whether Mr Smithies was a minister acknowledged by the Wesleyan Church in England. The second was that he had to be attached 'peculiarly' to the Perth Chapel. Finally, the government needed to be assured that Reverend Smithies would be wholly supported by the stipend provided, plus the donations of his congregation.[140]

The Wesleyans then informed the Governor that they intended to send the details of the application, and its refusal, to the Secretary of State for the Colonies in England, obviously hoping that Hutt's decision might be reversed. The reply from the Governor was to the effect that it would be more appropriate if the Wesleyan committee prepared a 'memorial' to be sent to London, accompanied by all the correspondence, a recommendation the committee accepted.[141]

Governor Hutt's responses to Reverend Smithies led to an acrimonious and inconclusive debate in the *Perth Gazette* concerning the apparent failure of the government to provide stipends for all denominations.[142] The first letter from 'a Wesleyan' described Governor Hutt's act as 'stillborn' and the last referred ironically to the members of the Legislative Council as having 'an inclusive spirit' and all worshipping in the same church. 'Thus an Act of Council has been opposed and nullified, and memorials rejected to serve these disinterested gentlemen'. These long letters suggested considerable hostility between some of the Wesleyans and members of the Church of England.

The Wesleyans undoubtedly failed to meet the original requirements of the act concerning the number of supporters belonging to their church. Their attempt to secure a stipend was always going to depend on being granted special consideration. Governor Hutt's refusal to grant a stipend to Reverend Smithies began before the dramatic drop in colonial revenue. The Governor, via the Colonial Secretary, used a variety of explanations for his refusal, suggesting that he found himself unable to persuade the council members to adopt a more positive attitude towards the Wesleyan interests. The Executive Council proved unwilling to consider a special grant of a stipend for the Wesleyans, according to Clause 3 of the act.

The same rules were followed when appeals for a stipend came from the Church of England, but with greater success because the majority of the population defined themselves as members of this church. While the Wesleyans were being denied a stipend for their minister, the Governor at first responded positively to an appeal from Reverend Wittenoom for a clergyman's stipend at Fremantle. The government promised that he would be provided with £100, and the local population promised another £60 when they appointed a competent person. They were instructed to appeal for advice concerning this appointment from certain Anglican bodies in England.[143]

This positive response was based on the certainty of sufficient local support, one of the conditions for providing a stipend. However, this stipend was still being refused in May 1842 because the Governor had been informed that Reverend King, recently arrived as the appointee for Fremantle, was receiving money from persons 'out of the Colony'.[144] Reverend George King, who arrived in 1841, was sent out as a missionary by the Society for the Propagation of the Gospel.

Reverend Mitchell faced the same problem. Captain Irwin's appeal for a stipend for Mitchell at this time was at first refused on the grounds that Mitchell was really an employee of a missionary body in England. However, it was implied that, if he were appointed to a church with established trustees, the question of his stipend would be reconsidered. This was achieved by appointing Mitchell clergyman for the church at the Upper Swan.[145] Reverend William Mitchell was eventually granted a stipend backdated to 1 September 1842.[146] However, this was then withdrawn because the Governor believed that Reverend Mitchell was still receiving an allowance from the Colonial Church Society in England.[147]

The debate about the right of the Wesleyans to claim a stipend for Reverend Smithies was kept alive during 1843 by a series of letters to the *Perth Gazette* by someone calling himself 'a passing Ishmeelite [sic]'.[148] While the Biblical allusions in these letters make it difficult to follow the argument, they clearly supported the claim for a stipend for what the writer called 'a very successful Christian Church'. The Wesleyan Church also had some support from the editor of the *Perth Gazette*, who published the correspondence passing between the Wesleyan Society and the Governor in 1843. The first was a letter from William Tanner, who was a local landowner and owner of *The Inquirer*.[149] Tanner believed that, since the chaplain for the Upper Swan had received a stipend, so should Mr Smithies. Included here was the Governor's reply that Reverend Smithies 'was not particularly attached to Perth' so that he had to refuse his claim.[150]

A little later the paper published a copy of a 'memorial' with 209 signatures of people who claimed that it was their intention to attend divine service at the Wesleyan Chapel. This was followed by a second letter to the Governor from George Johnson, Secretary of the Wesleyan

Society, who complained that he had had no response to the request made six weeks earlier. Governor Hutt's reply to these appeals was also published here. He claimed that the matter had to be given full consideration in the council. He rejected the calls for a stipend for Reverend Smithies because the signatures on the application indicated that many of the people who signed the memorial belonged to other Christian denominations.[151]

The provision of financial support for building houses for clergymen was also slow to eventuate, but allotments of land were granted to the three major religious groups in Perth, Fremantle or Bunbury in 1843 and 1844. In 1844, the Church of England wrote requesting that the Governor grant the trustees of their property four allotments of land for clergymen's dwellings, and they identified the land they thought most suitable. The Colonial Secretary confirmed that grants would be made to the Wesleyans,[152] the Roman Catholics[153] and the Church of England.[154]

The Colonial Secretary also received a petition at this time from 'the Inhabitants of the Town of Fremantle', calling on the government and the Legislative Council to provide further support for ministers of religion in Fremantle. The appeal included almost three pages of signatures.[155]

By 1843, Governor Hutt was using several excuses to delay the payment of money for church buildings, including that the buildings had to be finished before payment could be made. He referred to the necessity for the Legislative Council to examine the estimates of revenue and expenditure, finally admitting that the government was finding it difficult to meet all the requests from the various church bodies. By early 1844, the government's financial situation had further deteriorated. In May 1844, the Colonial Secretary informed the Roman Catholics, who had asked for a subsidy for their church building, that the government could not provide any further assistance at that time, a notice to this effect having already been placed in the *Government Gazette*. This letter reassured the Catholics that they would be informed 'when the funds at the disposal of the Government shall admit of such an advance'.[156]

The notice in the *Government Gazette* revealed the nature of the problem facing Governor Hutt in his attempt to assist all religious bodies. It stated that it was probable 'that the inhabitants in the several Districts of the Colony may have it in contemplation to erect places of Public Worship, and to apply for Minister's stipends, relying on the promises held out to them' under the provisions of the Church Building and Stipends Act.

The Governor's ruling was that 'in the present state of public funds it will be impossible for any such aid to be afforded; and, therefore, no application can be entertained until further notice'. However, he was prepared to honour those arrangements already made.[157] This lack of revenue was an insurmountable problem. In June 1844, a new act was passed to repeal the Church Building Act, 'except so far as its continuance may be necessary for the payment of sums heretofore promised'.[158]

The clergymen of the Church of England in outlying areas, where the population was small, faced difficulties similar to those confronting the Wesleyans. They had too few church members to provide any significant financial assistance to their minister, and too few members to qualify for assistance in the form of a stipend. The number of Church of England clergymen in Western Australia reached five when the very energetic John Ramsden Wollaston arrived in 1841, with the promise of a stipend as a colonial chaplain. He arrived at Perth and travelled to Picton, 105 miles south of Perth, to take up land in the area settled by the Western Australian Company. There he built St Mark's Church, which was opened in December 1842.[159]

His first application for a stipend was refused but he was subsequently promised one when the Picton church was completed, if he had enough support from the community.[160] This proved difficult, as the settlement in the south-west of the colony struggled to survive. When Governor Clarke arrived in early 1846, he responded positively to the appeal for financial help from Reverend Wollaston, who was servicing several groups in the Wellington district. The Governor now instructed him to serve the Albany district as well as those at Wellington and Sussex.[161]

Wollaston wrote of the distances he had to travel and the difficulties people had in attending distant churches in the absence of roads, and referred to the absence of poor people from his services. He had so far received some assistance from the local people but he thought that there ought to be some organised system for the payment of clergymen who were struggling with such difficulties.[162] In early 1848, Wollaston was made chaplain at King George's Sound and provided with a stipend.[163]

For four years, the requests for subsidies for church buildings and for stipends for ministers were a major part of Governor Hutt's correspondence with religious bodies. His 1840 act, designed to provide support to all denominations for the building of churches and for the provision of stipends, proved difficult to put into effect. This was partly because of the shortage of government revenue at certain times, but was also the direct result of the conditions for support set out in the act, which determined the question of stipends largely on the basis of the size of the population supporting a particular church. While the act provided the possibility of giving special consideration to claims that did not meet these requirements, such claims were always refused.

It is apparent that Hutt intended to assist the churches equally, as revealed by the subsidies given for the building of churches. However, the provision of stipends involved an agreement to furnish ongoing support, which would be a yearly charge on the limited revenue of the colony. The Wesleyans were very insistent about what they claimed were their rights, regardless of the rules about the number of their committed worshippers. The Governor could have made an exception and satisfied their claims, using Clause 3 of the act. His constant refusal to do so may be explained by the lack of support from the members of the Legislative Council, all adherents of the Church of England, who could point to the limited amount of public revenue.

In spite of all these difficulties, five churches subsidised by the government were built in Perth and Fremantle during Governor Hutt's period in office. The repeal of the act in 1844 revealed that the original plans to provide church-building assistance, and stipends, depended on sufficient colonial revenue, with the result that the Catholic Church would have to wait for its subsidy payment until 1850.

While assistance was provided for church buildings, only a small amount was available for stipends, all of them for the Church of England. However, this apparent preference for the Anglicans was about to be undermined by the introduction of new marriage laws. The clergy of the Church of England would all be seriously disturbed by the introduction of marriage registration, the required presence of the sub-registrar at every marriage, and the new right to marry with only a sub-registrar's license.

5

First marriage laws, 1841

Governor Hutt, who remained in office from early 1839 until he left the colony on 19 February 1846, arrived not only with new ideas, but also with specific instructions about how some of the problems in the colony might be solved. Because of his support for Wakefield's theories, he introduced some radical legislation to resume undeveloped land so it could be sold on the market; he attempted to improve relations with the Aboriginal population; and he had also been instructed to change the marriage laws, to bring them into line with the new laws in England. Many of these decisions, including his passage of the 1841 marriage acts, made him unpopular with the established landowners and the supporters of the Church of England.

Governor Hutt introduced two new marriage bills in April 1841, not long after he had undertaken to provide assistance for the building of churches, and, in May 1841, the first colonial laws concerning marriage in Western Australia were passed. This was twelve years after settlement. The public was introduced to the issue of marriage laws by the editor of *The Inquirer*, Francis Lochee, who had commented on Reverend Smithies' claims that he was entitled to conduct marriages. In that article, Lochee also wrote about the recent changes in English law and advocated their introduction in Western Australia.

Far be it from us to advocate anything like interference on points of conscience; let those who do not wish to marry according to the forms of the Church, and from which no ordained minister can deviate, be married...by a magistrate, or by a minister of their own denomination, as it may best please them; but at least let such magistrate, and such minister be properly appointed for the purpose, and equally authorised, to the exclusion of all others. It has already been done in England, and why not here?[164]

The first new law passed by Governor Hutt for the registration of marriage was essentially a version of the new English law passed in 1836. Civil marriage now became possible and allowed marriage with only a sub-registrar's license. The act also established a system of marriage registration. The first colonial Marriage Act concerned the registration of marriage by lay officials, along with the registration of births and deaths.

According to the report in *The Inquirer*, when Governor Hutt moved the first reading of the bill for the Registration of Births, Deaths and Marriages, which became law in May 1841, he stated that

the bill was similar to one lately passed in England, and was there imperatively called for by the public to supply the place of those registers kept by clergymen in the various parishes. It had also been found necessary to introduce it here. He would only observe, that although a registrar was to be appointed, and that he would be so far a government officer, he would be no additional charge on the revenue, as he would be paid entirely from the fees of his office.[165]

The act allowed the Governor to appoint a colonial registrar to keep a General Register of all Births, Deaths and Marriages, and also allowed the appointment of so-called sub-registrars to officiate in both Perth and country districts.[166] The first Registrar of Births, Deaths and Marriages was George Frederick Stone, appointed by the Governor in September 1841. At the same time, Stone was also appointed a sub-registrar for various areas near Perth and for Fremantle.[167] This meant that the new act came into force at the end of September 1841, after this necessary appointment was made.

Under this act, the Governor was empowered to make all the necessary regulations, to be duly reported in the *Government Gazette*, concerning the keeping of records and the obligations of the Registrar to provide information to the Colonial Secretary. Before any impending marriage, the sub-registrar had to be informed of certain personal details concerning the individuals involved. The license gave permission for the marriage to proceed within three months, and was to be read out at the marriage by the person officiating at the ceremony. The wording of this license included a statement that the sub-registrar had been given notice of the marriage, and it had been authorised by him.

The sub-registrar also provided books for the registration of marriage once the service was completed. These marriage registers from each area had to be submitted to the Governor on a yearly basis. Marriages had to be recorded with the signature of the sub-registrar who was present at the marriage ceremony, as well as the signatures of the couple involved and also those of two 'credible witnesses'.[168] The rules about recording births and deaths, set out in the same act, provided the basic instructions for what would become an important group of colonial administrators.[169]

Later that year, Governor Hutt thanked the members of the Legislative Council for the care and attention they had bestowed on important subjects. He said that he might name particularly the Act for the Registration of Births, Deaths and Marriages. While this act would furnish valuable statistical details to the government, it

> provides at the same time an incontestable record, which will be found hereafter of vital consequence as regards the security of property to each individual in the community.[170]

He was referring here to the recently introduced births, deaths and marriages registers, the future importance of which he rightly predicted. He believed, he said, that this act, along with the act to promote the building of churches and chapels, and to contribute to the maintenance of ministers,

> places the forms and outward securities of religion on a firm, because just and liberal, basis, at a time when it was yet in your power to do so without coming into contact with the complicated interests of a more advanced stage of society.

Hutt apparently believed that the introduction of radical changes to the marriage law would be more readily accepted in the Colony of Western Australia than in England.

Immediately following the introduction of the Registration Bill in the Legislative Council, Governor Hutt introduced a second bill, also passed into law in May 1841, setting out the procedures to be followed in the solemnisation of marriage in the colony. These two acts need to be considered together in order to reach a full understanding of the law. Whereas the Registration Act set out the rules to be followed by the colonial administration, the Solemnization Act informed the public generally about how a marriage should be conducted. This act defined the role of the clergy of all the churches, who would still conduct most of the ceremonies.

Those people wishing to marry needed to know what the law required, including their obligation to provide information to the sub-registrar in order to obtain a marriage license. The act specified that the minimum age of marriage without parental approval was twenty-one years for a man and eighteen years for a woman.[171]

This explains why the changes in the laws concerning registration and solemnisation of marriage often followed closely, one upon the other. The clergy in each district still kept their own marriage records, but the details also had to be entered in the government register.[172] The collection of records was straightforward because, under this 1841 act, all marriages had to be attended by a sub-registrar.

The first clause of the Solemnization Act was designed to reassure the Anglican clergy of the continuing importance of their marriage customs as well as their continuing role as marriage celebrants. The 1841 Western Australian Solemnization of Marriage Ordinance stated that 'all the rules prescribed by the Rubric concerning the solemnization of Marriage shall continue to be duly observed by every person in Holy Orders of the Church of England, who shall solemnize any marriage in the colony of Western Australia', and that they were to be conducted in a 'place of worship', whether or not it was a church.[173] The only new conditions were that a sub-registrar's license had to be obtained and the sub-registrar had to be present at the wedding.

There was also an alternative in the form of a sub-registrar's certificate, the details of which appeared in Clause 6 of the Marriage Solemnization Act. This certificate was to be provided in the case of people who intended to marry but who attended churches in different districts. For example, if one marriage partner lived in Perth and the other in Fremantle, a certificate would be provided for each clergyman, who would read the notice of the intended marriage for three Sundays. This certificate took the place of banns and allowed any objections to the marriage to be heard. The cost was five shillings for each certificate, a total cost therefore of ten shillings, the same cost as a sub-registrar's license.

The wording of the certificate was slightly different from the license, but was still essentially a statement from the sub-registrar giving permission to marry. The person officiating at the marriage had to return a signed form to the sub-registrar declaring that he had read the appropriate notice aloud for three Sundays before the ceremony. This provision allowed these Church of England marriage participants with a 'certificate' to marry without paying the cost of banns, presumably an outcome intended by the Governor, to make it easier for the poorer members of the Anglican community to marry.

Governor Hutt's marriage acts seemed straightforward enough, although they differed in one particular from the English acts, in that they no longer allowed the issuing of a bishop's license.[174] This had been part of the practice in the Church of England in the colony – a marriage license was an alternative to the declaration of banns, and had been granted by the Governor acting as a bishop's surrogate.

This was a matter of grave importance because this license, for which the Governor made no charge, had allowed marriage participants to avoid paying three guineas to the Church of England for the cost of banns.[175] At least half of all marriages in the colony had previously been conducted with a governor's (bishop's) license. Under the new laws, the alternative for Anglicans who wished to avoid the cost of banns, was the procuring of a registrar's certificate. More importantly, those Anglicans who were paying for banns now had the additional cost of a license. It became apparent in subsequent debates that these so-called 'intrusions' into customary marriage practice were regarded as highly offensive by the Anglican clergy.

But, equally upsetting for a church that had previously solemnised all marriages was the concession to people who were not members of the Church of England, similar to that made in the 1836 English law. This was the radical clause granting freedom to all those who were not members of the Church of England. They could now be married by their own clergy, in a church of their choice.

> ...it shall be lawful for the parties to adopt any form or ceremony they may think fit; provided always that no marriage shall take place without the production of the Sub-registrar's license or certificate, where such officer

shall have been appointed, as herein after provided – nor unless with open doors in the place of which notice has been given to the Sub-registrar, and in the presence of the Sub-registrar or his deputy, and of two or three credible witnesses...[176]

They had to be prepared to swear that there was no impediment to the marriage.

An additional freedom was also introduced in that it was now possible to marry in the office (usually the house) of a sub-registrar. According to Clause 8 of the act, 'any person may, after license or certificate duly obtained, contract and solemnize marriage according to the provisions of the Act at the office of any Sub-registrar'. This allowed the contract of marriage to be undertaken without the presence of any religious celebrant.

Clause 5 listed the information that had to be provided by the participants to the sub-registrar, including the name of the place in which the marriage was to be solemnised. At first, George Frederick Stone was appointed government Registrar, as well as sub-registrar for a district that included the area defined as Perth, Fremantle and some settlements along the river.[177] Later appointments of sub-registrars were made slowly over a considerable period. People in outlying areas had to apply to the nearest sub-registrar for a license and had to either marry in his presence, or be married by him.

This first introduction of civil marriage was the most radical change in the legislation and followed the recent change in England. The costs connected with civil marriage were relatively small, in comparison to the sum previously charged by the Church of England for the declaration of banns, frequently referred to as three guineas. This was believed at the time to be the cost in England although, as will be recorded below, it was later established that the sum charged in England was £3.

The schedule at the end of the 1841 act provided the detail about marriage costs. The main charges included ten shillings for the sub-registrar's license or certificate, which every marrying couple had to pay, £1 for marriage at the sub-registrar's office (or house) and two shillings and sixpence for the certificate for the married couple to keep as their private record. However, a sub-registrar was required to be present at every marriage, at the cost of five shillings. If this involved travel of any distance, the sum of nine pence per mile also had to be found for his trip there and back.[178] The total cost of marriage for those who did not have to pay for banns, or for the services of a clergyman, was therefore approximately £2.

Although the approval of the acts by the Secretary of State for the Colonies did not appear in the *Government Gazette* until 26 August 1842, the acts came into operation in the colony in September 1841. The Wesleyans were the only congregation with an established church in the Perth area when this act was passed, and Reverend Smithies moved quickly to conduct marriages according to the new colonial law.

In November of that year, he solemnised the marriage of an Aboriginal couple in the newly built Wesleyan chapel in Perth with some support from the community. According to the report of this marriage in the newspaper the *Perth Gazette*, the rite of baptism had previously been administered,

> and the duties they had mutually contracted fully explained to the newly married couple in a style suited to their limited comprehension. This is the first religious European ordinance in which the natives of Western Australia have participated; and, considering that these two aborigines have been, and are likely to remain domiciliated [sic] with the inhabitants of Perth, and that facility for their future civilization will be afforded by the local Government, we are inclined to hope favourably of this interesting experiment...A convenient cottage has been erected through the kindness of their Wesleyan friends, and furnished with suitable conveniences.[179]

This marriage was recorded in the new government marriage register.[180]

Three years later, Reverend Smithies administered the rites of baptism and marriage to another Aboriginal couple.[181] Then, in 1845, the *Perth Gazette* reported the marriage of a white settler to an Aboriginal woman in the Wesleyan chapel in Perth. This was claimed as the first matrimonial union between an Aboriginal and a European.[182]

As in England, these new rules allowed members of the Church of England to avoid the payment of fees to the church before the solemnisation of their marriage. The Church of England clergy soon began to realise that the new Marriage Act had reduced the sum they could collect for the publication of banns, since members of the Church of England could now also marry in their own church with a certificate, or in the office of the sub-registrar.

The marriage register for the period 1841–47 sets out the date and place of each marriage in the colony and identifies the people marrying, with details about their age, occupation and relatives. The signatures of witnesses and their addresses are included near the end of each entry. The last column provides the signature of the sub-registrar who witnessed the marriage.

There is no place in the entry for each marriage to record the signature of the person conducting the marriage ceremony, but the place of marriage is clearly identified. However, occasionally the name of the minister who conducted the marriage is written in the 'How Married' column. For example, Reverend George King's name appears in this column for marriages in October 1844 and March 1845, ignoring the usual detail about 'license or certificate'. Reverend J. K. Wollaston is identified as the celebrant for a marriage in the Busselton Shire in November 1847, one of the last under the Marriage Act of 1841.[183] Apart from a few entries, the name of the marriage celebrant is absent from the register but present on the couple's marriage certificate.

The evidence shows that in the period from October 1841 to November 1847, a few people chose to be married with a license in a sub-registrar's office or house in Perth or Fremantle, or at one of the larger country centres, thus avoiding the three guineas collected by the Church of England for the posting of banns. For example, in 1842, thirteen marriages out of a total of thirty-eight were conducted by a sub-registrar.[184]

The Wesleyans were able to adapt quickly to the new arrangements and, simply using a sub-registrar's license, married people of both European and Aboriginal descent in their churches at Perth and Fremantle. Bishop Brady did not return to the colony until January 1846. But, in June 1845 and in March 1846, the first two Catholic marriages were conducted by Father Joostens and by Bishop Brady in the Roman Catholic chapel in Victoria Street, Perth.[185]

According to the rules of the Catholic Church, as expressed in the book instructing the Catholic priesthood in all rituals, the marriage ceremony at this time was conducted in Latin.[186] However, it is unlikely that this requirement was enforced in the nineteenth century in Western Australia. An article in the *Catholic Encyclopedia* explains that the church displayed great tolerance towards the use of the vernacular, since the use of Latin 'was always disconcerting to the minds of the imperfectly educated'.[187] However, Latin was used for the books of Catholic marriage records.

It is worth observing that some of the few Catholics in the community at this time may have been familiar from their early childhood with the use of Latin in various church ceremonies. Whether in Latin or English, the short Catholic marriage ceremony was concluded with a benediction by the priest, translated as follows:

> We beg of you, O Lord, to turn your eyes towards these your servants. Let your goodness show through them your own design for the growth in number of the human race. They have been joined together by your authority; may they be kept together through your help.

The introduction of the new Marriage Act fuelled growing tension first of all between the leaders of the Church of England and the Wesleyans. Open hostilities between the Wesleyans and the Church of England had already begun in September 1840, after the laying of the foundation stone for the Wesleyan Chapel at Fremantle by Governor Hutt, just two months after the passage of the church-building assistance law, which provided up to £500 assistance from government revenue. The editor of *The Inquirer* reported that 300 or 400 people, including many Aboriginal people, attended the gathering. In his speech on this occasion, the Governor was very supportive of the Wesleyan initiatives and spoke of the importance of places of worship where the 'weak and wavering...might rally in the hour of uncertainty, and be encouraged by precept and example...' In his reply, Reverend Smithies was full of praise for Governor Hutt.[188]

In a Church of England service on the Sunday following Governor Hutt's speech in praise of the Wesleyans, Reverend Wittenoom attacked the followers of the Wesleyan faith, claiming they were responsible for 'the awful sin of schism and consequently deserving denunciation, ex-communication, and final perdition'.[189] This part of Reverend Wittenoom's sermon, and other claims he made, were reported in detail to Reverend John Smithies, who regarded them as offensive.

When Smithies replied to this attack in *The Inquirer*, he assured his readers that he was well informed about what Reverend Wittenoom had said in his sermon. He wrote that Wittenoom's sermon was directed at the dissenting world in general and the Wesleyans residing in Perth in particular. He claimed that he could not understand the reason for the attack, since Reverend Wittenoom had previously been welcoming and encouraging.

Smithies suggested in his long letter that Wittenoom had not acquainted himself with the history of the Wesleyan Church. In a personal attack on the Colonial Chaplain, he declared that

> we shall distinguish betwixt the minister and the people, and when the former passes the boundaries of prudence, charity, and goodwill to his fellow citizens, whether in the Pulpit or out of it, we shall regard him as in the above case as the aggressor...

In September 1842, the editor of *The Inquirer* published an article entitled 'The law of marriage', which revealed some continuing confusion about the nature of the changes introduced by the 1841 marriage acts, as well as a continuing reluctance to accept the intrusion of secular power into the marriage ceremony. The author stated that 'we are firmly of opinion that a marriage between a Dissenter and a member of the Church of England performed by a Dissenter is null and void'. It also asked whether marriages of various persuasions conducted by the Registrar were legitimate.[190]

A letter in the same edition of *The Inquirer*, from Reverend George King and members of the Church of England in Western Australia, stated that the new Marriage Act was ' "a heavy blow and great discouragement" to the cause of Christianity'.[191] The letter contained a long discussion about the history of marriage practices, and the following exhortation.

> The case stands thus: the law of the land will permit you to enter into the marriage by civil contract; but the Church can never be silenced, and she affirms, that though the state may permit this, the word of God instructs us otherwise, and marriage is a religious contract; therefore do not avail yourselves of the permission here given by the state.

This letter was followed three weeks later by one from Reverend Wollaston, repeating the claim that the act had been made not for Church of England members but for Dissenters. He stated that, while it might be legal, it was not acceptable to the church.

> The earnest desire of the Clergy is, that all the members of our Church, while they cherish every charitable feeling of tolerance towards their dissenting brethren, should act consistently with their profession; that they

should 'hold the faith in unity of spirit, in the bond of peace, and in righteousness of life'.[192]

This was a call for all Church of England members to follow the age-old pattern of declaring banns and marrying in a Church of England. The Governor realised that these statements suggested some confusion about the new marriage laws and instructed the Registrar to publish a summary of the solemnisation requirements.[193]

In the months that followed, it became apparent that the editors of the two major newspapers were taking opposite sides in the debate. On 10 December, an attack on the Church of England occurred when the editor of the *Perth Gazette* published a long letter, signed by 'an Observer', questioning the behaviour of people closely connected to the Colonial Church Society. The letter suggests that the author was present at a meeting of this body, when Frederick Irwin spoke against critics who had questioned the legitimacy of the society. The writer claimed that it was 'a burlesque on a missionary meeting, for there was no missionary there'.[194] He stated that a large sum of missionary money had been spent entirely in the Guildford area, although it would have been more 'respectable giving among themselves, ere they had gone a begging of their neighbors'. This was a reflection on the obvious wealth of the people who lived in this part of the colony.

The editor of *The Inquirer*, Francis Lochee, who was also a trustee of the Church of England, claimed that this critical letter was almost certainly the work of Reverend Smithies. He said that Smithies took 'every opportunity of manifesting his own virulent hatred of the Church establishment, and of encouraging others to sneer at…its institutions…'[195]

In a later editorial he declared that his claim that Reverend Smithies was the author of this attack must have been correct, otherwise he would have denied the charge against him. He also made some observations to the effect that John Wesley, the founder of Methodism, would not have approved of such sneering, and denied the claim made in the *Perth Gazette* letter that *The Inquirer* had been guilty of any misrepresentation of, or hostility towards, Wesleyans.[196]

'An Observer', replied to the editor of *The Inquirer*, referring to him as a person of 'fiend-like disposition' and hoping that the 'Wesleyan Missionary will not waste any more of his valuable time upon him'.[197] Presumably, at this point, some of the readers began to realise that this writer could not be Reverend Smithies.

While this dispute was continuing in *The Inquirer* and the *Perth Gazette*, the first yearly report of the Registrar of Births, Deaths and Marriages, including tables, was published in full in *The Inquirer* on 12 October 1842.[198] This clarified the reasons for the growing hostilities recorded between the Anglicans and Wesleyans in the previous two months. Referring to the report, the editor of *The Inquirer*, Francis Lochee, commented that

> the table of marriages exhibits a total of sixteen performances of ceremony not according to the rites of the church of England, which is a larger proportion...than we were prepared to find.[199]

He claimed that some of these were performed in places where there was no clergyman. He also claimed, without offering any proof, that several were Roman Catholic. He believed that there was probably no more than one member of the Church of England living within a reasonable distance of one of the ministers who was married by a sub-registrar.

Referring back to the debate in the letters column of his newspaper, he pointed out that the 1841 Marriage Act had 'been looked upon as interfering with religious ceremonies' and that some people claimed the legislation had been made for dissenters, not for the Church of England. However, he disagreed with this view, saying that the registration process had nothing to do with the ordinances of the church.

The figures explain the growing anxiety among the Church of England clergymen who had previously controlled all marriage practices. The 'marriage table' in the Registrar's report for 1842 was as follows:

Marriages solemnized according to the rites of the Church of England

By Sub-Registrar's licenses 19

By Sub-registrar's certificates 3

Total 22

Not according to the rites of the Church of England

In the Wesleyan Methodist Chapel 3

In Sub-Registrars' offices 13

Total 16

In other words, during the first year of its operation, although slightly more than half of the marriages were still occurring in the Church of England, only nineteen marrying couples had paid for banns at the cost of three guineas. And, in spite of the explanations provided by the editor of *The Inquirer*, the Church of England clergy were undoubtedly alarmed at the number who had disclaimed any religious affiliation and married in a sub-registrar's office.

The earlier dispute between the more conservative members of the Church of England clergy and the Wesleyans continued into 1843, now made more intense after the publication of the details of the marriage practices for the first year after the change of law. It was not that the Wesleyans had conducted many marriages, but that only nineteen couples had paid for Church of England banns, and that thirteen couples, obviously mostly members of the Church of England because of their predominance in the colony, had married in a sub-registrar's office.

Early in January 1843, the editor of *The Inquirer* published a long and fulsomely worded letter from Henry Trigg, then a well-known member of the Wesleyan body, who perhaps hoped to put an end to the ongoing dispute in the local newspapers. He was critical of the editor of *The Inquirer* for some of his over-blown language but, assuming that Smithies was the author of the original letter by 'an Observer', he stated that Smithies, too, might have been less provocative. He urged all those in the dispute to behave according to Christian teachings.[200]

But it seems that, according to some people, Trigg had been too forgiving towards the Church of England. Now a letter appeared in the *Perth Gazette* written by 'a Wesleyan', regretting that Trigg should have made a criticism of Reverend Smithies. He also asked how it was that Trigg knew the letter was written by Smithies. The letter writer claimed that there is a strong disposition in the colony

> to question the authority of any ministry, not under episcopal sanction…
>
> I would speak as a friend, and beg of Mr. Trigg to pursue that conduct he recommends to observe, namely, to retire to his closet, and there become a closer observer of the workings of his own mind; if he finds a root of bitterness there, root it out, or, in other words, wrestle with God in prayer till every unholy feeling is destroyed…[201]

Another letter by 'a Wesleyan', presumably the same person, appeared in the *Perth Gazette* a week later. Now the author stated that he did not believe Smithies was the author of the original letter, and criticised both the editor of *The Inquirer*, Francis Lochee, and Henry Trigg for making this assumption. He also attacked the hierarchy of the Anglican Church, which he said he would like to destroy.[202]

In the same edition, a writer calling himself 'A Hermit in Western Australia', referred to the 'religious wrangling' in the colony. He pointed particularly to an intolerant speech by Richard Nash, at that time Acting Advocate-General, at the previous meeting of the Church Missionary Society, and described an argument he had with Mr Nash. According to this account, Mr Nash maintained the principles of high church and state

> with so much zeal and pertinacity, and condemned all dissenters in such vehement language, that I began to suspect he was some great dignitary of the Church in disguise, on a mission of proselytism to this Colony.[203]

In the following week, the situation became even more interesting, as the writer who had earlier called himself 'the Observer' and had been identified by Francis Lochee and Mr Trigg as Reverend Smithies, now appeared again in the columns of the *Perth Gazette*. He referred to these assumptions and then identified himself as a person 'as strongly church as most men in the place, and will defend true church, state, and country to the last'.[204] In other words, it was he, not Reverend Smithies, who was the author of these recent attacks on the Church of England.

He then asked whether it followed that, because ' "an Observer" has written against some abuses in our Mother-Church, he is therefore' not a member. 'Is it to be believed that the church has no one individual member who would endeavour to reform and amend what appears [to be] error?' As if to prove his point, he then made a strong criticism of the Church of England appointment of Reverend Postlethwaite to the Upper Swan, a distance of only six miles from Reverend Mitchell, when other areas were being neglected. He questioned whether these gentlemen should be receiving a grant of £100 each from the colonial government.

The hostilities in the press gradually subsided as information became publicly available about the operation of the new marriage laws. By October 1842, the Registrar of Births, Deaths and Marriages advised Governor

Hutt that

> the Act of Council having been now a full year in effect, and therefore
> sufficiently made known to the public, the smallest penalty of twenty
> shillings should be enforced in every instance of neglect in future to
> register a birth, death or marriage within one month of the date thereof.[205]

Hutt instructed the Registrar to inform sub-registrars of this decision to
begin implementing this clause of the Marriage Act.

For the following three years, from October 1843 to October 1845,
the Registrar provided a report of the number of marriages in the colony,
along with increasingly complex statistical details about births and deaths.
The highest number of forty-four marriages occurred in 1842–43 for the
period of one year ending on 30 September. Twenty-three couples married
according to the rules of 'the Established Church [sic] and twenty-one with
only a Sub-registrar's license', the only license now required by law. Of this
second group, five married in the Wesleyan Methodist chapel and sixteen
in a sub-registrar's office.[206]

In 1844, the Registrar reported that the number of marriages solemnised
not according to the rites of the 'established church' was 45.9 per cent of the
total number of marriages.[207] In 1845, he provided figures for the number
of marriages in each district, with nineteen of the thirty-four marriages
occurring in Perth.[208] The number of marriages dropped considerably
towards 1847, a period of economic difficulty in the colony. The decrease
in the number of marriages that occurred in 1844, and which continued
for some years, was attributed to these difficult economic circumstances.

In his seventh annual report, the government Registrar, George Frederick
Stone, explained this reduced rate of marriage as due to reluctance on
the part of the poor to marry, implying a new kind of responsibility and
independence on the part of the colonial working class. He wrote that

> forethought as to their ability to maintain a family is commonly observed
> among our lower class. They do not marry to rush into poverty and distress
> and endure the poignant scorn of their equals. They do not calculate on
> charity as a source of subsistence, knowing full well they must look to
> their own exertions alone for the needful support of their children; they
> have no poor-laws to fall back upon, the Government professing to relieve

no distress, however pinching, except abject destitution occasioned by sickness or decrepitude.[209]

While John Hutt remained as Governor, the complaints of the Church of England clergy were to no avail. On 28 April 1843, for example, Reverend George King wrote a letter of protest about the 1841 marriage acts to Governor Hutt, referring to the inconvenience caused by the sub-registrar at the marriage ceremony and claiming that the Church of England regarded the solemnisation of marriage as a sacred rite. Hutt replied that the system of registration had been introduced in England and all the colonies, 'in order that proper Tables may eventually be prepared in every place', and that no change was possible.

He was less dogmatic in answering the rest of the letter. He said that

> the last paragraph of your letter I feel more difficulty in replying to. There can be no doubt that marriage is not considered by the Law of England a sacred rite, – and even supposing that it were so considered, the Act of Council does not prevent it being so looked upon in the case of members of the Church of England. It is those who choose to dispense with the rubric and ceremonies of that Church to whom the Act declares that they may be married according to what form they please provided that in every case a Sub-registrar is present...[210]

The two marriage acts introduced by Governor Hutt pleased members of the Wesleyan Church, who could now marry with a sub-registrar's license in their own chapels. When Bishop Brady returned to the colony, just before the arrival of Governor Clarke in 1846, he solemnised a marriage in the Catholic Church. But he would shortly express strong Catholic opposition to the Registration Act and the presence of the sub-registrar at the solemnisation ceremony.

The disagreements between the Wesleyans and the supporters of the Church of England concerning marriage laws took place between a very small group of people, most of whom knew one another by sight. When Governor Hutt left the colony in February 1846, there were still less than 5,000 settlers in the whole colony. They were divided between Perth, Guildford, Fremantle, York, the Vasse and Albany, with a few in other more outlying areas.

The distances between these districts in the colony were great, while the roads were poor or non-existent. There was no night lighting and travel was often dangerous, even in daylight hours. Only people with a considerable income could afford the means of travel and communication, including horses, wheeled vehicles or small boats. There was growing anxiety about the slow pace of economic development, the dramatic reduction in government revenue and the shortage of labour. This problem would be solved in 1850 by the introduction of convicts.

When Governor Hutt retired from his position in February 1846, he was well aware that his policies about church buildings, stipends and changes to the marriage laws had caused considerable divisions in the community. These divisions were about to intensify. When Governor Clarke arrived in the colony just before John Hutt departed, it was the clergymen of the Church of England who mounted the first sustained attack on Governor Hutt's marriage laws. They approached Governor Clarke in the hope that they could secure further changes to the law to satisfy Church of England interests. This proved unavailing but, after Governor Clarke's untimely death, the new Acting Governor, Frederick Irwin, was more than ready to listen to their proposals for change.

6

Changes to marriage laws, 1847

Governor Clarke, an Irishman and member of the Church of England, like so many of the official figures in the colony, arrived on 26 January 1846, just before the departure of Governor Hutt. Very soon, the colony entered on a period of some political uncertainty because of the illness of the new Governor from July 1846 and his death in February 1847. The Commandant of the Armed Forces, Frederick Chidley Irwin, then became Acting Governor for sixteen months until the arrival of Governor Charles Fitzgerald in August 1848.

Clarke's death was especially unsettling because Peter Brown, who had been the Colonial Secretary from the time of first settlement, also died in November 1846, soon after Governor Clarke became ill.[211] Brown was replaced by George Fletcher Moore, the Advocate-General, which position was now filled on a temporary basis by William Mackie. There was an interregnum of six months before the newly appointed Richard Robert Madden arrived in May 1847 to take up the position of Colonial Secretary.[212] He was also an Irishman, but a Roman Catholic, and previously active as a slavery abolitionist.[213] He had a lifelong interest in the Irish insurrectionary movement and, in the colonial situation, was particularly protective of the interests of Aborigines.

Richard Madden arrived just as new marriage bills were introduced in the Legislative Council and had begun to excite further debate in the community. He left the colony in January 1849 for a period of leave, because his eldest son had drowned in Ireland.[214] After a short time in Ireland, Madden decided not to return to Western Australia, a decision approved by Earl Grey.[215]

Richard Madden's departure from Perth in January 1849 was the occasion for an address to him emanating from the Catholic community.[216] According to an unidentified writer to the newspaper, his going was much regretted by people of all religious persuasions except by 'the few expiring members of the old Government faction', including the previous Lieutenant-Governor Irwin, 'under whose rule the colony so universally groaned'.[217]

Four years after his return to Ireland, Richard Madden wrote a letter to the Vicar-General of the Diocese of Dublin, in which he commented on his period as Colonial Secretary in Western Australia. This letter provides an unusual perspective on the political situation in the colony during Madden's short term in office.

> On my arrival in the Swan River Settlement, of which I was Colonial Secretary, I found Dr Brady contending single-handed against the entire local Government, every member of which, with two exceptions, was bitterly opposed to Catholicity. The Colony was administered by Irish Orangemen for the interests of Orangemen. Lord Grey knew this, and being determined to break down the Government of a faction, sent out a Roman Catholic as Secretary, the first Catholic ever appointed to that office in the Colonies – myself...From the time of my arrival, I took care that Dr Brady and his mission were no more troubled, disturbed or warred with.[218]

The Orange Order, so disliked by Colonial Secretary Madden, was established by Protestants in Northern Ireland in 1795, in opposition to the Defenders, a Catholic secret society. An earlier Orange institution had been established in 1688 to support William of Orange, when he became King of England. These Irish Protestants opposed Catholic emancipation, which occurred in the first third of the nineteenth century, just as the Western Australian settlement was beginning.

It is certainly clear that most of the people who held positions of power in the colony were committed members of the Church of England, many of them with an Irish background. At the beginning of Richard Madden's period in office as Colonial Secretary, Frederick Irwin was the Acting Governor and most of the members of the Executive and Legislative councils were of Irish origin. The Legislative Council included John Septimus Roe, George Fletcher Moore, William Mackie and George Leake.

As a Catholic, Richard Madden was clearly disposed to see these people as actively promoting the interests of the Church of England at the expense of other religious groups in the community. However, given the brevity of his term of office, he seems to have exaggerated his own role as arbiter in conflicts over religious issues.

But it is indisputable that some of the dominant figures in the Church of England hierarchy were responsible for the changes to the marriage law in 1847. Soon after the arrival in February 1846 of Governor Clarke, a close friend of Frederick Irwin, the Church of England clergy began to voice its strong opposition to Governor Hutt's 1841 marriage laws. On 10 March 1846, Reverend George King began a series of protests, apparently acting as spokesman for his fellow clergymen. He said that these marriage acts had been regarded by the clergy, since their first enforcement, 'as grievously and unnecessarily burdensome'.[219]

He had three specific complaints. The first was that 'encroachment upon the due discharge of our legitimate duties consists in the necessity of receiving a certificate from the Sub-registrar to authorise us to publish the banns'. The second complaint in this letter was about 'the necessary presence of the Sub-registrar at the ceremony'. This was not only difficult because of the distances and cost of travel but 'at all times an inconvenience to the officiating minister'. Finally, he complained about the 'necessity of receiving a license from the Sub-registrar when the banns are not published'.

Reverend King continued with remarks about the anomalous position of the clergymen, who had well-defined obligations according to the rules of the church, but could not obtain a church marriage license because of the absence of a bishop. He thought that, 'since the Rubricks [sic] of the Church had been confirmed by Act of Parliament, there must surely be no need to impose additional stringent regulations'.

His suggestion to Governor Clarke was that, if he and the Legislative Council found it inconvenient to remodel the legislation, the inconveniences might be removed by nominating the respective clergy as the sub-registrars in the various districts. He claimed that

> the people would thus be relieved from their present expenses of double fees, and the clergy would be enabled to apply for licenses to His Excellency or the quasi surrogates by him appointed as the representative of Her Majesty.

His letter concluded with a claim that the Bishop of Australia had written to him saying that the appointment of a bishop for Western Australia was under consideration.

Governor Clarke replied in apologetic but critical vein. He said that Reverend King's letter had occasioned 'considerable embarrassment' because the government endeavoured to meet the wishes of the Church of England clergy.[220] However, there could be no question that the appointment of registrars had been made in order to ensure a correct record of marriages solemnised in the colony, so that the statistics of the colony could be developed. There was no way this could be changed. He next asked Reverend King whether he was aware of the duties to be performed if clergymen became sub-registrars. They would not only have to attend marriages in their own churches but also in the chapels of all other denominations. He asked Reverend King whether it would be consistent with church rules for a Church of England clergyman to do this.

Reverend King consulted at length with his colleagues and eventually prepared a petition to be presented to the Governor, which was signed by Reverends Wittenoom, Wollaston, Mitchell, King, Postlethwaite and Mears. They claimed that the marriage laws had caused serious inconvenience and should be altered. Their objections to the 1841 acts were set out in this petition as follows:

> First, that the substitution of the Sub-registrar's notice for the publication of banns as enjoined by the Rubrick [sic] is considered inconsistent with the conscientious discharge of the ordination vows of the Clergy of the Church of England.
>
> Secondly, that the compulsory license of the Sub-registrar for the celebration of the marriage according to the rites of the Church of England is uncanonical and imperfect.
>
> And thirdly, that the necessary presence of the Sub-registrar at the celebration of the marriage is felt as an inconvenience to the officiating minister and a grievous tax to the community.[221]

The Governor replied to Reverend King and asked him to inform the other ministers of his response. He said that to change the Marriage Act in the manner suggested would go a great way to change its 'spirit and character... and would be inconsistent with the principle upon which it was framed'. This principle was to treat all religious denominations equally. Governor Clarke indicated that he was sympathetic to the Church of England viewpoint, but concluded his letter by saying that there could be no alteration at present.[222]

Reverend King did not regard Governor Clarke's reply as the final word. He argued in his next letter that the difficulties of making changes, which the Governor had foreseen, 'vanish into insignificancy compared with the abiding inconvenience to the clergy, which this anomalous Act of Council entails'.

He said that one of his colleagues had referred to the marriage ceremony as unconstitutional and humiliating. Since the only resource available to the clergy of the Church of England lay in an appeal to the legislature

> I cannot relinquish the hope that the clergy of Western Australia shall feel in this matter, that their rulers have lost none of that distinguishing characteristic which has long ennobled our fatherland; constituting our Kings and Queens, nurturing fathers and nursing mothers of the Church by law established.

He concluded by observing that the fact that the church was not recognised as 'established' in the colony should be no objection to acting on their petition, since the South Australian Marriage Act, which embodied their demands, had been found acceptable.[223]

By the middle of July, Governor Clarke was reported to be 'too unwell to be troubled' and he would die early in the new year.[224] The Governor's reply to this last letter by Reverend King was written instead by George Fletcher Moore, the Attorney-General of the colony. A note signed by Moore, as an instruction to his secretary concerning the nature of the reply, appeared across the original letter. It read as follows: 'The Government sees no reason to alter the decision made in a former consideration of the same subject'.

The Colonial Secretary Peter Brown was now also ill, and these illnesses closed the matter for that time. After Brown's death in November, when George Fletcher Moore became Acting Colonial Secretary, he acted as spokesman for Governor Clarke, who was no longer able to answer his correspondence.

Soon after Richard Madden's arrival as the new Colonial Secretary, protests had begun about the failure of the colonial government to provide adequate help for the Roman Catholic Church and the Wesleyan Church. On 10 June 1847, George Leake, a member of the Legislative Council, presented a petition he had received from the Roman Catholic Church claiming that they had not received the same assistance as the Church of England for their building program.[225]

One week later, a similar petition from the Wesleyans was presented to the council[226] and, a few days later, the council had a memorial from the Wesleyans setting out the details of the funds they believed they were entitled to claim. The council rejected both of these claims, although William Mackie supported the Wesleyan claim. A Wesleyan Church 'supporter' wrote to The Inquirer in the following week, protesting the government's action in voting against these 'legitimate claims'.[227] These requests were to no avail, until some of the claims were eventually reconsidered by the next Governor, Charles Fitzgerald, more than two years later.

Soon after the appointment of Frederick Irwin as Acting Governor, Reverend Wittenoom, Colonial Chaplain, made another plea for changes to be made to the marriage laws. He sent a memorial to the Executive Council

> praying on behalf of the members of the Church of England that the Marriage and Registration Acts should be amended, so as to leave them the same privileges as under the Marriage Act in England.

The Executive Council agreed that this should be done.[228] This reference to privileges in the English act referred to the right to solemnise marriage with a bishop's license (a license previously provided in the colony by the Governor acting as a bishop's surrogate) instead of a sub-registrar's license, and the requirement that the publication of banns should be controlled by the Church of England clergy.

It can be assumed that William Mackie was responsible for drafting the new marriage bills in 1847 since he was the Acting Advocate-General for a short period before the arrival of Richard Madden as Colonial Secretary. A comment on the passage of the bill in November by a writer who identified himself as 'a Liberal' refers to the original marriage bill as 'the bantling [brat] of the Acting Advocate-General'.[229] Since there appears to be no surviving copy of the original bill, its contents must be determined from the brief records of Legislative Council proceedings, and from the rather limited reporting of the Legislative Council proceedings in *The Inquirer* and the *Perth Gazette*.[230]

The public debates in the newspapers reveal that the 1847 change to the marriage laws, planned by these powerful political figures, increased religious tension in this small community. These debates reveal the beliefs and ideas circulating in the community and dividing the settlers over questions of religious belief, including the issue of whether or not the Church of England was the 'established church'. It is apparent that those engaging in letter writing were not always well informed about English law, and disagreed among themselves about the rights and obligations of secular authorities. There were general attacks on the dominance of the Church of England in the field of marriage, but also a strong protest about secular intervention in marriage practice.

One of the first attacks on the 1847 bill appeared as soon as it was presented to the Legislative Council, well before the second reading. The writer of this article, the editor of the *Perth Gazette*, Elizabeth Macfaull,[231] was critical of the decision to introduce a new marriage bill, making the claim that the earlier 1841 act 'was generally appreciated by the community', and that in introducing a new marriage bill, the Advocate-General 'has descended to the most ridiculous and injurious interference imaginable'.[232]

Macfaull began with the question of the introduction in 1841 of the Registrar's license.

> We are told, considerable difficulty has already occurred with the various Ministers of religion in Perth in respect to the Sub-Registrar's licence... and have they not, as members of the universal Church of Christ, an equal claim to be exempted?

This was a reference to the fact that many members of the Church of England were marrying with a ten-shilling license rather than paying three guineas to the church for the cost of banns.

> And, after all, what is this obnoxious license? Merely a license from a responsible legal (not religious) officer appointed by the Crown, enabling parties to marry according to any religious rite they think fit to adopt, without attempting directly or indirectly, to interfere with the rigid observance of any ecclesiastical license or forms applicable to such

religious rites. The act says to the public, you may marry, according to what religious ceremony you please, but the State requires for secular purposes, that you adhere to certain legal forms, which, to avoid cavil or complaint, are applied to all without exception...We confess that we always looked upon the existing Marriage Act as peculiarly well adapted to the circumstances of a young colony, where the prejudices of either Churchman or Sectarian had not taken root. We, therefore, incline to the view the proposed amended act as, either the precipitate result of a love of change, or an ill-timed concession to the bigoted clamour of a, over sensitive and intolerant clergy.

It also became apparent that, while the Roman Catholic clergy had come to terms with Hutt's marriage-license fee of ten shillings, they were alarmed to discover that William Mackie was proposing to increase the fee to three guineas. In three letters to Richard Madden, the Colonial Secretary, Bishop Brady (or Father Joostens on his behalf) referred to the government planning to put a 'prohibitory' law upon marriages conducted in the Roman Catholic Church in the shape of a 'three guinea' license. In his letter on 10 July 1847, he said that he had been reluctantly compelled

to announce to all members of the Catholic Church that, should such an unheard of measure be adopted, he would be forced to act contrary thereto as being opposed to the law of God and its Church.[233]

More readers of the two local newspapers were made aware of the planned changes to the Solemnization of Marriage Act after the second reading of the new bills in the Legislative Council on 24 July 1847. In introducing the new bills, William Mackie said that the framers of the 1841 act had totally overlooked the fact that the law of England fixed the cost of banns, while colonial law enforced the cost of registration. This was obviously a great disadvantage for those members of the Church of England who chose to pay for both banns and registration. He proposed that 'members of the church [of England] should not be compelled to take out the Sub-Registrar's license or certificate, thereby doing away with the fees allowed for those documents'.[234]

He also said that he disapproved of the system of civil marriage allowing people to marry with only a registrar's license or certificate, the method chosen by many members of the Church of England who could not afford the cost of banns. He described this alternative as an objectionable clause of the 1841 act, which allowed 'people to marry at any hour of the day or night, in a back parlour, for the sum of 10 shillings'.

There were several new clauses introduced on 24 July 1847, two of which were passed without any disagreement being recorded. One concerned the change of name of sub-registrars to registrars and that of the Registrar to Registrar-General. The second concerned the change of a woman's age of consent from eighteen to twenty-one years. The proposal that an episcopal license should be introduced as an alternative to the sub-registrar's license, to be available only to members of the Church of England, was also accepted. This was a return to English practice before 1836, when the so-called bishop's license was an alternative to marriage by banns. This practice was carried out in the colony from 1829 to 1841 in the form of a governor's license. It had not been allowed under the 1841 Marriage Act. In this 1847 colonial bill, it was proposed that the registrar would record the episcopal license as an alternative to the one he would otherwise have granted.

The other main part of the proposal was that the cost of both the government registrar's license for those of other religious persuasions, and the license issued by 'someone with Episcopal authority' within the Church of England, would be the same. The costs of marriage would be equal for all denominations in that the fee for an episcopal license, or for a registrar's license, would be three guineas, the same, it was claimed, as the cost in England. Members of the Church of England would therefore pay this sum to the church rather than to the colonial authorities.

This planned charge of three guineas for a license was more than six times the original cost of a sub-registrar's license. It seemed, according to this bill proposed in 1847, that the Church of England would now receive all payments made for a marriage license for their members, while the Dissenters, so-called, would maintain the same level of government revenue by a huge increase in their payments.

However, this proposal met some opposition in the council when Mr Leake moved that the cost of both kinds of license be reduced to one guinea. The Advocate-General, George Fletcher Moore, then intervened and suggested a compromise of two guineas. He stated that one of the reasons the Roman Catholics were protesting against the bill 'was that, by the rules of their Church, they were obliged to have banns and obtain a dispensation, at the cost of three guineas, in addition to the license required by law'[235]. This change was passed on the casting vote of the Acting Governor, Frederick Irwin.

The date set for the third and final reading of the act, usually regarded as simply a formality, was 29 July. However, the third reading had to be postponed. The Legislative Council sat on the date originally set for the third reading, but George Fletcher Moore referred to an oversight concerning the fee of two guineas for a license. He had discovered that the fee according to English law was actually £3, while all the earlier discussion in the council had assumed that the sum was three guineas. He suggested that the act be recommitted.

In retrospect, it appears that Moore was becoming increasingly concerned about some of the new proposals in the marriage law, and was looking for an excuse to have it reconsidered. Apparently, even William Mackie was still doubtful. He agreed to the act being reconsidered, 'not on account of the fee; but for the purpose of assimilating it to the English Act & for the sake of uniformity'.[236]

The marriage question was discussed again on 5 August and a committee consisting of William Mackie, George Leake and Walter Andrews was then set up to consider further changes to the marriage law. On the same day, a memorial from the Roman Catholic body, protesting about the marriage bill, was laid on the table. The report of this committee was read by Mackie in the council on 12 August and declared to be the first reading. The second reading, when some debate might occur, was finally set for 2 September.[237]

In the intervening period, the debate in the press continued, and it was inevitable that the issue of the 'establishment' of the Anglican Church would reappear. A letter in the *Perth Gazette*, from someone identified only as a 'Liberal', discussed this question. He wrote that 'however the assertion may surprise clergymen of the English church, I state, without fear of contradiction, that church is not yet duly established in Western Australia; there is no Bishop'. Referring to recently proposed changes to the Marriage Act, he said that

> it is equally certain there exists no power in the colony to appoint Surrogates
> for the purpose of granting three guinea Licences. It, therefore...behoves

our clergy to manifest less hostility, and display more good humour, liberality, and condescension towards dissenters; and also to give way in trifles in order the better to preserve essentials. [238]

This writer claimed that William Mackie, a staunch supporter of the Church of England, was responsible for the introduction of the new Marriage Bill, when the existing 1841 marriage law had everything to recommend it.

[It] does not interfere with the vital religion of the church, it does not subvert any of its canons or rubricks [sic]. There is the publication of banns, the religious service, the fee to the officiating minister; everything in fact, but the power to grant licenses; everything but that whereby the church may make a nefarious charge, wherewith to revel in luxury and ease. And yet this liberal little act is to be ruthlessly repealed, to meet the mistaken views of cold unbending high churchmen.

He concluded by saying:

I utterly deride the idea of ministers of the Church [of England] requiring a Bishop's license. It is only a subterfuge to obtain fees. It may be a prelude to further impediments being thrown in the way of Dissenter's [sic] marriages.

The importance of the control of marriage by ecclesiastical authorities resurfaced a week later when *The Inquirer* published an article for consideration by members of the Church of England, prefaced by a statement from the publisher that 'We have been induced to print the following observations for the consideration of the members of the Church of England'.[239] The article claimed that some misunderstanding existed as to certain aspects of the 1841 Marriage Act in relation to the Church of England. The writer claimed that the 1841 act, in requiring a sub-registrar's license before marriage could take place, violated the ecclesiastical law about marriage requirements, 'For surely no act of Council can supersede the authority of ecclesiastical law'. However, this claim was undermined by the writer himself in a later passage, when he stated that 'It is clearly a misnomer to say the Church of England is established in this colony, in the common acceptation of the term'.

Both the Roman Catholic clergy and those of the Church of England had always imposed their own ecclesiastical rules about marriage. The more conservative members of both churches believed that these rules could not be ignored. Apart from the cost of the license, the Roman Catholics believed that the marriage procedures were contrary to Roman Catholic ecclesiastical law.[240]

More generally, the Roman Catholics protested about the growing power and intrusion of lay authorities in the ceremony of marriage, always previously regarded by these 'ancient churches' as solely the responsibility of their clergy. Catholic protests were becoming more frequent, perhaps with the encouragement of Richard Madden. In retrospect, it is apparent that some of these protests applied equally to all secular marriage acts, both English and colonial, including the Marriage Act passed by Governor Hutt in 1841.

After consideration by the committee, the bill was presented again in its amended form on 2 September 1847. It dealt with changes to the law with regard to marriages in the Church of England, while subsequent clauses set out the requirements for people of other denominations. These clauses were extremely complex and confusing. According to Clause 3, marriage could be

> solemnized by persons in holy orders of the Church of England according to the rites and rubric of that Church:– Provided always that the Registrar's certificate if tendered shall be used and stand instead of publication of banns...[241]

The certificate costing £2 would be read out for three Sundays, taking the place of banns.

However, Clause 11 indicated that the registrar was not permitted to issue any licenses for marriage in the Church of England. These certificates would now be issued by the Church of England clergy because of another important change. The new marriage law gave the right to grant licenses to the church, as had been the case in England with the original bishop's license.

This was the most important change enshrined in this new ordinance, passed in the Legislative Council on 9 September 1847. According to Clause 4, licenses for marriage according to the rites of the Church of England without banns may be issued by any person having episcopal authority or the jurisdiction of Ordinary within the colony, or in the absence of such jurisdiction or authority, by the Governor or any other person appointed for that purpose under the hand of the Governor, and of whose appointment shall be given in the Government Gazette...

This license would cost £2, 'to be appropriated in like manner as fees for the like license in England'.

These licenses issued by the church would replace the registration licenses issued by the registrar, although the couple marrying had to provide the same information that would otherwise have been provided to him. After the marriage, the Registrar-General would be provided with copies of all these special Church of England licenses. The new fee of £2 for each registration would belong to the church.

However, the right to issue licenses was not granted to the clergymen of other churches. Referring to these marriages, Clause 11 stated that every registrar had 'authority to grant licenses for marriage in any place of worship...or in his office...' provided that he did not attempt to issue any licenses to be used for any marriage according to the rites of the Church of England.

These legal changes pleased the dominant Anglicans in the colony, who had achieved two of their three major goals. They had returned the control of their marriage procedures to their clergy and had recovered some of their lost revenue. But they would continue to complain about the required presence of the registrar at the marriage ceremony.

Two other changes in Mackie's original bill were retained. A woman's age of consent was changed from eighteen to twenty-one years, effectively a greater restraint of her freedom.[242] Under another short act passed at the same time, the title of 'sub-registrar' was changed to 'registrar', with a 'Registrar-General' at the top of the hierarchy.[243]

This 1847 Solemnization of Marriage Act also dealt with the issue of the possible illegality of marriages conducted before the passage of the 1841 act. Clause 21 stated that 'all marriages celebrated in this colony before the passing of the said Act hereby repealed...shall be [deemed] valid...' This clause was intended to deal with the uncertainties that had arisen about the validity of marriages performed in the colony between 1836 and 1841.

During the discussion on the bill, William Mackie sensibly made the first reference to Jews and Quakers, in order to explain to people who were puzzled by the exemption of these two groups from the requirements of the bill. He explained that

> Quakers would not allow marriage to be considered as a sacrament, and always perform it in a private house, not at their place of worship; Jews did the same; and if parties were too poor, some richer person lent them the use of his house for the performance of the ceremony.[244]

As the debate on the marriage law finally drew to a conclusion, the Advocate-General, George Fletcher Moore, presented a long protest for insertion in the Legislative Council minutes, objecting to the new acts largely because they departed so radically from the laws of England. He identified himself as among those who supported most of the previously existing law introduced by Governor Hutt.[245]

As the proceedings in the Legislative Council on the new Marriage Act drew to a close, it became apparent that neither of the so-called 'ancient churches' represented in the colony were satisfied with the act. On 9 September, Bishop Brady of the Catholic Church protested to the Legislative Council members via a note handed on from the Colonial Secretary and also to the Governor in a letter addressed to the Colonial Secretary.[246] He stated that the Catholic Church would not be able to observe the enactments of the new marriage bill as several of them were contrary to the canons of the Roman Catholic Church, 'which canons were binding on the conscience of the members of that religion'.[247] He referred to the requirement to register a marriage as well as to the cost, and to the presence of the registrar at the marriage ceremony, claiming that these disabilities were pressing on Roman Catholics in a manner unknown in any other part of the British dominions. The Advocate-General described these claims as 'an untruth from beginning to end'.

Nor were the alternatives available to members of the Church of England in the new Marriage Act satisfactory to the more conservative members of its clergy, some of whom may have advised William Mackie on the original proposal. Reverend Wollaston expressed doubts about conducting marriages of couples with only a registrar's license, and without the declaration of banns. He wrote a letter to *The Inquirer* stating that there was a great difference between secular laws and rules and those imposed by ecclesiastical authority 'with which the Clergy have voluntarily bound themselves...'[248] He claimed that the clergy could not dissent from the 'Articles and Rubrics' of the church 'to the observance of which...we have solemnly pledged ourselves'.

Referring to his own experience, he said:

> I received English ordination, and I do not see how my removal to any other part of the world...can, of itself, be a sufficient excuse for my not adhering to solemn and deliberate engagements, as far as the altered circumstances in which I am placed will allow me. If, as is admitted, a faculty or license to the Clergy of the Church of England can be granted only by spiritual authority, and there is no such authority in the country, why should my scruples against the use of the Sub-Registrar's certificate or license be thought deserving of censure; especially since marriage is now made by law a civil contract, and there is no longer any necessity, in order to get legally married, to apply to the Church of which I am a minister?

In 1847, the dominant individuals of the colonial government decided to change the marriage law in a way they believed would restore both control of marriage practices and greater funding to the Church of England. All this was finally achieved by the passage of two acts amending the 1841 law.[249] By 9 September 1847, both the bills were finally passed in the Legislative Council, and the last clause of the Solemnization of Marriage Act stated that 'it would come into force on the first day of November next'.[250] The new act was set out in the *Perth Gazette* on 9 and 16 October, including the details from the schedules.

However, there was some administrative confusion, caused perhaps by the length of time that the matter was under discussion in the Legislative Council. It was not until 26 November 1847, that the public could read of the Acting Governor's declaration that the act was in force. The *Government Gazette* published his instructions concerning 'acts requiring to be done by persons desirous of solemnizing marriage after 1 November 1847, under the provisions of the new Marriage Act of Council, 10th Victoria, No. 18'.[251]

On 2 November 1847, the Registrar General, George Frederick Stone, wrote to the Colonial Secretary that, although the new Marriage Act had been declared to be in force, no registrar had been supplied with a copy of the act or with any printed forms. He was therefore unable to carry it into effect. He suggested two months' postponement in order to get necessary forms from the printer.[252] The first marriage using the new printed schedule occurred at the registrar's office in Fremantle on 14 December 1847. While many people still chose to marry in the registrar's office, there was an increase in the number of those who chose marriage by episcopal license in a Church of England.

During the next year, the written marriage-registration form differed quite widely. Sometimes it was the old form that was used, sometimes the new; occasionally the marriage celebrant cited the appropriate act. In spite of his protests, Bishop Brady found himself able to solemnise several marriages, which he recorded longhand, using no form at all.[253] In spite of the hostile debate about marriage laws, the clergy of all religions managed to accommodate themselves to the changes and marry their parishioners.

Several members of the government hierarchy, supporting the interests of the Church of England, tried to direct all the funds for Church of England marriage licenses into the hands of the church. After protest, the revised bill, passed by the Legislative Council, had reintroduced a registrar's certificate. But since the costs were the same, many Church of England members chose an episcopal license, thus providing a substantial sum for the church, since this religious group made up the majority in the population.

As a result, there were now three marriage acts on the statute books. These were the original Registration Act introduced by Governor Hutt in 1841, as well as the act containing amendments passed in 1847. The original Solemnization Act of 1841 was repealed and replaced by the Solemnization Act of 1847. Governor Fitzgerald arrived in August 1848 with instructions to change the marriage law to achieve 'the most perfect impartiality' between the different religions.

This attempt by dominant political figures to satisfy the clergy of the Church of England by returning most of the control of marriages to the church authorities, as was the case before Hutt's marriage acts of 1841, was apparently largely unpopular. In September 1848, the Registrar-General, George Frederick Stone, referred in very general terms to the popularity among all religious denominations of the system of registration, and the activity of the registrars. But he expressed deep regret that the useful working of the system should have been put to hazard by an alteration in the principles of the Marriage Act. In justice to the registration, and the gentlemen striving to carry out its details successfully, I would report that since the repeal of the original Marriage Act, and substitution of the present Ordinance, extreme dissatisfaction throughout the Colony is the marked result.[254]

The most conservative clergy of the Church of England, who were opposed to any 'secular intrusion' in the solemnisation of marriage, continued their objections. The Non-conformists opposed the new law because of the increased cost of marriage registration. But the strongest opposition now came from the Roman Catholics. By the middle of 1848, these opponents of the new legislation prepared to protest to Governor Fitzgerald, who was soon to arrive in the colony.

7

Towards a solution, 1849

The next two governors in Western Australia were from Protestant families in Ireland, following the pattern set by the wealthy settlers and powerful political figures from the time of first settlement. Governors Fitzgerald and Kennedy would dominate the political scene in the colony from 1848 until 1862. Governor Charles Fitzgerald, born and brought up in County Clare in Ireland, had risen from the position of cadet in the British Navy to command a ship engaged in the suppression of the slave trade. He had a period in office as the Lieutenant-Governor of the Gambia before his appointment to govern Western Australia. He arrived in August 1848 to confront the problem of an ailing economy in a colony of less than 5,000 settlers.

The ten years before Governor Fitzgerald's arrival had been a time of considerable economic and social dislocation. Many people joined in calling for the introduction of convicts, since one of the problems of the time concerned the shortage of labour. The growth of the economy had come to a halt and government revenue had dropped dramatically between 1842 and 1848. Religious tensions in the community had been fuelled by changes to the marriage law. The secretaries of state for the colonies must have been increasingly annoyed at the number of protests and memoranda sent to London by people in the colony representing various religious interests.

After the sudden departure of Richard Madden in January 1849, four men occupied the position of Colonial Secretary, before Frederick Barlee arrived with Governor Kennedy in 1855.[255] Barlee stayed in this position for twenty years, becoming increasingly powerful as a decision-maker, and responsible for organising an efficient colonial administration.

When Governor Fitzgerald arrived in August 1848, he received welcoming addresses from various groups in the community, each expressing the hope that their interests would receive his full consideration. These groups included the small Congregational Connexion, the Roman Catholics, the Wesleyans, and a group defining itself as 'We, the undersigned Magistrates, Clergy, Landholders, Gentlemen and others, inhabitants of the Swan Districts', presumably mostly those of the Church of England community.

The addresses were published in the *Government Gazette*, along with Governor Fitzgerald's placatory replies.[256] The address from Bishop Brady warned that the Roman Catholics had a problem in connection with the marriage laws:

> We reserve for a more fitting occasion an application to your Excellency on the subject of an existing grievance, which we labour under from the operation of the recent Marriage Act...[257]

In his replies to the welcoming addresses, Governor Fitzgerald made no immediate promises but, as soon to be revealed in the Legislative Council debates, he had been instructed to make further changes to the Western Australian marriage law.

From August 1848, Governor Fitzgerald, at first dependent on Richard Madden to write his letters, responded with great tolerance to the considerable correspondence of Bishop Brady, who was undoubtedly optimistic that Governor Fitzgerald would be more accommodating to the interests of the Roman Catholic Church than either Governor Clarke or Acting Governor Irwin. Brady began a long correspondence with the new Governor, asking for financial assistance for Catholic schools, for a stipend and for church-building money. He also wanted land for church buildings and cemeteries, and changes to the Marriage Act.[258]

Governor Fitzgerald's opening address to the members of the Legislative Council, and therefore to the people of Western Australia, was warmly approved by the editor of the *Perth Gazette*, who reported that the Governor 'gives evidence of his anxiety to promote the welfare of their country'.[259] For the first five years after 1850, he was responsible for the administration of the newly introduced convict system. Although the convicts were controlled by a separate administrative structure, the rapid population increase they entailed also led to a huge growth in the work of the colonial administration.

The British Government also agreed to pay the fares of an equal number of free settlers, and the first ten ships arrived before 1854.[260] There were doubts expressed at the time about the colony's capacity to employ all these people, many of them from the Poor Houses of England and Ireland. However, the decision was made to continue despatching them on the understanding that their support in the colony, if they could not be employed, would be paid for out of colonial revenue.[261] Governor Fitzgerald made decisions on a daily basis about the myriad problems of housing, food and employment for the new arrivals, all recorded in a vast correspondence.

Not long before the first convicts and assisted immigrants began to arrive, there was a curious report of an unusual marriage in England, which helped prepare the readers for the influx of immigrants. The following report appeared in *The Inquirer* in June 1849, entitled 'An Emigration Marriage':[262]

A young woman, aged 22, being taken ill of typhus, was removed to the workhouse at Devonport, where, by attention, she soon recovered. After her restoration to health, she expressed a desire to emigrate to Australia, if the guardians would advance the sum of £2 10s., which is necessary to be paid to the Emigration Society for outfit previous to sailing, and which money is returned to them on disembarking; and the guardians having received a most satisfactory character for her from the governor of the workhouse, they agreed to do so; and she accordingly went to the office to inquire about her passage.

Whilst waiting there, however, she was accosted by a respectable person, who asked her business, and if she were going to emigrate? She replied in the affirmative, when he rejoined, 'So am I; and if you have no objection, I'll marry you previous to sailing.'

She replied that she was obliged for the offer, but thought it was very extraordinary and premature, seeing that he knew nothing about her; upon which he remarked that he liked her honest countenance. At length, the matter was most seriously entertained, and she referred him to the service she had lately left. He at once started off to the address, and received such a satisfying character that, on returning, he immediately purchased the license, and the hasty couple were married on Christmas-day. It may be added, that previous to the wedding, he spent £20 for his wife's outfit, paid her passage, and returned the £2 10s. to the guardians, with many thanks.

In 1848, Earl Grey, the Secretary of State for the Colonies, repeated the earlier advice to Governor Hutt. He instructed the newly arrived Governor Fitzgerald

> that the most perfect impartiality should be exercised towards the adherents of different religions. I would again caution you against doing or permitting, as far as your influence extends, anything which might tend to increase the irritation against each other which unfortunately appears to exist in the minds of both Roman Catholics and of the Protestant members of the community.[263]

It was customary for laws passed by the Legislative Council to come into force in the colony before despatches had been received from the British Government notifying the colonial government that they had been either allowed or disallowed.[264] The news of the passage of the earlier 1847 Marriage Ordinance had taken a considerable time to reach London, and it was late 1848 before the reply from the Secretary of State for the Colonies was received. The act had already been in force for twelve months when it was disallowed by Earl Grey, the Secretary of State for the Colonies. By that time, Governor Fitzgerald had taken up his new position, his arrival on the *Trusty* reported on 12 August. It was to him that the letter of refusal was addressed.

The objections of Earl Grey to the 1847 Marriage Act did not consider any of the problems raised by critics in the colony, but concerned the issue of the validity of marriages performed in the period before the passage of the 1841 act. As explained earlier, the new English laws, passed in 1836 in England, and in force from 1837, allowed civil marriage, and required the appointment of a government registrar. These laws were not applied in the colony. It was therefore possible that some marriages conducted between late 1836 and 1841 might have been regarded as invalid, since the colony had previously followed English law in its conduct of marriages.

In his despatch, Earl Grey said that

the 21st clause of the Act No. 18, repealing the previous marriage ordinance of Western Australia, appears to be open to considerable objection.

It gives validity to all marriages celebrated in the Colony before the passing of the law which the Act No 18 has been framed to repeal 'in whatever form or place, and by whosoever, the same were solemnized', provided only that no lawful impediment existed at the time of the marriage.

This clause has probably been inserted to meet some particular cases and, with regard to these cases, may be just. But its language is so broad that it might be held to give the force of marriage to some actions, which do not in any degree deserve to be so legalised and might consequently be productive of very considerable injustice, by raising various questions as to the validity of regular marriages subsequently contracted by the same parties.

He wanted the clause altered before he could give his approval, during which time the Marriage Ordinance should be suspended.[265]

This despatch from London was dated 8 June 1848 and Governor Fitzgerald replied to it on 1 November 1848. However, we know that the 1847 act continued to be used because the marriage register sometimes recorded this act as the one under which a particular marriage was being conducted. One such example may be found in the marriage register on 6 May 1850.[266] The act was therefore in force from November 1847 until June 1850, when Governor Fitzgerald proclaimed his new Marriage Act. He chose to ignore the instruction to disallow the 1847 act, presumably because he needed time to prepare his new marriage law. He probably also wanted to avoid the confusion likely to arise if the 1841 marriage law was resurrected. The 1847 Marriage Act therefore survived from November 1847 until May 1850.

In November 1848, when Governor Fitzgerald replied to Earl Grey, acknowledging receipt of the despatch containing the objection to a clause of the existing marriage law, he signalled his intention to change the marriage law.

I beg to inform you that the present Ordinance enacted by my predecessor is one generally complained of by all denominations of Dissenters without exception. It is my intention to instruct the Advocate General to frame one placing all denominations of Christians precisely on equal terms, thus as I hope carrying out your Lordship's instructions, as to observing the most perfect impartiality to all denominations.[267]

Governor Fitzgerald now faced several related issues connected with the registration and celebration of marriage. He had to change the clause about the validity of previous marriages in the 1847 Solemnization of Marriage Act, as instructed by the Secretary of State for the Colonies, before it could be approved. But, as his letter to Earl Grey makes clear, he apparently intended to make other changes to satisfy members of the Catholic and Dissenting churches.

The correspondence before Governor Fitzgerald's arrival indicated that the Roman Catholics not only deplored the continuing preference of the colonial hierarchy for the Church of England, but also considered the requirement to pay registration fees and the presence of the Registrar at marriage ceremonies as 'unwarranted intrusions' by the colonial state. The Non-conformists regarded the additional registration fees as a means whereby colonial revenue could be increased, while more funds would flow to the Church of England from the introduction of the special Church of England license.

Local complaints about the unsatisfactory nature of the 1847 Marriage Act began soon after Fitzgerald's arrival in August 1848. In September, he received the first long letter on this subject from the Roman Catholic Bishop Brady, who was replying to a letter already sent to him by Governor Fitzgerald on 26 September, asking that he explain what he saw as the impediments for Roman Catholics in the marriage acts.[268]

The bishop set out what he called 'the objectionable clauses of the Marriage Acts', saying that he assumed the changes in 1847 were designed to remove the hardships and disabilities experienced by the Church of England and other denominations. But instead of removing these disabilities entirely, the new marriage bill took them off 'by exceptions and exemptions, and by imposing greater hardships and disabilities on another portion of the community'. In the following four pages of his letter, the bishop criticised seven specific clauses in the 1847 act.

Bishop Brady claimed that clauses 3, 4 and 5 made 'all publication of banns in the Catholic Church or even dispensation or a license granted by a Catholic Bishop or ordinary still null and void'.[269] Referring to his earlier experience, he explained that, under the law of New South Wales, all publications of banns, dispensations or anticipations of marriage were considered lawful and duly registered if under his signature as a missionary priest whereas, in Western Australia, no marriage could be conducted without a registrar's certificate.[270] He advised that Clause 14 should be reversed so that, as in New South Wales, the certificate of the bishop or clergyman officiating at the marriage would be exhibited to the Registrar-General, and not the other way around.

He referred also to the 'painful circumstance' on the occasion when Father Joostens married two people without realising that the registrar had to be present. It seemed particularly important to him that the presence of the registrar should no longer be required for marriage solemnisation, given the vast distances to be covered. His second objection was to Clause 11, which allowed any person to present themselves to the registrar for marriage 'regardless of their Christian duties'. In other words, the power of the Catholic Church over members of their flock could be subverted.

The bishop claimed that the Catholic ritual was different from that laid down in the act. He said that Clause 19, concerning the consent for marriage for persons under twenty-one years, was both ambiguous and injurious to the Catholic community, while clauses 24 and 27 were equally oppressive. He pointed out that the Church of England had been granted the right to solemnise marriages by banns and dispensations granted by its own clergy instead of by the registrar. These exceptions were not being granted to the Catholic Church. As a result, the Catholic priests would be considered guilty of felony if they proceeded according to the rites of their own church. The Governor replied first of all that he would use his best endeavours 'to remove all reasonable grounds of complaint'.[271]

In his reply, Brady refuted recent claims made by the registrar that his presence at the marriage ceremony would impart at least an appearance of order and decorum and would discourage clandestine marriages. Bishop Brady responded that neither of these claims 'had any connection with the Catholic Church'.[272] He was glad the registrar had admitted that his presence could be inconvenient and referred again to the practice in New South Wales, where the registrar relied on the certificate of marriage provided by the clergyman.

He referred again to Father Joostens' experience and named the married couple who had been fined for marrying without the presence of the registrar. If this could happen in Perth, 'at the seat of Government', how much worse might it be in the country, where it was so much more difficult to obtain the services of a registrar?

Before Bishop Brady had finished his correspondence with the Governor, the editor of *The Inquirer*, Arthur Shenton,[273] raised the issue of marriage legislation. He referred to the 1847 Marriage Act as even more unpopular than that of 1841, since all parties, 'whether Roman Catholics, Dissenters or Churchmen', viewed it with equal distrust. These religious bodies all had a prejudice in favour of marriage considered as a divine sacrament.

[I]t cannot be wondered that the trammelling of their rites by the introduction of civil forms and the intrusion of lay registrars, should have not met with so much indignation from every denomination of Christians.[274]

On 26 April 1849, on the occasion of the second reading of his new Marriage Solemnization Bill, Governor Fitzgerald told the Legislative Council members that he found much discontent prevailing on the subject of the Marriage Act among all sects but the established Church.

To the Roman Catholics, the presence of the Registrar was offensive in a religious point of view; with them marriage was a sacrament, and in extreme cases where parties had lived together without the performance of this rite, and one should be on a death-bed, the delay caused before the Registrar's presence could be obtained, and the marriage celebrated, might be attended with consequences fatal to the spiritual welfare of such parties; that was the opinion of the Church of Rome. The Wesleyans complained of the injustice of charging an extra forty shillings to all who were not members of the Church of England. The Independents considered they were indirectly compelled to support the Church establishment by paying marriage fees, and that moreover the high scale of these fees tended to discourage matrimony. To meet all these objections, and to preserve at the same time the secular advantages of registration, was the intention of the present bill.[275]

In this speech, Governor Fitzgerald did not mention any complaints from the dominant Anglican interests, perhaps because he had already negotiated with them concerning their major objections. While some of the clergy continued to deplore the collection of information by the registrar, and the payment of a registration fee, this problem had been largely resolved by the introduction in 1847 of a clergyman's license. In any case, they knew that the Governor was bound to support the work of the registrar, who collected statistical information for the government. This meant that the only remaining issue for the Anglican interests, if they could keep the existing clauses of the 1847 act, was the undesirable presence of the registrar at the marriage ceremony.

Governor Fitzgerald said that he had had a despatch from Lord Grey, Secretary of State for the Colonies, exhorting him to pay particular attention to the equalisation of all measures towards religious sects, and he considered that, if the offensive elements could be removed, it would tend to preserve peace and harmony among the community.[276]

Governor Fitzgerald now provided a rather unusual solution to all these disagreements. The 1847 Marriage Solemnization Act would remain in place for Church of England marriages. This meant that the Anglican clergy retained the right, introduced in 1847, to issue the registration license. In the new Registration Act, described below, the Governor no longer required the presence of the registrar at the marriage ceremony. To the satisfaction of most Anglicans, the Governor was limiting the so-called 'intrusions' of the colonial government into ecclesiastical marriage practices.

In addition to this, he introduced another Bill for Marriage Solemnization, referring only to those who were not members of the Church of England. Marriages could be conducted

> by a Priest or Minister of the Roman Catholic Church, duly empowered by his Superior, or by an Ordained Minister of the Presbyterian Church of Scotland, or by an Ordained Minister of the Wesleyan Methodist Society duly appointed by the British Conference of the Wesleyan Methodists, or by an ordained or officiating minister of the Congregational or Independent Denomination, or by an ordained or officiating minister of the Baptist Denomination...[277]

The Baptist and Independent celebrants had to be licensed on the basis of an overseas recommendation, because of the absence of local authorities in these denominations in Western Australia.[278] This was simply a restatement of the existing situation, granted originally by Governor Hutt in 1841.

The act also allowed the solemnisation of marriage before the provision of a registrar's license. The clergyman conducting the marriage had to write immediately to the registrar to certify that the marriage had taken place, and provide all the details of the parties involved, along with his own signature and the signatures of the marriage partners and witnesses.

Governor Fitzgerald also addressed the problem identified by the Secretary of State for the Colonies concerning the validity of marriages between 1836 and 1841 in a short separate act, which amended Clause 2 of the existing Solemnization Act. Earl Grey approved the change in a despatch sent in 1850, in which he referred 'to the clause I objected to now being dealt with by your clause 2'.[279] This clause, referring to the marriages solemnised between 1836 and 1841, allowed their legitimacy if they were 'followed by cohabitation and repute of marriage'.[280]

When the new Marriage Bill was presented to the Legislative Council, the clerk read a letter from the Roman Catholic bishop objecting to Clause 8 of the bill, allowing the registrar the right to sue for the cost of registration, still set at £2. Bishop Brady was less accommodating than most Anglicans, who had made some concessions about the secular requirements of the colonial government.

The bishop, still adamant about ecclesiastical laws, pointed out that the church was forbidden by the Council of Trent from exacting any money for the

> Sacrament of Marriage…The reason for such a general rule is first, that no obstacle or impediment be thrown in the way, to prevent the contracting parties from receiving the nuptial blessing and grace attached to the sacrament; secondly, in order to prevent unlawful unions; and thirdly, in favour of the poor.

He said that the members of the church were generally of the poorer class of people, and did not have the means to pay the cost of registration. Added to this, the district registrar might be at a great distance, when parties to a marriage might be anxious to avail themselves of the passing visit of a priest in the most distant districts. It would be, then, a very hard case if the bishop, or any of the clergy, was called upon to confer the sacrament of matrimony and to recall certain parties to their duties, and could not proceed without having obtained a license or a receipt for registrar's fees — what an awful predicament! 'The priest would have to sacrifice the sacred duties of his ministry — for the temporary advantage of a Registrar's fee'.[281] The Catholic Church was still objecting to the cost of registration, and the presence of a registrar at the ceremony, a requirement soon to be removed.

An amended version of the Marriage Registration Act was introduced immediately in a third bill. This act repeated the instruction that ministers who solemnised a marriage now had to sign certificates providing the details of the marriage, also to be signed by the parties to the marriage. One copy was to be sent to the district registrar. In this act, it was stated clearly that the registrar was no longer required to attend the ceremony. The minister was entitled to receive a fee for his work, quite apart from the cost of registration.[282]

Naturally, the records of marriages were entered into the government registers in the English language, but a separate record was kept by local parishes for their private archives. The Catholic priests at New Norcia, for example, recorded the details in Latin, and these included some marriages between persons of European and Aboriginal descent.[283]

Although they were passed in May 1849, these three new acts were not proclaimed until 13 June 1850, after approval from the Colonial Office in London.[284] Governor Fitzgerald's intervention to change the marriage laws was timely and satisfying to most of the dissenting Protestants, and even the Roman Catholics managed to accustom themselves to the cost of registration. Although they had been able to avoid marriage in the Church of England since 1841, neither church had ever previously been named in a Marriage Act.

In April 1849, Brady thanked the Governor for his new bill 'designed to obviate for the future any further difficulties which the former Acts placed in the way'.[285] Three days later, he blessed the Governor and thanked him for 'his kind manner of expression'.[286] But when he had time to read the new bill more carefully, it still proved unsatisfactory. In another letter on the same day, Bishop Brady objected to Clause 8, repeating his earlier claim that it would place the Catholic clergy in a difficult position if the registrar's fees had to be paid before the marriage. He wanted this requirement removed, since it was an obstruction to the sacrament and because he wanted to prevent unlawful unions and act in favour of the poor.[287] The Governor assured him that the changes he wanted made had already been included in the new bill, referring obviously to the right of the clergyman to inform the registrar after the marriage had taken place.[288]

A few days later, Bishop Brady found something else 'derogatory to the Catholic priesthood' in the new bill. This was a reference to marriages being deemed to be of the same force as those conducted by the Church of England. He suggested a new form of words that did not imply some special status for the Church of England. He also sent the Governor a copy of the marriage certificate he wanted to be allowed to use.[289]

The Governor was now becoming impatient with this renewed criticism. He pointed out that Bishop Brady had advised him that the New South Wales act was worthy of his consideration, yet now the bishop was critical of the use of words which were also contained in that act. He said that in the new act all religious denominations would be placed on the same footing as the 'established church'.[290]

Clearly, the new act, referring to the conduct of marriages by clergy who were not members of the Church of England, allowed them to perform the service without first obtaining a license and without the presence of the registrar. However, the registration fee, whether provided beforehand or charged after the marriage, remained £2. There were no new cost schedules printed in any of the acts passed by Governor Fitzgerald.

Governor Fitzgerald went a long way to satisfy the complaints of the Catholic Church, although the costs remained the same. However, his retention of the 1849 act, as it referred to Anglicans, suggests that he believed that the Church of England, as the 'established church' in the colony, had some priority over the other denominations. In retrospect, the muddled nature of the solutions he provided cast doubt on his claims to establish 'perfect impartiality' between all the denominations in the marriage law.

Governor Fitzgerald may also have added to perceptions of bias in favour of the Church of England, perhaps even giving weight to the argument that it was treated like the 'established church', when he passed an ordinance to regulate the temporal affairs of the Church of England.[291] This act was framed by Archdeacon Wollaston to provide for the management of each Anglican Church in the colony, by appointing 'trustees elected by the parishioners, and assuring each incumbent a dwelling place, garden and glebe'.[292]

Governor Fitzgerald provided £20 each for Catholic schools in 1851 and, in the following year, he provided grants for schoolmasters in these schools. However, he responded with reluctance to calls in 1851 for more equal treatment for clergymen. He granted only £50 each to the Wesleyan minister, Reverend Smithies, and to the Roman Catholic Bishop Brady.[293] By this time, Wittenoom's salary had risen to £350, and the other four Church of England clergymen were receiving £100 in financial support from the colonial government. However, these relatively smaller sums may have been decided in light of the small number of Wesleyans and Catholics in the community.

Apart from Bishop Brady's belated correspondence, there were few criticisms of Governor Fitzgerald's marriage acts, perhaps because of the growing interest in the problems to be faced by the colony with the coming of convicts and assisted immigrants. These issues began to dominate the columns of the local newspapers. But two objections to the marriage acts appeared in the last part of 1849. The first was a letter to *The Inquirer* by someone signing himself 'an Independent', who claimed that Baptists and Independents 'were stigmatised' in the Solemnization of Marriage Act, made for those who were not members of the Church of England.[294] This was a reference to the fact that, before a couple from one of these groups could marry, they had to obtain evidence from England that their chosen minister was ordained.

Another long protest came in the form of an editorial comment from the editor of *The Inquirer*, Arthur Shenton, a member of the Church of England, but capable of considerable detachment. The author referred 'to the extreme simplicity and comprehensiveness' of the English Marriage Act of 1836, which allowed civil marriage and introduced compulsory registration.[295] He contrasted this act with the colonial act of 1849,

> that precious result of the labours of our legislators, who, having passed, amended, or repealed diverse Acts, each attempt being more confused and contradictory than its predecessor, at last retired from their labours with an air of the most placid content, leaving, as an apple of discord, an Act in whose provisions confusion worse confounded reigned supreme; understood by none, disliked by all, productive of inconvenience in its immediate working, and the culpable cause of future mischief, it stands the luckless monument of Western Australia's legislatorial folly.[296]

Among other things, he revisited the earlier appeal to Governor Clarke that all clergymen should act as registrars. He was also critical of the confusion apparent in the use of different marriage certificates. This confusion was certainly visible in the marriage register at this time, presumably because new forms had not been prepared before the law was declared to be in force.

Arthur Shenton's comments were soon shown to be justified. The complex marriage laws, proclaimed on 18 June 1850, were an administrative nightmare. The 1841 Registration Act remained in place although amended by two new acts, one in 1847 and one in 1849. The Solemnization Act of 1847 remained in place for the solemnisation of marriages by the Church of England, although one other brief and separate amendment to this 1847 Solemnization Act clarified the issue raised by the Secretary of State for the Colonies, Earl Grey, concerning the legitimacy of earlier marriages. A new solemnisation of marriage law had also been introduced especially for those who were not members of the Church of England. This meant that there were now six laws still in place covering the issues of the registration and solemnisation of marriage.[297]

In spite of confusion over the marriage laws, Governor Fitzgerald had apparently achieved general approval from the public during his period in office. Before he left the colony in July 1855, he received several positive memorials. His reply to one of these reflected his personal satisfaction with his work as Governor. He said it was

> a source of much pleasure to me that, although on my arrival I found every interest in the colony in a state of great depression, nevertheless I leave it rapidly advancing in every element of prosperity, and free from those difficulties which embarrassed the first 21 years of its existence.[298]

The confusion now surrounding the marriage law would be successfully resolved by Governor Kennedy, who followed Governor Fitzgerald in 1855. The dominance of the Church of England was about to be undermined.

abroad, determinable at the pleasure of His Majesty, or any of His Majesty's Heirs and Successors, shall, by reason of any future demise of the Crown, be vacated, or become void, until the expiration of eighteen Calendar months next after any such demise of the Crown as aforesaid.

By His Excellency's command,
PETER BROWN,
Colonial Secretary.

Colonial Secretary's Office, Perth,
November 18, 1837.

TENDERS in Triplicate will be received at this Office on Friday next, the 24th Instant, for the supply of the undermentioned Victualling Stores, required for the use of His Majesty's Colonial Schooner *Champion*. The Stores to be delivered, at the risk and expence of the Contractors, on the deck of the *Champion*, and to be subject to the approval of her Commander :—

(25) Twenty-five lbs. of Tea.
(8) Eight gallons of Vinegar.
(41) Forty-one gallons of Rum.
(44) Forty-four gallons of Peas.
(116) One hundred and sixteen lbs. of Sugar.

By His Excellency's command,
PETER BROWN,
Colonial Secretary.

Colonial Secretary's Office, Perth,
November 18, 1837.

HIS Excellency the Governor directs that the following Table of Precedency, which has been ordered to be observed in Her Majesty's Colonial Possessions, should be published for general information :—

1. The Governor, or Lieutenant Governor, or Officer administering the Government.
2. The Lieutenant Governor (not administering the Government), or the senior Officer Commanding the Troops, if he is to succeed to the Administration of the Government in case of the death or absence of the Governor, Lieutenant Governor, or Officer administering the Government. In the event of hostilities, the senior Officer in Command of the Troops will take this Precedency, under any circumstances.
3. The Bishop.
4. The Chief Justice.
5. The Members of the Executive Council. Their relative precedency, amongst themselves, is established in each case by His Majesty's "Instructions" to the Governors of Colonies.

6. The President of the Legislative Council.
7. The Members of the Legislative Council.
8. The Speaker of the House of Assembly.
9. The Puisné Judges.
10. The Members of the House of Assembly.
11. The Colonial Secretary (not being in the Executive Council.)
12. The Commissioners or Government Agents of Provinces or Districts.
13. The Attorney-General.
14. The Solicitor General.
15. The senior Officer in Command of the Troops, except in cases already provided for.
16. The Archdeacon.
17. The Treasurer, Paymaster-General, or Collector of Internal Revenue
18. The Auditor General or Inspector General of Accounts
19. The Commissioner of Crown Lands
20. The Collector of Customs
21. The Comptroller of Customs
22. The Surveyor-General

(17–22 bracketed: not being Members of Executive Council.)

23. Clerk of the Executive Council.
24. Clerk of the Legislative Council.
25. Clerk of the House of Assembly, &c., &c., &c.
26. In Courts for the Trial of Piracy, the Members to take rank according to the order in which they are designated in His Majesty's Commission; except in the case of the Naval Commander-in-Chief (where there is one), to whom, as matter of curtesy, the Chair, on the right of the President of the Court, is assigned.

By His Excellency's command,
PETER BROWN,
Colonial Secretary.

Colonial Secretary's Office, Perth,
November 18, 1837.

HIS Excellency the Governor is pleased to direct it to be notified, for general information, that the accession of Her present Gracious Majesty Queen ALEXANDRINA VICTORIA to the Throne of the United Kingdom of Great Britain and Ireland and its Dependencies, will be proclaimed, in front of the Government House, Perth, on Monday next, the 20th instant, at 1 o'Clock P. M.; where, and at which time, all Civil and Military Officers, as well as the Inhabitants generally, are directed to give their attendance.

By His Excellency's command,
PETER BROWN,
Colonial Secretary.

Colonial Secretary's Office, Perth,
November 18, 1837.

BY accounts which have been received from England, the Governor has been apprised of the demise of

Governor Stirling's 'Table of Precedency', published in the Western Australian *Government Gazette*, 18 November 1837, p. 130.

Marriages at Fremantle

17 Edward Wood of Fremantle Bachelor and Rose Read of Fremantle Spinster were married at Fremantle by Licence this Twentieth day of May 1839 by me
J.B. Wittenoom Colonial Chaplain

This Marriage was solemnized between us
In the presence of us

- Edward Wood
- Rose her X mark Read
- J. Duffield
- M. A. Pengilly
- S.K. Pengilly

18 John Davis of Fremantle Bachelor and Eleanor Frances Thomson of Fremantle Spinster were married at Fremantle this Seventeenth day of February 1840 by me
J.B. Wittenoom Colonial Chaplain

This Marriage was solemnized between us
In the presence of us

- John Davis
- Ellen F. Thomson
- John H. Stockpole
- C.L. A. Thomson
- Adelaide Thomson

19 William Owen of Fremantle Bachelor & Adelaide Thomson of Fremantle Spinster were married at Fremantle by Licence this eleventh day of April 1840 by me
J.B. Wittenoom Colonial Chaplain

This Marriage was solemnized between us
In the presence of us

- William Owen
- Adelaide Thomson
- S. Curtis
- A. Glindon
- E. Back

20 William Samson of Perth Bachelor and Elizabeth Mary Pace of Fremantle Spinster were married at Fremantle by Licence this Eighteenth day of June 1840 by me
J.B. Wittenoom Colonial Chaplain

This Marriage was solemnized between us
In the presence of us

- W. Samson
- E. M. Pace
- George R.
- W. H. Sholl
- J. S. Roe
- C.H. Bland
- W. B. Andrews

An example of marriage records kept by the Church of England between 1830 and 1841.

In the Year of Our Lord 1839–42

21. John O'Connor Corporal in Her Majesty's 21st Regiment Bachelor & Judith Ryan of Perth Spinster were married by me at Fremantle this twenty first day of July 1840

Revd M. B. Brown H. Govt Resident

This Marriage was solemnized between us

In the presence of us

J. G. O'Connor Corpl 21st Rt.
Judith her X mark Ryan
John Haggarty
J. R. Pengilly

---

22. Henry Chapman of the Basse River, Bachelor & Amelia Glindon of Fremantle, Spinster were married at Fremantle by Licence this thirtieth day of December 1840 by me

J. B. Wittenoom Colonial Chaplain

This Marriage was solemnized between us

In the presence of us

Henry Chapman
Amelia Glindon
Anthony Curtis
Susannah Curtis
Edwd Back
William Owen
Wm S. Rogers

---

23. William Horatio Sholl of Perth Bachelor & Jane Crocker of Perth Spinster were married at Fremantle by Licence this seventeenth day of March 1841 by me

J. B. Wittenoom Colonial Chaplain

This Marriage was solemnized between us

In the presence of us

Wm H. Sholl
Jane Crocker
Revd M. B. Brown
Lionel Samson

---

24. Francis Helpman of Fremantle Bachelor & Anne Pace of Fremantle Spinster were married in Fremantle Church by Licence this fourteenth day of December 1842 by me

G. King

This Marriage was solemnized between us

In the presence of us

Frank Helpman
Ann Pace
Revd M. B. Brown
W. Samson

See number 21: Marriage by the Government Resident at Fremantle.

The second Wesley Church on the corner of Murray Street, Perth, partly funded by the colonial government. The foundation stone was laid on 30 December 1840 and the church was completed by the end of 1841. Courtesy the Battye Library and Perth City Council

An early sketch of St John's Roman Catholic Church in Victoria Avenue, Perth, partly funded by the colonial government. The foundation stone was laid on 16 January 1844 and the church was completed in 1845. Often called the pro-cathedral, the church now has a front door. Courtesy the Archives of the Roman Catholic Archdiocese of Perth

The old Anglican Cathedral, Perth, partly funded by the colonial government. The foundation stone was laid on 6 January 1841 and the church was opened on 22 January 1845. The church was consecrated by Bishop Short in 1848. Courtesy the Battye Library

The Courthouse and Gaol built in Beaufort Street, Perth, first used in 1857, part of which has been incorporated into the museum complex. Courtesy the Battye Library

The back of the original Supreme Court building of 1837, showing the additions built in the 1860s. Courtesy the Battye Library

Marriage Regulations.

The Clergy are desired to note the following facts in reference to Marriages :—

1. The Church of England recognises Divorce for one cause only, viz., infidelity to the marriage vow.

2. The authority of the Clergy to celebrate marriages rests upon the fact that they are licensed by the Bishop to do so in accordance with the rites of the Church of England.

3. The being placed upon the list of the Registrar-General is necessary only to secure recognition of the marriage as a civil contract.

4. Clergymen are bound to act in accordance with the laws and customs of the Church in the celebration of marriages.

The Bishop has therefore framed the following Regulations for guidance of the Clergy :—

1. Under no circumstances can the guilty party in a divorce suit be re-married during the lifetime of the other party to the marriage.

2. In the case of the innocent party wishing to re-marry, application must be made to the Bishop for his permission, and no such marriage shall be allowed without the license of the Bishop to that effect. Such license will only be issued when evidence sufficient to satisfy the Bishop that the party is innocent has been submitted to him.

3. The Holy Communion shall not be administered to the guilty party in a divorce suit, his (or her) evil living being open and notorious, until the said party shall have declared himself (or herself) to have truly repented and amended his (or her) former life.

4. The Holy Communion shall not be administered to the guilty party in a divorce suit who has re-married during the lifetime of the other party, except after an openly avowed repentance.

5. Marriages shall be celebrated by the Clergy only in Churches and rooms licensed for the holding of services, excepting where no such building is within five miles of the residence of one of the parties wishing to be married.

Marriage regulations concerning the remarriage of divorced persons. Taken from the The Year Book for 1897, Anglican Diocese of Perth, p. 59.

Western Australia.

ANNO QUINQUAGESIMO QUINTO

VICTORIÆ REGINÆ.

❊❊

No. XX.

AN ACT to amend the Law relating to the Property of Married Women.

[Assented to, 18th March, 1892.]

WHEREAS it is desirable to amend the law of Property and Contract with respect to Married Women: Be it enacted by the Queen's most Excellent Majesty, by and with the advice and consent of the Legislative Council and the Legislative Assembly of Western Australia, in this present Parliament assembled, and by the authority of the same, as follows: — Preamble.

1. (1.) A MARRIED woman shall, in accordance with the provisions of this Act, be capable of acquiring, holding, and disposing by will or otherwise of any real or personal property as her separate property, in the same manner as if she were a feme sole, without the intervention of any trustee. — Married woman to be capable of holding property and of contracting as a feme sole.

2. EVERY woman who marries after the commencement of this Act shall be entitled to have and to hold as her separate property and to dispose of in manner aforesaid all real and personal property which shall belong to her at the time of marriage, or shall be acquired by or devolve upon her after marriage, including any wages, earnings, money, and property gained or acquired by her in any employment, trade, or occupation in which she is engaged, or which she carries on separately from her husband, or by the exercise of any literary, artistic, or scientific skill. — Property of a woman married after the Act to be held by her as a feme sole.

Western Australian Statute 55 Vict., no. 20, 1892, 'An Act to amend the Law relating to the Property of Married Women'.

8

Marriage problems settled, 1856

Governor Kennedy, who followed Fitzgerald in July 1855, was born in County Down, Ireland, and educated at Trinity College, a Protestant university in Dublin attended earlier by George Fletcher Moore. He had been an army officer, a poor law inspector in Ireland, and Governor of the Gambia and Sierra Leone. Governor Kennedy arrived in the ship the *Avalanche* in late July 1855, and was welcomed with a seventeen-gun salute at Fremantle and a celebratory meal with local dignitaries at the local Francisco's Hotel,[299] events that had been arranged beforehand.[300] His predecessor had not yet left the colony and was being praised and farewelled at this time by various groups in the community.[301]

By the time Governor Kennedy took over from Governor Fitzgerald, the most chaotic period caused by the introduction of convicts had passed. The first of over 9,000 convicts arrived in 1850 and the last ship carrying this human cargo arrived in 1868. The government also paid the fares of more than 7,000 free immigrants, many of them single women, as well as many large families, all expected to work for their living.

Like his predecessor, Kennedy was deeply involved with the administration of the convicts with ticket-of-leave status, who worked in the community under local administration. He was active in concentrating the new convict workforce in the area around Perth, putting them to work on building roads, draining swamps and also beginning work on the first stages of Government House on St George's Terrace. He resolved several problems involving serious mismanagement and fraud at various levels of government, assisted by the new Colonial Secretary, Frederick Barlee, who had been his private secretary in

Sierra Leone. Kennedy remained in Western Australia as Governor until February 1862.

When Governor Fitzgerald left the colony in 1855, the population was growing dramatically and the number of Roman Catholics in the community had increased more rapidly than any other religious group. In 1848, the census recorded a total settler population of 4,622 people, of whom 406 were members of the Roman Catholic faith. By 1859, the total population had risen to 9,942, while the Catholic worshippers now numbered 3,354.[302] The balance of the population had gradually shifted away from the dominance of a few families with their indentured workers. By the time Governor Kennedy left the colony, the majority of the population consisted of convicts, ex-convicts and recently arrived immigrants.

Governor Kennedy's introduction and passage of new marriage laws was much less problematic than it had been for earlier governors. This was partly because the main political interests of the population had shifted considerably, due to the vast changes occurring in the economic and social life of the colony. The absence of major problems connected with changes to the marriage law may also have been due very largely to the absence by this time of so many of the key figures in earlier debates.

The two most influential Church of England clergymen during those years had been John Burdett Wittenoom, Colonial Chaplain from 1829, and Reverend John Ramsden Wollaston, who was appointed Archdeacon in 1849. Wittenoom died in 1855[303] and Wollaston in the following year.[304] The new Church of England Colonial Chaplain was George Purvis Pownall, who had been appointed originally as one of the clergymen to service the convicts, and had been living at York. The first Church of England Bishop, Matthew Blagden Hale, did not arrive in the colony until January 1858.[305]

The Roman Catholic Church went through a period of upheaval at this time. John Brady, Roman Catholic Bishop, remarkable for his constant correspondence aimed at promoting Roman Catholic interests, left the colony permanently in 1852, after a period of intense conflict with his Coadjutor-Bishop, Dom Joseph Serra. Bishop Serra was then absent from the colony from 1853 due to ill health, leaving Rosendo Salvado as Coadjutor-Bishop of Perth. Serra returned in January 1855 but left permanently in 1859, when his place was taken by Martin Griver as administrator. Griver had been in the colony since 1849.

Reverend John Smithies of the Wesleyan Church, who had been one of the most outspoken critics of government policy concerning earlier marriage laws, left the colony and settled in Van Diemen's Land in early 1855.

The political landscape had also changed in dramatic fashion before the arrival of Governor Kennedy. Frederick Irwin, Commandant of the Armed Forces since 1829, and twice holding the position of Acting Governor, left the colony and returned to England in 1852. In the same year, George Fletcher Moore, a powerful figure from the time of first settlement, also left for England, because of the illness of his wife. Richard West Nash, a leading member of the Church of England, left the colony in 1849 and died in London in the following year.

Other key figures in the Legislative and Executive councils died in the colony around this time. George Leake, who was the first director of the Western Australian Bank and an appointed member of the councils from 1837, died in Perth in 1849. Henry Sutherland, Colonial Treasurer and Collector of Revenue, died in 1855. At the first meeting of the Legislative Council in 1856, when the new marriage bills were passed, only two of the old guard, John Septimus Roe and William Mackie, were still present. A powerful member of the Church of England, and the Commissioner of the Civil and Criminal Courts, William Mackie retired soon after the arrival of Governor Kennedy, and died in 1860.

Not long after Kennedy's arrival in July 1855, the issue of the marriage laws resurfaced. Governor Kennedy repealed the previous registration and solemnisation of marriage laws by passing two new acts, which would remain in force for nearly forty years. In the Legislative Council debate, Governor Kennedy, in his introduction, stated that the new bill had been taken mainly from the one passed in New South Wales in the previous year, with other colonies also following instructions from England. In retrospect, the new Solemnization Act seemed to provide satisfactory solutions to all the recent criticisms.

However, there was one continuing problem. During the discussion of the bill, Marshall Clifton, one of the members of the Legislative Council, suggested that the bill be delayed until the expected appointment in the colony of a Church of England bishop. He claimed that, if the bill became law, the Church of England would face particular difficulties over the requirement to publish banns before marriage. Perhaps he was hoping to retain the Church of England privileges, contained in both the 1847 and

1849 marriage acts, allowing the Church of England clergy to issue their own marriage licenses, an alternative process to the publication of banns. Governor Kennedy's bill removed these special rights, and the marriage procedures were to revert to the original practice of declaring banns.

Marshall Clifton said that

> a Roman Catholic Priest for instance might celebrate a marriage within a few hours after application and for a small fee, while a clergyman of the Church of England could only do so after the publication of Banns...[306]

To avoid this delay, a member of the Church of England had to go to the expense of obtaining a license and being married by a registrar. This meant, according to Clifton, that although the marriage was valid, there was no 'religious solemnity' surrounding the event.

The Colonial Secretary, Frederick Barlee, replied that the object of the bill was to put the Church of England on the same footing as the other denominations except as to banns, 'and he much doubted if a Bishop had the power to alter in that respect'. William Mackie, Commissioner of the Civil Court, who had not yet retired from office, supported Frederick Barlee. He claimed that the requirement of banns rested on ecclesiastical law, 'which the Bishop had no power to alter'.

There was no serious public discussion of marriage laws in the local press before the passage of the new bills in June 1856. The editor of the *Perth Gazette* only recorded that the marriage bills under consideration appeared 'simply to consolidate the Law on the subject'.[307] The editor of *The Inquirer* made some brief, critical comments about the increased severity of the penalties for not recording births and deaths according to the law, but made no mention of marriages.[308]

The Solemnization of Marriage Bill was passed with the detail consolidated into one act. The new act was radical in one respect, in that there was no mention of any Christian denomination, since all rules now applied equally to everyone except Quakers and Jews. Any minister of religion could solemnise a marriage as long as he was registered in the colony.

At the same time, the next Registration Ordinance was introduced by Governor Kennedy, repealing previous ordinances[309] and setting out the rules to be followed in much more detail. The Governor could now appoint assistant district registrars, which would help to avoid the delays that worried Marshall Clifton, while duplicate copies of local registers had now to be sent to the Registrar-General. A schedule of fees chargeable by all registrars was set out.

Another important change was that the Registrar-General was now required to list the names of all ministers of religion desiring to be registered to celebrate marriages. In order to inform the public, these names were to be listed annually in the *Government Gazette*.[310] Both these acts were passed by the Legislative Council on 12 June 1856 and became law on 1 August of that year. Governor Kennedy felt confident that they would receive the approval of the Secretary of State for the Colonies.

The new acts dealt indirectly with many of the issues causing earlier conflict. The process of marriage registration had been the most frequent source of conflict. The new acts declared that, before marriage, the participants had to sign a declaration either before the registrar, or before the minister of religion, claiming that they knew of no impediment to their marriage (Schedule D).[311] The age of marriage without a parent's consent had been fixed at eighteen years for a woman and twenty-one years for a man in the first colonial Marriage Act of 1841. This was changed to twenty-one years for both men and women in 1847, and this age was retained in all subsequent Western Australian marriage acts in the nineteenth century.

If people objected to being married by a Christian minister, they could be married by the district registrar in the area where they normally resided. In this case, they also had to sign a declaration that they objected to being married by a minister of religion (Schedule B). The cost of the actual marriage service by a registrar was £2. At the end of the marriage ceremony, the participants and the person who conducted the ceremony all signed the document known as the Certificate of Marriage (Schedule E).

The Registration Act, Clause 28, clarified the issue of cost, the cause of much agitation in previous marriage law, making clear that the charges imposed by the various churches would not concern the government. But

> nothing herein contained shall affect, or be deemed or construed to affect, the right of any officiating minister to receive the fees usually paid for the performance of any religious rite of baptism, burial or marriage. [312]

In other words, the churches could make their own rules about the costs of a marriage service. Quakers and Jews, first mentioned in marriage law in

Western Australia in the 1847 Marriage Act, were again declared exempt from some of the main clauses of the ordinance and could marry according to their own practices, but their marriages had to be registered.

The cost of marriage registration had been a central issue in all previous debates about changes to the marriage laws. This had been raised from ten shillings in Hutt's first Marriage Act in 1841 to £2 in 1847. Governor Fitzgerald had made no change to this cost in 1849. The cost of registration to be paid to the government was now returned to the 1841 cost of ten shillings, as clearly set out in the schedules at the end of the Registration of Births, Deaths and Marriages Act.

Governor Kennedy's acts of 1856 obliged everyone to pay the registration costs to the registrar before marriage, without any concessions to members of the Church of England who, after 1847, had become accustomed to paying the registration fee to the church. Apart from the charge of £2 if the registrar conducted the marriage ceremony, the registration fee of ten shillings was the only government charge imposed for marriage in a church or private house. (The Governor was given the power to issue special licenses to allow a marriage in a private house.) This settled the question of registration costs for the rest of the century.

Governor Kennedy became increasingly unpopular at this time because of the passage of several laws including one limiting the distillation and sale of liquor, which annoyed sections of the local community, who organised a meeting of protest. The Governor wrote two long letters to the Colonial Secretary, claiming that the sale of liquor 'had grown to be a monstrous evil, neutralizing all reformatory measures'.[313] He also claimed that the protesters were mainly ex-convicts and that he did not think that 'educated men in the Colony would advocate change to the Legislative Council'.[314] He was accused of abusing his power, and calls were made for the introduction of a more representative government.[315] Governor Kennedy conveyed these wishes to the Secretary of State for the Colonies in London, asking whether the representation in the Legislative Council could be increased. Henry Labouchere, who was now the Secretary of State, answered that he was 'not disposed at present to increase the number of members'.[316]

But no major protests were levelled at the new marriage acts. It has been claimed that Kennedy's attempts to exercise greater control over public revenue, and over the supervision of the increasing number of convicts

in the community, made him generally unpopular.[317] However, it must
be assumed that the new marriage acts of 1856, introduced by Governor
Kennedy, were welcomed by most sections of the community. They were
not only decisive in ending the confusion surrounding the law, they also
finally ended the dominance of the Church of England in the marriage
practices of the Colony of Western Australia.

These laws would remain in place until the 1890s, by which time some
new marriage laws had been passed in England. The number of marriages
recorded in 1856 reveals that those of Catholic religious persuasion now
exceeded those of the Church of England, as this table shows.

Western Australian marriages, 1856

Church of England	27
Roman Catholic	29
Wesleyan	20
Independent	14
Married by the district registrar	9
Total	99

The difficulties faced by many married people would soon be transformed by the introduction after 1863 of divorce laws, and laws affecting
the distribution of property, the custody of children and the provision
of financial support. These changes in the law reflected changes made in
England and were introduced following instructions to colonial governors.
The social transformations in England leading to these changes were not
being experienced in the same way in the Colony of Western Australia,
nor necessarily understood by the colonial population.

Before considering the divorce law in detail, it is necessary to try to
understand the experiences of many unfortunate married women in colonial
Western Australia. While many marriages were recorded in the diaries and
letters of the early settlers, these accounts usually stressed the difficulties
of establishing homes rather than questions of domestic harmony. In the
nineteenth century, these personal subjects were not normally topics for
public discussion.[318]

We know that, in the difficult circumstances of early settlement, some
of the poorer families were unable to fend for themselves. One of the
first ordinances in the colony, defined simply as 'an enactment by a local

authority', was that of 1845, 'to provide for the Maintenance of and relief of Deserted Wives and Children, and other Destitute Persons...'[319] This ordinance, introduced by Governor Hutt, was believed to be necessary because of the growing evidence of destitution in the small community, and because of the government's very limited revenue from which to provide for the poor. It was also the case that the usual pattern of extended families had been greatly disturbed by the process of emigration to Western Australia, so that it was often difficult to establish family relationships.

The all-embracing nature of the 1845 ordinance was apparent in the first clause, which stated that

> in the case of every poor and destitute person, not able to work, his or her father or grandfather, mother or grandmother, and children, being of sufficient ability, shall at their own charges relieve and maintain every such destitute person...

The amount of relief to be provided to a destitute person by a relative was to be decided after an assessment by two justices of the peace. These justices were given the right to summon people and order them to provide support. If they proved recalcitrant, they could be fined or imprisoned. According to the colonial law of 1845, husbands were bound to support their wives and children, but the distances between colonies and the poor systems of communication made it difficult to enforce the law. It was also the case that the problem of family poverty was exacerbated if men were imprisoned for failing to obey this law.

This 1845 act also tackled the complex issue concerning the legal status of children and whether they were legitimate or illegitimate. The act made fathers responsible for the support of their so-called 'bastard' children, and obliged them to contribute sums of money for their welfare. In the second half of the century, there were several other acts especially designed to prevent the destitution of unmarried mothers and their illegitimate children.

The population imbalance in the Colony of Western Australia left many men in an anxious search for a wife. With the introduction after 1850 of male convicts and free immigrants, many of them women, there are accounts of men choosing a wife from one of the immigrant ships and marrying her immediately. These immigrant women had no personal resources and many of them undoubtedly hoped that such a marriage would provide security, and the opportunity to have a home and a family. In some instances, they ended up among the many women who had to seek government poor relief for themselves and their children, sometimes requiring entry into the women's poor house.[320]

For the last half of the century, a large part of the cost of poor relief went to support women who were married but reduced to destitution, usually with several children to support. There were several clearly identifiable reasons why a woman might seek government assistance, especially if she could not leave her small children to go out to work. If a husband died, was put in prison or was unemployed, the provision of poor relief was essential for survival. There was no other government welfare system operating at this time, and most women had no relatives in the colony. The Colonial Secretary also received many appeals for poor relief from women whose husbands had deserted them, in many cases leaving Western Australia for other colonies. This was especially so after the discovery of gold in Victoria in the 1850s.

But the worst outcome of marriage for many women was the experience of domestic violence. The extent of such violence is difficult to determine since there were relatively few cases brought before the courts. According to English law, women had no personal resources because anything they owned became their husband's property after marriage. It was therefore difficult to bring a complaint before the court with the help and advice of a lawyer. There were, however, several charges of violence brought before the Western Australian Criminal Court in the period between 1833 and 1872, and three of these cases provide examples of the kind of behaviour occurring in this relatively poor and ill-educated community.

The first example is that of Thomas Dent, who was charged with assault and battery on his wife, Elizabeth Dent, on 18 December 1832. Dent was brought before the court in January 1833, when he was accused of beating and wounding his wife 'and then and there to her other enormous things did, to the great damage and hurt of her'.[321] Thomas Dent admitted that he had punched his wife, who had been calling him names, promising never to hurt her again. He was found guilty and sentenced to three months' imprisonment with hard labour.

In a later case, the prosecutor waxed eloquent in his declaration concerning the criminal behaviour of John Allison. He referred to Allison as a person of wicked, depraved and abandoned mind and disposition, and wholly lost to a due sense of morality, decency and religion...who...offered his wife for the sum of ten pounds to provide sexual services to Cornelius Bradman.[322]

Allison was found guilty and given a sentence of six months' imprisonment.

In 1872, John Drabble's crime against his wife earned him a sentence of life imprisonment. The prosecutor referred to Drabble, otherwise called Joseph Mellor, as

> not having the fear of God before his eyes...and seduced by the instigation of the Devil, feloniously, wilfully and of malice aforethought did kill and murder one Elizabeth Drabble, otherwise called Elizabeth Mellor, against the peace of our Lady the Queen and her Crown and Dignity.[323]

All these crimes were committed in the presence of witnesses who appeared before the court to give evidence. The absence of witnesses in most cases of violence in marriage relationships undoubtedly meant that, for many women, the violent behaviour of their husbands had to be suffered in silence. Nor was there any solution for the problem a woman faced if her husband appropriated all her savings and left her destitute. This property was his, according to law.

A court case in 1867 provides an example of another kind of solution to the problem of destitution. Joanna Foley had married Jeremiah Foley on 29 April 1865. Two years later, in May 1867, she was charged with bigamy in that she married Joseph Cole on 18 April 1867, knowing that her 'former' husband, Jeremiah Foley, was still alive. When asked in court whether she had anything to say, she replied as follows:

> I knew my former husband, Jeremiah Foley, was living at the time I married Joseph Cole on 18 April. The week before I was married to Cole, I asked my former husband to come home to Newcastle and live with me. He said 'No, I will not,' as he was not able to support me, and my family by my first husband. [Clearly, she married three times.] He said he would have no further claim upon me, and that I might do the best I could to support myself and my children.[324]

Apparently, Joanna Foley thought that the best option available to provide adequate support for herself and her children was the presence of a husband. Her punishment for the crime of bigamy was twelve months' imprisonment with hard labour.

We have seen that, while no specific instructions were given about marriage law before 1841 in Western Australia, the detailed instructions to the newly appointed Governor Stirling, in the document from the Colonial Office of 5 March 1831, included the direction that no law was to be passed permitting 'Divorce of Persons joined together in matrimony'.[325] It would be another thirty years before the question of divorce law was once again referred to in colonial despatches.

After the passage of the 1857 English divorce legislation, the Colonial Secretary, Lord Stanley, sent a copy of the act to each Australian colony, advising the governors that they should consult their Legislative Councils about introducing a similar measure. The Colony of Western Australia, established in 1829, had to wait until 1863 for the passage of its first divorce law. However, Governor Kennedy's marriage acts of 1856 permanently resolved one aspect of ongoing colonial conflict based on religious differences. The year after Kennedy left the colony, Governor Hampton would introduce a divorce law, something previously unknown in the Colony of Western Australia.

9

Divorce law, 1863

Governor John Hampton,[326] who followed Governor Kennedy in February 1862, gained a medical degree at Edinburgh in 1828, and worked as a ship's surgeon, including on several convict ships sailing to Van Diemen's Land. He was the Comptroller of Convicts in Tasmania from October 1846 until his appointment as Governor of Western Australia in February 1862. Before he and his wife left the colony in November 1868, the end of the convict system in Western Australia had been announced.

Governor Hampton's reputation was tarnished because of an inconclusive inquiry into his administration of the convict system in Van Diemen's Land. When Captain Henderson, Comptroller of Convicts, left the colony in 1862, Hampton took control of the Western Australian system for a short time, and then tried, unsuccessfully, to have his son appointed to the position. In the second half of the 1860s, criticisms of Governor Hampton's autocratic style of government increased colonial demands for a more representative system of government.

However, the new Legislative Council was not introduced until 1870, after Governor Frederick Weld[327] arrived in the colony to replace Governor Hampton on 4 March 1869. The bill to establish a system of representative government was passed on 1 June 1870.[328] Under the new act, twelve members elected by male property owners would sit in the Legislative Council along with official and nominated members. But, before the Legislative Council became more democratic, it would be called upon to pass the new divorce law in the Colony of Western Australia.

Before the first divorce legislation in 1863, wives were bound to cohabit with their husbands, the implication of the words 'till death us do part' in the marriage ceremony. In practical terms, this cohabitation was secured in most cases because a husband could control his wife's property and her earnings. If she attempted to separate from him, she could be deprived of the money she earned to support herself.

However, in some cases brought before the Criminal Court, women were granted the right to leave a violent husband. The English law passed in 1839, known as Serjeant Talfourd's Act, gave power to the courts to grant the mother access to her children and custody of those below seven years of age.[329] This law was also introduced in Western Australia in 1844, when Governor Hutt passed an act for adopting and applying certain imperial acts, including an act to amend the law concerning the custody of children.[330]

From this time, women could also seek assistance from a Magistrate's Court. As we have already seen, in 1845, the government introduced an ordinance

> to provide for the Maintenance and Relief of Deserted Wives and Children,
> and other Destitute Persons, and to make the property of Husbands and
> near Relatives, to whose assistance they have a natural claim, in certain
> circumstances, available for support.[331]

Charges of assault could also be brought against a violent husband according to laws applying to all assault cases in the community. However, it is apparent that these laws were frequently ineffective in offering support for many abandoned women and children.

From the early 1860s, many women sought protection and assistance by applying for entry into the women's poor house. In the 1860s and 1870s, women with children frequently applied for entry because their husbands had deserted them, threatened them with violence, or taken all their resources and left them penniless.

In 1849, the newspaper *The Inquirer*, by publishing a report from the *Hampshire Advertiser*, provided an example of the kind of cruelty endured by many married women and indicated the sorts of questions considered by ecclesiastical courts in England. This was nine years before these ecclesiastical courts were replaced by civil courts. The report, which can be interpreted as an ironic comment, read as follows:

> Husbands are indebted to the Ecclesiastical Court for approximating to
> a definition of what constitute 'legal cruelty' in the married state. In the

case of Bialbablotzky versus Bialbablotzky, Dr. Lushington has made an important step. The wife prayed a divorce on the ground of cruelty; and the learned Judge considered the charge to be made out, 'the husband having on two occasions inflicted upon his wife severe punishment – on one occasion with a horsewhip, on another with a cane.'

In a recent trial, the judge intimated, negatively, that to push a wife about, or even, if we remember rightly, to inflict a blow, was not legal cruelty; Dr. Lushington now pronounces affirmatively, that to 'punish a wife' with horsewhip or cane does amount to legal cruelty. You may 'punish,' but the law, by the Judges, draws the line at the cane and the horsewhip.

This disposes of the popular fallacy that a man may beat his wife with 'a stick no thicker than his thumb.' The thumb is probably too thick, and canes and sticks we conceive to be obsolete. You may hustle your wife, at any period, out of the room, or push her against chests of drawers – you may bully her, swear at her – you may order her and 'punish' her – you may do all this and plead judicial authority for it; but the cane is interdicted. To such a point has the civilization of England advanced, that the stick is no longer a legitimate instrument of marital influence.[332]

Just as the marriage laws in the colony copied those passed in England, a divorce law in Western Australia was finally introduced under instructions from the Colonial Office some seven years after the first change occurred in England.[333] In introducing the divorce bill, Governor Hampton was following Colonial Office instructions and revealing very little about his own views on the question of divorce. His introduction of the bill in 1863 was followed immediately by strong protests from the Roman Catholic Church.

The first reading of the 1863 Divorce Bill in the Western Australian Legislative Council occurred on 10 June and the second reading on 25 June, with no report of any discussion in the minutes of the council. However, before the bill was read a third time and passed on 8 July 1863, Governor Hampton referred to a 'memorial of protest' from Father Martin Griver, administrator of the Roman Catholic Church, which was currently being circulated to all Roman Catholic clergy for their signatures. Father Griver had not followed either of the usual procedures of addressing the memorial directly to the Governor, or requesting a member of the council to present it to the Governor. As a result, Governor Hampton moved that the memorial be read in the House since he 'was anxious that everyone should have the most ample field for expressing their opinion on the acts of the Government'.[334]

He then dismissed the claim in the memorial that the bill had been hurried precipitately through the council, pointing out that there had been a notice in the *Government Gazette* to the effect that the bill would be brought forward.[335] This notice had been followed by an interval of fourteen days between the first and second readings. Moreover, he said that the measure was by no means a new one since, as long ago as April 1858, a despatch had been received by the Governor from the Secretary of State as to the assimilation of the law respecting divorce in the colony as closely as possible to that in force in England.[336] However, in spite of being prepared to listen to criticism, Governor Hampton apparently allowed no further time for debate. The bill was read a third time and passed.

Both the *Perth Gazette* and *The Inquirer* printed a copy of this Catholic memorial, including a list of the eight Roman Catholic clergy who had signed it. The memorial stated that the church was 'extremely grieved' at the intention of the colonial state to pass the divorce law, which the priests regarded as 'tending to produce grave consequences and contrary to the doctrine of Christ'.

They gave four specific objections to the bill. The first was that they believed married people would no longer bear with one another's faults if they were offered the possibility of divorce. The second objection claimed that people would marry with little care if they could escape from their marriage. They also claimed that there would be more frequent separation of families and abandonment of children, who would become a burden on the colony. Finally, the representatives of the Roman Catholic Church stated that its existing tolerance of mixed marriages would have to be reconsidered, presumably because they believed that the marriage of people of different denominations would be more likely to lead to divorce. The memorial was followed by a list of biblical quotations, apparently supporting the church's opposition to the Divorce Bill.[337] In spite of the increase in the number of Roman Catholics in the community, this memorial failed to influence the decision of the government.

The Divorce Act contained considerable administrative detail, as well as complex instructions for lawyers and married couples concerning petitions for divorce. The preamble of the act stressed the importance of copying English law[338] 'as far as the same are compatible with the requirements of the Colony'.[339] It recognised that there were close family connections between people of the two countries, and argued that the law should be designed to prevent conflicts and problems arising when both laws might have to be considered.

The first clause of the Divorce Act officially established a Court for Divorce and Matrimonial Causes, while later clauses set out many details about the powers of this court and its mode of operation. Western Australia was the only colony to follow this path, since the other colonies added the divorce law cases to the list of those being heard in their Supreme Court. The Chief Justice of Western Australia was to preside over the Divorce Court, while the Registrar and other officers of the Supreme Court were obliged to attend its sittings and assist in its proceedings. All the barristers who were entitled to practice in the Supreme Court were also available for petitioners to the Divorce Court.

After the passage of the 1880 Supreme Court Act, these original arrangements were changed to transfer the business of the Divorce Court to the Supreme Court. This complex 1880 act was designed to detail the operations of the Supreme Court in the field of divorce, but not to affect divorce law itself.[340] In his introduction to the 1880 bill, the Attorney-General said that his task had been 'considerably lightened by its being a modification, condensation, and, to a great extent, a mere transcription of English Acts'.[341]

This bill had been introduced, he said, so that the Western Australian Supreme Court 'should be technically adjusted to those of the higher Courts of England'. There was considerable discussion of technicalities, including reference to the fact that there were many more separate courts in England than in Western Australia, where the only existing separate court was that dealing with marriage. Divorce cases were therefore held in the Court for Divorce and Matrimonial Causes from 1863 until 1880 and, thereafter, in the Supreme Court.

The first part of the divorce legislation to offer help to married women did not actually involve an appearance before the Divorce Court.[342] While several acts referred to earlier provided the possibility of assistance from a magistrate to women who were deserted or assaulted, it now became possible for a magistrate to assist in the protection of a woman's property. The desertion of a woman by her husband allowed her to apply to a 'Police

Magistrate, Resident Magistrate, or Justices at Petty Sessions' for an order to protect her personal property and earnings from her husband.

The Perth Magistrate's Court, also known as the Perth Police Court or the Court of Petty Sessions, had been established to hear cases not requiring a judge or jury, although a case could be referred to a higher court. Magistrate's Courts were established in all districts of the colony soon after settlement, in order to solve minor cases. There were, for example, ten resident magistrates listed as part of the civil establishment in the *Blue Book* of 1869.[343]

In the new Divorce Act of 1863, Clause 13 declared that

> A wife deserted by her husband may at any time after such desertion apply to the Police Magistrate or to the Resident Magistrate of the district wherein she resides...or...to Justices in Petty Sessions...for an order to protect any money or property in the Colony she may have acquired or may acquire...against her husband and his creditors...

The following clauses dealt with various complexities connected with property issues, including those concerning dealings with other interested parties. The magistrate could also direct that the husband pay alimony to his deserted wife or to trustees on her behalf. In these circumstances, the wife was regarded as a 'feme sole [sic]'[344] in legal terms and therefore responsible for her own financial affairs, over which her husband no longer had any control.

This meant that, even without appearing before the Divorce Court, a woman could now get a magistrate's order for protection of her property or earnings, according to clauses 13–15 of the 1863 divorce law. This appeal to a Magistrate's Court was the cheapest option for a woman with some property who needed some form of protection from her husband so that she could provide support and maintenance for herself and her children. These clauses began the process of unravelling the laws of many centuries, which had given husbands control of the earnings and personal possessions of their wives.

We come, next, to the two possible solutions to the complete breakdown of marriage, both involving the ending of the marriage partnership, and both of them available under certain circumstances after a petition to the Divorce Court. The first possibility was to petition for judicial separation, a matter to be decided by the Divorce Court. This did not allow for remarriage, and could be obtained 'either by the husband or the wife, on the ground of adultery, or cruelty, or desertion without cause for two years and upwards'.[345] In the case of judicial separation, the court could order that the husband pay alimony to his ex-wife as long as she lived. It could also, according to Clause 32, 'make such provisions in the final decree, as it may deem just and proper with respect to the custody, maintenance, and education of the children'.

As part of this petition, other questions of property settlement could be decided by the court. According to Clause 41, in a case of judicial separation or dissolution of marriage because of the adultery of the wife, if 'the wife [was] entitled to any property either in possession or reversion', a settlement could be made by the court for the ultimate 'benefit of the innocent party, and of the children of the marriage, or either or any of them'. Clause 43 dealt with the same issue and seemed to leave all options about property settlement available for consideration by the court, in the interests of 'the children...or of their respective parents'.

The second option available before the Divorce Court was dissolution of marriage and the rules were set out in clauses 23 to 28. The husband could present a petition to the court claiming that his wife had committed adultery. A wife, on the other hand, had to provide evidence of her husband's 'incestuous adultery, or of bigamy with adultery, or of rape, or of sodomy, or of bestiality, or of adultery coupled with such cruelty as without adultery would have entitled her to a divorce *a mensa et thoro* in the Ecclesiastical Courts in England' before the passage of the recent legislation. According to Clause 28, the marriage could be declared dissolved if the judge was satisfied that the case was proved.

An early amendment to the Divorce Act in 1871 clarified certain aspects of the situation concerning the allocation of a weekly sum that the divorced husband should pay for the support of his wife and children. The original act had assumed that husbands would have sufficient property to secure 'such gross...or annual sum of money' as to the court might 'deem reasonable', suggesting that the petitions for divorce were designed to suit people with substantial incomes.[346] This 1871 amendment gave the Divorce Court power to order the husband to pay his wife a monthly or weekly sum, subject to change on certain grounds, if he had no resources except his weekly wage.[347]

Clearly, the wife who petitioned for divorce had the more difficult task of proving her husband's guilt, since an accusation of adultery alone against a man was not enough to obtain a conviction. According to the original act of 1863, after three months to allow for the possibility of an appeal against the findings of the court, those people whose marriages had been dissolved could marry again. In the amendment to the Divorce Act, passed in 1871, this waiting period was extended to six months.

The records of the Divorce Court for the period 1863 to 1899 allow for some statistical conclusions about the frequency of divorce, and the gender of those petitioning the court for either judicial separation or dissolution of marriage. The Divorce Act was passed in July 1863 and the first two petitions were filed in 1864. The first, by Sarah Duffield, occurred on 29 March 1864, when she requested judicial separation from her husband, John Cole Duffield, on the grounds of cruelty. On the same day, Adelaide Isaacs petitioned for judicial separation from her husband on the grounds of cruelty and desertion.

These two petitions came before the Divorce Court but are not recorded with the rest of the cases for the period from 1865 to 1899. However, the details can be found in the list of petitions and also in particular record books.[348] The particulars of all other cases that came before the court for the period 1865 to 1899 follow one another in order in the divorce files.[349] In some cases, especially in the early years, these files did not include all the details of the case. In particular, the decision of the judge was not always recorded.

After a petition was lodged, considerable preparation had to be made before the case could be heard in the court. The divorce petition index provides the dates when all the relevant details and information gathered were presented to the clerk of the court, including the lawyers' statements on behalf of the petitioner and the defendant.

Letters were despatched to require that the petitioner and defendant attend the hearing on the first appointed day, and copies of marriage certificates, birth certificates and other legal documents were found for presentation before the court. Information was gathered about defendants to see whether they had the resources to pay court costs and legal fees.

Until the passage of the Married Women's Property Act in 1892, the husband always had to pay the legal fees. Lawyers were reluctant to take responsibility for presenting a case for a male or female petitioner if the husband had few financial resources. In most cases of dissolution of marriage on grounds of adultery, the co-respondent (the partner in the adultery) was required to pay the court costs. The lawyers would therefore also investigate the income of the co-respondent before accepting the case.

Some of the case reports in the divorce records indicate that the legal fees for this work lay between £20 and £30, while the court costs reached £40. The total cost of a case before the Divorce Court was therefore the equivalent of a year's income for many men in the community.[350]

In cases involving adultery, the co-respondent was ordered to appear, sometimes with witnesses identified by the petitioner. While it was legally necessary for these instructions to be despatched, they were often ignored by the intended recipients. Charges were frequently not defended either by the respondent or co-respondent. Occasionally, a petitioner was unable to attend because of the cost of travel to Perth, in which case the submissions were presented to the court in his or her absence. In one case, the petitioner lived in England and was seeking divorce from her ex-convict husband. This case was negotiated over time between the two countries, as permitted under clauses 48–50 of the 1863 Divorce Act.

The lawyers advised their clients as to the likely success of their petition and whether, for example, a woman had enough evidence to petition for dissolution of marriage. Although they must have heard many different accounts of domestic conflict, their submissions made before the court, detailing violence, ill-treatment and desertion, always contained the same phrases and terminology, presumably the language that the lawyers knew would satisfy the demands of the court.

The issue of gender relations in all its complexity was finally confronted in Western Australia after the passage of the first divorce law in 1863. This law seemed to legislate in favour of men, who could achieve a divorce more readily than a woman. But there were momentous shifts in family relations enshrined in this act, in that men now had to accept legal responsibility for the support and education of their children, if an order to this effect was issued by a magistrate, after judicial separation or after dissolution of marriage. This responsibility of male parents for child support was extended in subsequent legislation.

How far, then, would the introduction of the first divorce law in Western Australia go to improve the situation for married women and their children? It is customary for historians to point to the continuing position of disadvantage suffered by married women after the passage of the Divorce Act. They refer particularly to the fact that a woman had to prove adultery and at least one other listed offence before she could be granted dissolution of marriage. Men had only to prove adultery. The alternative for women was to seek judicial separation.

Historians have been preoccupied with this unequal gender distinction in petitioning for divorce. There is usually the implied assumption that, had they been offered the opportunity, all women would have preferred dissolution of marriage rather than judicial separation. While this may be true, these assumptions have tended to crowd out any detailed consideration of the truly radical nature of the relief offered by the new act. An examination of the specific clauses of the Divorce Act of 1863 reveals that it offered three possible solutions to marriage problems for both men and women. Two of these solutions, an appeal to a magistrate or a petition for judicial separation, were only ever used by women. They both offered some chance of security for a woman with children.

In order to understand the operation of the Divorce Act, the following chapters, divided into three time periods, will consider the extent to which petitions were used by men and women. Did women apply to a magistrate for protection of their property? Why were there so few petitions for dissolution of marriage from either men or women until the late 1890s? What changes were made to the law in the period between 1863 and 1900, and why was their effect on the operations of the law so profound? Who benefited most from these new laws?

10

Divorce law and the courts, 1863–79

The decades after the passage of the divorce law saw great change and dislocation in the colony. From 1850 to 1870, the total population rose from just under 5,000 to almost 25,000. This number included 9,669 male convicts and 7,827 free immigrants, most of whom were women. The majority of these convicts and immigrants were from the poorest sections of English and Irish society, with no personal resources and no relatives in their new home. The importation of convicts ended in 1868, but for two decades they were still being only gradually absorbed into the community.

The convicts who were already married left their wives in England or Ireland, and very few of these women chose to accept the free passage, offered by the British Government, to rejoin their husbands. One of the earliest recorded petitions, which came before the Divorce Court in 1865, was settled in London. Isabella Graham Robson, residing in England, petitioned for judicial separation from William James Robson, a ticket-of-leave convict residing in Australia, partly on the grounds that he had deserted her.[351]

The convicts and ex-convicts in the community, all of them men, made up approximately two-fifths of the total population by 1870. The absence of wives, and the struggle of both freed convicts and free immigrants to establish new lives for themselves, suggests long periods of isolation and social dislocation. The convicts were a mixed lot in terms of age. Already in 1869, soon after the convict system ended, there were many ex-convicts from the earlier 1850s who were seeking permanent support in the Old Men's Home, also known as the Invalid Depot, which was established in that year at the foot of Mount Eliza. On the other hand, many young unmarried ex-convicts undoubtedly sought a wife as soon as they were free and had established themselves in the community.

This chapter will consider the operations of the Magistrate's Courts and the Divorce Court between 1864 and 1879. Changes to the divorce law in 1880, as described in the previous chapter, meant that all divorce proceedings would from then on be heard in the Supreme Court.

The business of the Perth courts was conducted in several different buildings. In 1857, the courts shifted from the old Courthouse built in 1836 to the new building in Beaufort Street, containing a courthouse and gaol. When this became overcrowded, the old Courthouse was used again. In 1879, the old Commissariat building on the site of the present Supreme Court building became a courthouse. When the building of the Supreme Court began in 1895, sections of the court shifted again to the old Courthouse and to Trinity Church Hall. The present buildings of the Supreme Court were completed in 1903.[352]

The first question to consider is whether or not an appeal to the Magistrate's Court after 1863 proved a cheap and sensible alternative to an appeal to the Divorce Court. It is not possible to establish the number of charges of a specific nature brought before all magistrates in the colony in any one year. This is partly because of the large number of cases overall, but also because not all of the charge books survive. The examples provided below refer only to the Perth Magistrate's Court for limited periods.

The magistrate in Perth heard charges on several days every week and delivered his verdict after a few minutes' consideration. Serious cases were referred to the Criminal Court but cases such as drunkenness, disorderly behaviour, assault, trespass and other minor offences were heard almost immediately by the magistrate. In 1863, the divorce law added a new kind of case to these hearings.

According to official records, the court costs to the plaintiff, the person bringing the case before the court, depended on the cost of the summons. The cost of summoning defendants varied greatly, depending on whether they lived in Perth or at some more distant address. A summons not exceeding ten shillings attracted a magistrate's fee of sixpence, a clerk's fee of sixpence and a bailiff's fee of two shillings, a total cost of three shillings to be paid by the plaintiff. The highest charge, for a summons costing 100 shillings, attracted a total fee of twelve shillings.[353]

However, the surviving records of the Magistrate's Courts only occasionally indicate what the plaintiff was required to pay in court costs. On many occasions, the magistrate directed that the costs should be paid by the defendant. All of this was complicated because the court costs for a woman's complaint against her husband would have to be met by him anyway, since he controlled their joint income. In general, it can be assumed that, if skilled workers were paid between six shillings and ten shillings a day for six days a week, the unskilled were earning approximately five shillings per day. The costs for the Magistrate's Court would therefore be manageable if the defendant was employed.

However, women seeking poor relief were granted only one shilling a day in government support for themselves and their families, probably barely enough to survive outside the poor house. This may explain why the Superintendent of the Poor Houses sometimes went to the police to report on a husband who had deserted his wife. Presumably, he also paid the costs. If the case were successful, the woman and her family would cease to be a charge on poor relief funds.

In the records for the Perth Police Court for the short period of eight months from April to December 1868, all the cases brought against men following complaints by their wives were for assault or for desertion and failure to provide support. There were no cases for protection of their property, as allowed under the Divorce Act. There were four cases of assault, three of which were dismissed because the wife declined to proceed. The details recorded do not explain this change of heart but it may have been the result of intervention by other family members or, perhaps, the husband's promise never to reoffend. In one case in this period the assault charge was followed by a fine and the requirement to promise to keep the peace.

In this same period, there were three cases of desertion, two of which were punished with a period of imprisonment with hard labour, while one husband had to agree to pay a weekly sum to his wife for her maintenance, to be paid regularly to the clerk of the court. It is difficult to see what advantage accrued to a wife and family if a husband was put in gaol.[354]

In a later period, from January to December 1875, the records of the Police Court reveal the same pattern. There were nine cases of assault by a husband on his wife, with six dismissed without charge. One husband was bound over to keep the peace, while one was remanded and reconsidered, resulting in him being required to pay his wife six shillings a week. In the final case the husband was remanded with no conclusion recorded. Of the two cases of desertion, one husband was gaoled with hard labour and one required to pay a fixed sum every week.[355]

How, then, do these cases relate to the new ruling contained in the 1863 Divorce Act? The section in the act dealing with the power of the Magistrate's Court stated that

> A wife deserted by her husband may at any time after such desertion apply to the Police Magistrate or to the Resident Magistrate of the district wherein she resides...or to Justices in Petty Sessions...for an order to protect any money or property in the Colony she may have acquired or may acquire...[356]

The limited number of cases of desertion in the two periods examined above do not fit this description, since all the women were seeking support without any mention of protecting their own property. However, there were some cases before the Magistrate's Courts fitting this description, because Emma Collins, the only woman to petition for divorce during the period before 1879, claimed that on 19 September 1872, she obtained an order from the police magistrate in Perth protecting her property from her husband on the grounds of desertion, which her husband refused to sign. Obviously, the power of the magistrate was not sufficient to compel the offender to conform to his ruling. In this case, as we shall see below, Emma Collins, who had received a legacy from England, was able to proceed to lodge a petition for dissolution of marriage.[357]

The lack of evidence from the Magistrate's Court concerning applications for the protection of property suggests that very few deserted women had any property. A few women like Emma Collins, who did make an application of this sort, found that the magistrate's ruling could be ignored, presumably because the decisions of the magistrates were not adequately policed. This conclusion is confirmed by evidence from the 1880s, when most of the women petitioning for judicial separation before the Divorce Court had already appeared in the Magistrate's Court. They all gave evidence that the magistrate's decision had been ignored by their husbands.

This raises the next question concerning the availability of petitions to the Divorce Court. As referred to in the previous chapter, the proceedings before the new Divorce Court were much more expensive than an appeal to a magistrate and were clearly not available to many men or women, because the lawyers would not undertake a case unless they could assure themselves that the husband or the co-respondent could pay the legal fees and court costs.

Women were much more likely than men to seek to end their marriage during this first period from 1863 to 1879. Those women whose husbands had financial resources could persuade a lawyer to prepare a petition for them. In a successful case before the Divorce Court, the defendant was obliged to pay the costs. The women almost always sought judicial separation, which was the most likely to succeed. An examination of the statistics in terms of gender will provide an outline of the changing patterns over time.

In the first sixteen years, from 1864 to 1879, there were twenty-four cases brought before the Divorce Court, eighteen of them from women seeking judicial separation. One woman petitioned for dissolution of marriage. Before the end of 1879, only five men petitioned for dissolution of marriage, the only kind of petition men ever made.

Petitions to the Divorce Court, 1864–79

Gender	Men	Women
Judicial separation	0	18
Dissolution of marriage	5	1
Total	5	19

Most of the married men in the community had small incomes and would have found it difficult to persuade a lawyer to undertake the work for a petition to the Divorce Court for dissolution of marriage. However, if a husband could persuade a lawyer that he had strong evidence from witnesses that his wife had committed adultery, his case could well be accepted.

The court costs were usually passed on to the co-respondent, sometimes with successful claims for compensation paid to the husband. This meant that the lawyer had to investigate the financial situation of the co-respondent before he would accept the case. However, as this would be more time-consuming and difficult than investigating the financial resources of a petitioner, it may have been undertaken with reluctance.

One example of a male petition was that of Robert Thompson,[358] who petitioned on 2 October 1879 for dissolution of his marriage with Susan Thompson on the grounds of her adultery with a man named Albert Francisco. The Thompson marriage took place in January 1874 and they had two children. As was usual in these cases, Robert Thompson provided details of the name of the co-respondent and had witnesses who could support his evidence. He made no application for the custody of his children, but applied for £2,000 in damages from Francisco.

The newspaper reports of the trial provide all the detail about the adulterous behaviour of Mrs Thompson and Albert Francisco, who made little attempt to conceal their activities. Captain Miles of the *Clarence Packet*, a small boat sailing to Cossack, informed Thompson of his wife's behaviour in sharing a cabin with Francisco for the whole trip. Two other witnesses provided additional evidence. The court also heard evidence of his wife's excessive purchase of liquor, about which her husband reprimanded her harshly. However, it was concluded that he was in general a good husband.[359]

The records include a heartbroken letter to the petitioner from his wife, pleading for him to take her back and promising never again to commit adultery. He was apparently unmoved, since the trial continued. She made no attempt to defend herself in court but Francisco denied the charge. Thompson was granted dissolution of marriage, with the co-respondent to pay the costs. The question of damages had to be decided by a jury, and nineteen names were listed as members of the 'common jury'.[360] Franscisco was ordered to pay £700 to the petitioner.

The greater number of petitions filed by women in the first sixteen years after the law was passed shows that offences against women were more frequent and complex than those against men. The few male petitioners all sought dissolution of marriage on the grounds of adultery by their wives. All but one woman in this period petitioned for judicial separation on the grounds of assault, violence of various kinds, desertion, failure to provide support, and adultery by their husbands. Many women were simply desperate to escape from their marriage situation, something now possible for the first time.

A successful petition for judicial separation on the grounds of cruelty, desertion or adultery allowed a woman to separate from her husband, retain custody of her children and receive a regular payment of alimony, an option available only to those whose husbands had some capital. The preparation for the court case always involved careful consideration of the resources of the defendant, who would be required to pay the costs of the court appearance and the legal fees. Most of these petitions provided evidence of the most inhumane treatment of women by their husbands. In this early period, most of the women involved had been married for many years and had several children.

One of the earliest charges was brought against Francis Henry Vincent, well known in the colony at this time because of his long period as the superintendent of the Aboriginal Prison at Rottnest. In 1842, he had been charged 'with undue severity, and inflicting such a degree of chastisement upon a native as occasioned his death'.[361] However, the case was dismissed.

On 11 February 1868, Louisa Vincent petitioned for judicial separation from her husband, Francis Henry Vincent, the elder, of Fremantle.[362] Louisa Vincent, originally Louisa Hume, spinster, married Henry Vincent on 19 October 1831. In her evidence before the Divorce Court, she explained that she had lived with her husband at Fremantle and Rottnest Island until 14 December 1860. She had three sons and three daughters. For the previous twelve years, she had suffered greatly from his violent temper: 'He treated me with great harshness and cruelty while living at Rottnest, frequently shaking and abusing me in the presence of my daughters'.

When Henry Vincent resigned his appointment as superintendent at Rottnest on 31 December 1866, they returned to Fremantle. From that time on

> his conduct towards me has been much worse and more violent. He has repeatedly during that time struck and threatened me, and addressed to me and my daughters very disgusting language too bad for me to mention.

On 2 January 1867, while they were in temporary lodgings, his conduct 'was violent and abusive in the extreme, and he struck me twice in the presence of our daughters'.

She described how, when they moved to another house, he became more violent, on one occasion pulling the skin off her ears and making them bleed. He pulled her out of bed at one in the morning, and when she went to her daughter's room, 'he turned her and her two adult daughters out of their room to sit in the kitchen, and then locked her in the storeroom until morning'.

She claimed that Vincent had often, both at Rottnest and at Fremantle, 'turned me out of bed and made me walk up and down the room for hours and, if I attempted to sit down, forced me to continue walking'. He compelled her to take her meals in the kitchen and threatened to break her bones if she entered the dining room.

In December 1867, she was forced to leave his bed and sleep in her daughter's room. 'He told me to pack up and leave the house'. On 14 December, he asked her if she was ready to go. And then, 'taking me by the shoulders, pushed me down the passage and out of the house, having first thrown my box of clothing out of the house'. From that time, she had been living at the house of her son Francis Henry Vincent, the younger, and with Mrs Agett at Fremantle. She had never returned to her husband's house or cohabited with him from that time. She claimed her husband was 'naturally violent, but of later years, more hard, hasty and violent in language and customs'.

Louisa Vincent and her daughters left Henry Vincent's house in December 1867. Before the appeal for judicial separation was heard in the Divorce Court, he made a will leaving all his property to his second son. He offered to change his will to leave his property to his eldest son, and to the rest of his family, if his wife and daughters would return to him. In 1870, this will was the subject of an appeal to the Supreme Court by the eldest son. The discussion in the court concerned, inter alia, the question of whether Henry Vincent was suffering from delusions and might be considered insane at the time when he made the will in 1868.[363] There was no agreement in the court on this matter in 1870, but it provides a possible explanation for his violent and contradictory behaviour.

The court records provide considerable detail concerning Vincent's earnings and investments. He was required to give security to pay the necessary expenses of the court case before it could be brought before the court. The costs were recorded as £20 17s for his wife's lawyer and £30 for the court costs. It appears that he did not try to defend himself in court, where the case was heard on 12 August 1868. His wife was granted a judicial separation and £40 alimony per year. Louisa Vincent had been married to her violent husband for thirty-four years before she petitioned for a separation.

This petition for judicial separation reveals some of the characteristic responses of this early period. The petitioner is of middle age with an established family. She simply wishes to escape her existing situation, without any hope or desire for remarriage. She has been abused and humiliated by her brutal husband for most of her married life. Because of their financial dependence and the laws about child custody, women in these circumstances had previously been unable to escape their desperate situation.

The following case concerns the only woman's petition for dissolution of marriage before 1879.[364] The young Emma Collins, who had no children, was unusually fortunate in making an early escape from the violence of her marriage and finding sufficient cause to petition for a complete divorce. It was very difficult at this time for women to petition for dissolution of marriage because of the problem of proving two or more causes. Unlike many young women at that time who had arrived in Western Australia as immigrants, she had support from her parents. This provided her with a means of escape and, eventually, the courage to confront her husband.

Emma Woodhead married Peter Collins in Bunbury on 9 September 1867 when she was 'about 17 years of age', with the consent of her parents. According to her evidence, within a fortnight of the marriage, her husband began to ill-treat her, striking her and pulling her by the hair. He threatened her with violence, 'using the most coarse and insulting language' and frequently said that as soon as her father and mother left Bunbury, 'he would have her to himself and could do what he liked to her'. Finally, after a particularly violent beating, she returned to her parents, who supported her and with whom she stayed. They shifted from Bunbury to York and, for a considerable time, she heard nothing from her husband and he contributed nothing towards her support.

Emma Collins claimed that, about six months before the trial, Peter Collins became aware that 'she was entitled to a legacy and other monies in England' and he began to inquire about his wife. She explained that her husband refused to sign the court order she had obtained from a magistrate on 19 September 1872 in the hope of protecting her property. On several occasions after this, she offered to return to him if he would provide a proper home. This he neglected to do. She claimed that she believed he never had any intention of living with her again but that his sole purpose was, if possible, to obtain the receipt of the money falling to her.

The evidence then turned to claims of his adultery with a Mrs Crogan, whose husband was out of the colony. According to the evidence produced, they were living together in one room 'in a house called the Old Pier Hotel in Perth'. On 20 November 1873, Emma Collins sought a dissolution of marriage on the grounds of cruelty, desertion and adultery.

At the trial on 7 January 1873, the defendant denied all the charges. He said that there had been no cruelty; he had never refused to support her; and she offered to return to him only if he signed a document relinquishing his right and interest in her legacy and monies, which he had refused to sign. He claimed that his wife had condoned his adultery and he then claimed that she, Emma Collins, had committed adultery with two men.

She replied to his submission, claiming that she had not left him without due cause; that she did not hear from him for a long period (presumably implying his desertion and failure to support her); and that she did not condone his adultery and did not commit adultery herself. The court granted the first dissolution of marriage to a woman in Western Australia, and her husband was obliged to pay the costs, something he attempted to avoid. The lawyer's costs amounted to £21 13s 4d and the court costs to £40. This was the cost of the only application by a woman for dissolution of marriage before 1880.[365]

Before the passage of the Western Australian divorce law in 1863, women were almost invisible in the public records. They were present as shadows in the laws about marriage, but these laws were about the power of the state to control certain important defining activities, not about the behaviour of individual men or women. The names of women were certainly to be found frequently in the contemporary records about poor law relief and occasionally in the records of the criminal courts. Otherwise, there is little record of their daily activities or any account of their position in relation to men, except that women in high society appeared occasionally alongside their husbands at public celebrations.

Men were the chief actors in all the histories of politics, law-making, business activities, and exploration. Almost all the heroic figures of popular imagination were the men who occupied the high positions in religious and secular institutions. They were also employed in all the service industries like school teaching, policing and the colonial administration. The nuns of the Catholic Church were an obvious exception to this prevailing pattern, but marriage conferred invisibility on most women.

After the passage of the divorce law in 1863, many women were offered the opportunity to escape from a marriage of intolerable violence and bondage. The other possibility – to appeal to a magistrate to gain financial security from their husbands – was often tried but apparently seldom successful, presumably because an agreement signed before a magistrate could be neither compelled nor enforced. In 1879, a new amendment to the Divorce Act extended the assistance offered by the Magistrate's Court.

11

Divorce law and the courts, 1880–89

The convict system ended in 1868 in Western Australia and, in 1870, Governor Weld made the first moves towards a more representative system of government. He increased the number of members in the Legislative Council to eighteen, twelve of them elected on a limited franchise. This development inspired many people to seek even more radical changes. However, in spite of growing political protests throughout the 1880s, the control of government would remain in the hands of the Governor and the Executive and Legislative councils for another twenty years. After a long campaign, responsible government was finally introduced in 1890.

In this second period under examination, from 1880 to 1889, there was no overall increase in the number of divorce petitions, now part of the work of the Supreme Court. Part of the explanation for this undoubtedly lay in the continuing poverty in the community. Very few people could afford to appeal to the Divorce Court in the first two decades of its operation. But many women could now apparently take advantage of the increased opportunities offered by the Magistrate's Court to leave their violent husbands and seek financial support and custody of their children. This new opportunity was due to changes made to the 1863 act.

In 1879, the Legislative Council considered an amendment to the 1863 Divorce Act to increase the number of matters to be decided by the Magistrate's Court. The act contained detail about the costs to be recovered by the Divorce Court when disputes arose over court findings. However, the main purpose of the act was to deal with situations involving marital violence prior to a divorce. It increased the power of magistrates to offer a wife protection from her violent husband but also increased her power concerning the custody of children.

The 1879 act was introduced by S. H. Parker, Member of the Legislative Council for Perth, who was apparently aware of the failure of the clause in the original act concerning women's property. He said that the original act was being amended to fit more nearly the practices obtaining in England. The later provisions of this act expanded on the individual rights of married women in a situation of conflict with their husbands.

According to Parker, the main provision of the bill was to empower magistrates,

> If a husband shall be convicted summarily...of an aggravated assault... upon his wife, [to] order that the wife shall be no longer bound to cohabit with her husband; and...That the husband shall pay to his wife such weekly sum as the Court or magistrate may consider to be in accordance with his means...[366]

Full discretion was also given to the magistrate to order that the legal custody of any children of the marriage under the age of ten years should be given to the wife.

The 1879 act appeared to give a magistrate considerable new power. His decisions under the original 1863 act mainly concerned a woman's property. Now, if a husband was convicted of aggravated assault on his wife, and if the magistrate was satisfied that her life was in danger, she was no longer bound to cohabit with her husband 'and such order shall have the force and effect in all respects of a decree of judicial separation on the ground of cruelty'. In other words, the magistrate could give her permission to leave her husband and the husband had to pay her enough money for her support. She also automatically gained custody of her children under the age of ten years. The only qualification was that this would not apply if she committed adultery.

While this new act seemed to promise considerable opportunities for the poorer section of the community, the evidence from the records of the Magistrate's Courts suggests that, at this time, the decisions of the court were still not adequately enforced. For example, the charge book of the Perth Police Court for the year 1880 provides a profile of the cases concerning assault and desertion by husbands for a period of one year.[367]

There were twenty-seven charges brought by women against their husbands in 1880, with the details usually presented to the magistrate by the wife. Eleven of the charges were for assault and fifteen were for desertion and failure to provide support for a wife and children. One of the charges was for failing to comply with a previous order to pay maintenance.

The judgments reveal that six of the cases were dismissed, sometimes because the wife failed to appear or did not wish to proceed; three were withdrawn, possibly after the husband promised not to reoffend; and six were adjourned. In five cases, the husband was committed to prison for a short period (usually one month) with hard labour. One husband was fined, two were bound over to keep the peace, and four were required to pay a weekly sum to their wife in maintenance.

In that year, in the Perth Magistrate's Court, there were several repeat offenders. This was the outcome of a renewed complaint by a wife whose husband had failed to observe the magistrate's ruling on a previous occasion. One such offender, Harry Simpson, appeared before the magistrate on five occasions in 1880, either for assault or desertion. On three occasions, the case was dismissed, possibly because the magistrate saw both husband and wife as partly responsible for the quarrels. However, on one occasion, Simpson was fined ten shillings with five shillings in costs, and on the other he was gaoled for one month with hard labour. Obviously, the magistrate's decision made very little difference to the behaviour of Harry Simpson.

The six adjourned cases are of considerable interest. It can be assumed that adjournment occurred when the husband failed to appear, or when it was not possible for him to pay any maintenance. Women went to the Magistrate's Court when their husbands were in gaol, were too ill to work or could not be located. In these cases, the resident magistrate wrote to the Colonial Secretary to explain that the woman and her children had no means of support and to suggest that she be granted poor relief or entry into the women's poor house. The Colonial Secretary received these letters on a weekly basis from all over the colony. Relief in the form of money was usually provided for a period of two months before being reconsidered or, in some cases of extreme hardship, entry into the poor house was approved.[368]

This 1879 act was introduced to assist women who could not afford to sue for judicial separation through the Divorce Court because their husbands did not have sufficient income to pay the costs. But the number of men appearing before the court a second time indicates that many men continued to ignore a magistrate's ruling.

Most of the women who filed a petition for judicial separation claimed that they had signed an agreement of separation before a magistrate, but that the conditions had not been honoured by their husbands. For example, on 1 January 1886, Bridget Taaffe filed for judicial separation and stated in her petition that she had sought protection from the police and agreed to a deed of separation on 31 May 1883. According to her evidence, her husband had returned and threatened her.[369]

This case was typical of many, indicating that an appeal to a magistrate was the precursor to many subsequent appeals for judicial separation. Women tried the cheaper option in the hope of stopping their husband's violence, receiving regular financial support, or even separation. When this failed, or if the decision could not be enforced, they visited a lawyer to see whether they could petition the Divorce Court.

This was of course a much more expensive procedure. The women provided information about the family income and the lawyer advised them concerning the likelihood of a favourable outcome, in which case their husbands would be obliged to pay costs. This remained the case until the passage of the Married Women's Property Act in 1892.

From 1880 to 1889, the total number of cases before the Divorce Court reached fifteen, and in this period six men sought dissolution of marriage.

Petitions to the Divorce Court, 1880–89

Gender	Men	Women
Judicial separation	0	5
Divorce	6	4
Total	6	9

In the case of Bridget Taaffe, the judge in the Divorce Court made a most extraordinary speech about his perceptions of the required behaviour of married women. The petitioner married Francis Taaffe in Dublin on 13 January 1858 and had four children (her husband later claimed there were five, one of whom had died). Two of these children were now married and the youngest was fifteen. Bridget Taaffe gave evidence that they had come to Australia about twenty years before and that she had cohabited with her husband, a soldier, until May 1883.

When her husband was drunk, he beat her with a stick and assaulted her with his clenched fist. As a result, she had been compelled to seek protection from the police. They agreed to a deed of separation on 31 May 1883. She explained that she kept her children by running a greengrocery store at Fremantle. Her husband had left her for some time and then came to live in a house next door. He returned frequently to her house and, on one occasion, threatened her with a 7-pound weight. He had since threatened to break or remove all the furniture. She lived in fear of him coming to the house.

The report of the trial in the press provides much more detail about Francis Taaffe's brutal treatment of his wife and one of his daughters. In his response, he insisted on his innocence, and boasted of the medals granted him as a member of the Pensioner Force.[370] However, it is difficult to believe that he had not frequently threatened and molested his wife.

In his observations before he delivered his verdict on 18 March 1886, Judge George Frederick Stone made a long statement about the legal definition of cruelty. He claimed that the term 'cruelty' meant something different in the Divorce Court from the ordinary commonsense understanding of the term. Cruelty that would justify judicial separation was

> such cruelty as will place the life or the health of a person in danger, or that
> it is something, which renders cohabitation unsafe or likely to be attended
> by injury to the person or the health of the party complaining.[371]

He then discussed the details of the petition, claiming that the evidence was unsatisfactory and the witnesses unconvincing. He thought that, if a person could get a judicial separation from the court without giving convincing evidence that the violent conduct was likely to be repeated, it would soon be flooded with hundreds of petitions by parties treated in this way.

He also spoke at length about the obligations of a wife, implying that those who failed to meet these requirements deserved the ill-treatment they received. 'If a wife can secure her own safety by lawful obedience and a proper self-command, she has no right to come to the Court'. He quoted several earlier cases where the judge considered that the wife 'had not behaved well or dutifully towards her husband' and had therefore brought the problems on herself.

He then gave his considered opinion about the character of Bridget Taaffe, whom he described as

> a thorough businesswoman. She has several intelligent daughters and she
> has carried on a business to assist in the keeping of the household, but I
> do not think that there is evidence to show that the husband has neglected
> his duties as a husband and a father. I think he has also contributed his
> labour to the success of the household, but I think that his wife is a person
> of that character that she would resent any interference on the part of the
> husband in any matter of business and that, when she has been irritated,
> that irritation has risen solely from the want of tact and the length of
> tongue of the petitioner herself.

The judge made one concession and admitted that the husband was also a man of quick temper! But he claimed that it was Bridget Taaffe's duty 'to try to live peaceably with her husband and to put up to a great extent with his failings and shortcomings'. He dismissed her petition, but agreed to order a protection of her earnings. He also agreed to allow moves to appeal his finding. An appeal against the findings of the court was held almost immediately, but was dismissed. Bridget Taaffe had lost her case.[372]

Another case at this time was concluded successfully, perhaps because of the value accorded to evidence provided by witnesses. On 22 May 1886, Jessie Laurence[373] petitioned for judicial separation from Albert James Laurence. They were married in November 1864 at Goolwa, in South Australia. Eight children were born but only two survived. These were two boys, one now twenty and one only eleven. The family had lived at Goolwa, Glenelg, Melbourne, and in Perth. Jessie Laurence sought alimony from her husband, explaining that he was a landowner and land speculator who had recently sold a property worth £800.

Her husband had treated her with violence and shut her out of the house. She had gone to a magistrate and they had signed a deed of separation. He was supposed to give her £1 10s a week but she claimed that he kept a sum of money that she had taken from an account she had in a bank in Adelaide. He refused to return her money and refused to give her a weekly allowance. The evidence provided by her, and by the witnesses, tells a story of them living in cheap hotels and of his constant violence. She claimed that, as a result of his treatment, her health was impaired.

The cases of Taaffe and Laurence from the 1880s have some of the same characteristics as the earlier case involving Vincent. The women were middle-aged and had established families. They had been treated with violence for many years. They hoped that the Magistrate's Court, with its increased powers, would provide them with a solution. However, because the decision of the Magistrate's Court could not be enforced, they decided to make a claim for judicial separation, after consultation with a lawyer regarding the likely outcome.

Between 1880 and 1890, four women sought dissolution of marriage on the grounds of adultery plus either cruelty or desertion – or both. Some of them had also previously applied for a magistrate's order for some form of protection. It seems likely that lawyers were now advising their clients that a strong statement about the level of violence, coupled with adultery, would be accepted by the judge as sufficient cause for a successful outcome.

On 7 September 1886, Mary Ellen Lucille Harper[374] petitioned for dissolution of her marriage with William Lewis Ward Harper on grounds of cruelty and adultery. They were married on 3 November 1874, and had two daughters ten and eleven years of age. In her evidence, Harper claimed that she had been treated with cruelty and violence and that she had been infected with venereal disease. She accused her husband of adultery with person(s) unknown. He had deserted her in April 1883. The respondent was not represented in court and did not appear to answer the charges. The decision of the court was that he was guilty of adultery and cruelty, and a divorce was granted. She was to have custody of her daughters and receive alimony of £1 per week.[375]

During this period of ten years, there were still only six petitions from men, all seeking dissolution of their marriage on the grounds that their wives had committed adultery. All but one of the husbands could name the co-respondent. In some cases, the petitioner sought damages from the co-respondent. In most of the cases, neither the wife as respondent, nor her partner in adultery, appeared before the court to offer any defence. At this time, none of these male petitioners sought custody of his children. All were granted dissolution of marriage without much complication, and the co-respondent was obliged to pay the costs.

On 21 June 1886, for example, George Thomas petitioned for dissolution of marriage on the grounds of adultery by his wife, Mary Anne Thomas.[376] They were married at Fremantle in the Anglican Church on 6 May 1874 and continued to live in Fremantle. They had one daughter, who was now ten years old. The petitioner explained that he had gone to the North West as a station hand in 1880, and regularly remitted small sums of money to his wife. This ceased when he heard rumours about her and returned to Perth. He accused her in his affidavit of living 'as man and wife' with someone called Jordan. According to his account, she did not respond to his accusations. The decision of the court was that the marriage was dissolved and the petitioner should have such relief 'as may seem meet'. The question of damages was presumably decided by a common jury.

This case was typical of men's petitions generally. The petitioner knew the name or names of his wife's partner(s) in adultery. They had informants or witnesses to corroborate their story. They frequently made requests for damages, implying that a wife was of some economic value to her husband. Finally, the trial was brief and decided in the petitioner's favour with some damages awarded, although not usually the amount requested.

In conclusion, we can see that the total number of petitions before the Divorce Court did not change dramatically before the 1890s. From the passage of the act in 1863 until 1889, a total of twenty-eight women filed a petition for either judicial separation or dissolution of marriage. They were relying on the fact that their husbands would have to pay the expenses of the lawyer and the court. In the event of a successful outcome, they could separate from their husbands, they would be able to control their own earnings and property, and they would receive financial support for themselves and their children. In this same period, only eleven men petitioned for dissolution of marriage.

The explanation for this small number appears at first to lie in the prohibitive cost of a case. However, while the husband who petitioned for dissolution of marriage because of his wife's adultery would have to pay lawyer's fees, he would not have to pay the court costs since these were passed on to the co-respondent.

Perhaps equally important was the hostility of the Christian churches to divorce legislation. The Church of England could not prevent these petitions for divorce from members of their congregations, but their opposition may have been a factor of considerable importance among the more respectable and settled members of the community. However, many of the petitions for divorce came from people who had married in an Anglican Church.

The importance of this church opposition to divorce became apparent in 1897, when the Bishop of Perth followed Anglican practices elsewhere by introducing four new regulations for the guidance of the clergy concerning the remarriage of divorced people:[377]

1.   Under no circumstances can the guilty party in a divorce suit be remarried during the lifetime of the other party to the marriage.

2.   In the case of the innocent party wishing to remarry, application must be made to the Bishop for his permission, and no such marriage shall be allowed without the licence of the Bishop to that effect. Such licence will only be issued when evidence sufficient to satisfy the Bishop that the party is innocent has been submitted to him.

3.   The Holy Communion shall not be administered to the guilty party in a divorce suit, his (or her) evil living being open and notorious, until the said party shall have declared himself (or herself) to have truly repented and amended his (or her) former life.

4.   The Holy Communion shall not be administered to the guilty party in a divorce suit, who has remarried during the lifetime of the other party, except after an openly avowed repentance.

For several centuries, the question of divorce had assumed great importance in both the Church of England and the Catholic Church. A large proportion of the population in Western Australia during this period were Roman Catholics, due to the earlier influx of convicts and free immigrants from Ireland. They remained a large part of the community when the population more than doubled between 1870 and 1890. There were 23,315 people in the colony in 1870, not including the so-called 'full-blood Aborigines'. The number increased to 49,782 by 1891. During this twenty-year period, the number of Catholics increased from 6,674 to 12,464.[378]

The Catholic Church always had strict rules about the annulment of marriage except under very particular circumstances. This was sometimes allowed because the original marriage had not been carried out according to law, the marriage partners were too closely related, or one of them was already married.[379] But an annulment was different from a divorce because it implied that the marriage had never been valid or it had not been consummated. According to Catholic teaching, marriage vows meant that the couple were permanently united in the eyes of God and could not be separated. This view was not only supported by various biblical teachings but had been reinforced over a long period by a variety of ecclesiastical judgments.[380]

After vehemently opposing the introduction of the divorce legislation in Western Australia in 1863, the Roman Catholic Church introduced the same rules applied elsewhere for those who divorced and remarried. The divorced couple could continue to receive the church sacraments if they attended confession before communion. But those who remarried were excommunicated.

In the period before 1890, very few couples listed in the records of the Divorce Court were identified as having married in a Catholic Church. However, there were a few examples. On 24 July 1880, for example, Ellen Lakeman petitioned for judicial separation, and on 7 September 1886, Lucille Harper petitioned for dissolution of marriage.[381] There were undoubtedly other cases, which cannot be verified because some of the records identify the place of marriage but provide no details about the nature of the ceremony. However, it is apparent from the available evidence that divorcing couples came less frequently from the Catholic Church than from Anglican or other Protestant persuasions.

The reader may seek other possible causes for the small number of divorce petitions for the first twenty-seven years after the passage of the act. The activities of the Magistrate's Courts suggests that many more women needed to be rescued from unfortunate marriages, but that the Divorce Court was not an available option. Sometimes they had been deserted by their husband and he could not be found; sometimes a woman knew that her husband's resources were too limited to afford a lawyer.

But, in 1892, a new act was passed that would transform the patterns observable in the number and nature of the petitions. In spite of the concessions made to women who appeared before a Magistrate's Court or the Divorce Court, the common law arrangement that a woman's property belonged to her husband remained in place in Western Australia until 1892. In practice, this meant that only those women who had been granted a separation from their husbands by a magistrate, or had been successful in their petition before the Divorce Court for judicial separation or dissolution of marriage, could actually control their own property. The first act concerning the right of all married women to hold property was passed in 1892.[382] This would have a profound effect on the nature of the petitions presented by women to the Divorce Court.

12

Divorce law and the courts 1890–99

Western Australia began a rapid process of change after 1890. The new system of responsible government introduced in that year ended the power of a British governor over the Legislative Council. A more democratic system of voting was introduced, although at first involving only white men, while an elected parliament of two houses chose one of the leading elected politicians as the Premier. Western Australia would not entirely lose its colonial status until it became one of the states in the Australian Federation in 1901.

However, other remarkable changes occurred during this period, due largely to the discovery of gold and the subsequent gold rush. The population increased dramatically in ten years from 49,782 in 1891 to 184,537 in 1901.[383] Housing was needed for the increasing numbers of unemployed who returned from the goldfields while, on the other hand, the wealth of many established citizens began to increase enormously. As the social problems became more and more obvious, large numbers of people banded together to create charitable institutions.

The number in the poor houses grew and the attendant problems led to dramatic shifts in the definition and treatment of the poor. They were now increasingly identified in three different ways: as the old and infirm; as abandoned and neglected children; and, finally, as the unemployed. It was gradually understood that each group required different treatment, and the social services of the time began to be transformed. Among other changes, the Superintendent of Poor Houses undertook to establish what proved to be an efficient Employment Bureau.

The introduction of the Women's Property Act at this time demonstrates that a considerable change had occurred in the community in perceptions of gender difference. While some people deplored this shift towards greater equality, the bill passed both houses of parliament with apparent ease.

The Married Women's Property Bill was introduced in the Legislative Assembly in 1892 by the Member for York, S. H. Parker. He said that

> the Bill I am now asking members to pass, I bring forward as a matter of justice towards one half, and the gentler and nobler half, of the human race. I have no doubt that most members are acquainted with their own privileges, and the rights and powers which they exercise over property. They also know that under the common law in force here... married women have virtually no rights over property at all. The effect of marriage upon a woman is somewhat similar to the effect of a conviction in the case of a felon...As soon as the marriage ceremony is over, she loses every article of property she possesses.
>
> (Interjection: Quite right too.)[384]

Parker continued: 'I am astonished that any member should be bold enough, audacious enough, to give expression to such a sentiment in the House'. He made further remarks about the position of women, pointing out that

> whatever property she may inherit or acquire after her marriage is also taken from her. Almost the entire benefits of that property devolve upon her husband, and he can do pretty much what he pleases with it. True, if it is real estate, he cannot dispose of it without her consent, but as he can enjoy it during her life and, after her death, during the term of his own life, it seems there is very little left for the wife. With regard to personal property, every single penny that she possesses goes to her husband. If she joined her husband after the marriage ceremony with only twenty shillings in her pocket, she must hand it all over to her husband.
>
> (Interjection: Don't talk nonsense)

Parker denied that he was talking nonsense and proceeded in a calmer manner with an account of recent changes to property laws in England. The laws had been changed in 1870, 1874 and 1883, followed by dire predictions of the untold wrongs and miseries that would follow. However, there was no evidence of the accuracy of such predictions, and the English law of 1883 would now be introduced into Western Australia.

In discussing the details of the new bill, Parker pointed out that under existing common law, the guardians of young women of the wealthy classes could bestow property on them as part of a marriage settlement.

> This property is settled upon her and her children, and she has it to her own separate use, her husband having no power to interfere with it. He cannot touch it. It is not liable to his debts or his obligations in any way. He cannot gamble it away, or drink it, and leave the woman a pauper. Her friends take good care to tie it up safely, so that whatever happens, she may have the benefit of it, and be able to live in comfortable circumstances, whatever vicissitudes may happen to her husband's finances.
>
> This Bill simply proposes to make the law of the land what this law of custom is now amongst the wealthy or propertied classes…it does not introduce anything novel or revolutionary.

According to further remarks about the details of the bill, Parker pointed out that, after its passage, no marriage settlements would be necessary: women could keep all their own earnings and they could enter into contracts.

He finished his second-reading speech as follows:

> It means that, if a married woman has a drunken or gambling husband, who wastes his substance in riotous living, and the wife is a thrifty and industrious woman capable of earning her own living, and of maintaining herself and her children in decency, this Bill will protect her in her efforts in that direction, protect her from her drunken or thriftless husband and enable her to support herself and her children and bring them up as respectable citizens…

He concluded with the interesting observation that the changes would mean that a husband, when he married, would no longer be responsible for the accumulated debts of his wife. After some debate and disagreement, the act was passed with a large majority in the Legislative Assembly and with little debate in the Upper House.

Clause 1 stated that

A married woman shall, in accordance with the provisions of this Act, be capable of acquiring, holding, and disposing by will or otherwise of any real or personal property as her separate property, in the same manner as if she were a feme sole, without the intervention of any trustee.[385]

This complex act was followed by two amending acts in 1895 and 1896, which clarified some fine legal points raised by the original act.[386] These acts had the effect of giving women complete freedom in connection with their rights over earnings and any other property. A woman's obligation to remain with her husband had always largely depended on the issue of his ownership of all her possessions. If she had children, she could not separate from him because he owned her property and earnings. After the passage of the Married Women's Property Act, a wife was in a position to make an independent decision.

We come now to a consideration of the way in which the various possibilities under the Divorce Act were realised in the period from 1890 to the end of 1899. This new Property Act made redundant the original section of the Divorce Act concerning the power of magistrates to grant protection of women's property from their husbands. As we have seen, this section of the act had been generally unsuccessful because the Magistrate's Court did not enforce these decisions. As a result of the new Married Women's Property Act, such appeals for protection of property no longer came before the local magistrates.

However, after 1890, there is evidence that the additional powers on other matters granted to magistrates in the act of 1879 were increasingly enforced. In 1990, twelve women applied for assistance from the Perth Magistrate's Court. Eight claims were for desertion by husbands who had left their wives and children without any means of support; three of them had already appeared before the court and had failed to provide the support determined by the magistrate. Four other cases involved acts of violence.[387] For example, on 20 December 1890, the records give details of the case against Thomas Jeffcott. He had been taken into custody by two policemen and the case was heard on the day of his arrest. Jeffcott faced the following charge: 'You at Perth on 20 December did assault and threaten to cut the throat of your wife, Emma Davis Jeffcott, and she is in bodily fear'.

The person making the charge was his wife, and there were no recorded witnesses, except that the two policemen presumably arrived at some stage during the fracas. Jeffcott was bound over to keep the peace with a large surety[388] of £100, the approximate amount of money earned by a tradesman in one year. This decision would presumably deter Jeffcott from inflicting further violence on his wife.

In another case, in 1893, John Joseph O'Connell was charged before the Magistrate's Court with the desertion of his wife and six children, all under the age of ten.[389] He was ordered to pay twenty-five shillings a week to the clerk of the court, to provide adequate support for his family. In this case, the wife had the assistance of a lawyer, and the husband was also imprisoned for one month. This apparently satisfactory outcome, and the likelihood that it would be enforced by the supervision of the clerk of the court, suggests that the Magistrate's Courts were becoming increasingly sophisticated.

In 1896, there were further legal extensions to this pattern of protection and assistance for married women relating to the jurisdiction of magistrates. The MLA for North Fremantle, M. L. Moss, explained the purpose of the new bill on the occasion of the second reading in July 1896.[390] He said that the bill was a transcript of a similar act passed in the British parliament in the previous session and that it was an extension of the present act in the colony dealing with 'destitute persons'. This act reveals a determination to offer some relief to women who had too few resources to appeal to the Supreme Court, where the petitions for judicial separation or dissolution of marriage were now heard.

Under the new 1896 act, the power of the magistrate would be extended so that he could now make an order for judicial separation, 'which power had hitherto been limited to a Judge of the Supreme Court'. A woman suffering persistent cruelty or neglect, or whose husband had been convicted of an aggravated assault, could now apply to two justices for judicial separation. Moss commented that the Supreme Court appeal was beyond the means of many people. A case could still be referred to the Supreme Court by the magistrate.

'Whether or not she was intending to apply for a divorce', the court could rule that the woman no longer had to cohabit with her husband and that she might have custody of children up to the age of sixteen. The husband was required to pay a weekly sum for her upkeep, and one or both was required to pay the costs of the case. This requirement that a woman might be obliged to pay part or all of the costs was the result of a passage of the Married Women's Property Act in 1892 that gave women complete control of their property and earnings.[391] The rules would not apply to a woman shown to have committed adultery 'Provided that the husband has not condoned, or connived at, or by his wilful neglect or misconduct conduced to such act of adultery'.[392] But the court had the option of changing a decision after the presentation of fresh evidence.

This 1896 amending act was largely a repetition of rules set out in earlier legislation, especially that of 1879, which gave increased power to magistrates. This contemporary preoccupation with the way the Magistrate's Court could deal with problems in marriage, including assault, desertion and child custody, was a way of assisting women who could not afford a petition to the Divorce Court.

The repetition of this legislation suggests a search for a means to enable a magistrate to enforce his decision, presumably because of the number of women in the community who still had no means of support. Some of the clauses of these amending acts appear to have been designed to prevent destitute women and children becoming a drain on colonial revenue, since the cost of poor relief had become a high proportion of government expenditure by the late 1860s.[393] By 1896, the poorest women had hope of assistance by applying to a Magistrate's Court, including the possibility of a complete separation from their husbands.

An examination of some of the records of the Perth Police Court for the period after 1896 indicates that the number of people summoned before a magistrate had increased enormously with the rapid growth in population. Some of those summoned were men accused of deserting their wives, and leaving them and their children without means of support. In January and February 1897, for example, eight charges were brought before the magistrate. Some were dismissed, some were adjourned for consideration at a later date, and some of the men were obliged to pay their wives a fixed sum on a regular basis.[394]

By the following year, the cases appear to have increased, with more emphasis on the possibility of complete separation. The court records are much better preserved for this later period, and the pages recording the details of a particular case are often clipped together in one file. On 28 October 1898, for example, Octavius Dyson was accused of persistent cruelty to his wife, Maud Mary Dyson, and failure to pay a reasonable maintenance for his wife and infant children. As a result of his violence, she had already been forced to live apart from him. Dyson had previously appeared in the Magistrate's Court, in February 1897, and had been ordered to pay his wife £1 10s a week. This he had failed to do.[395]

Empowered by the 1896 act, Maud Mary Dyson now asked the magistrate to decide in favour of three things. She wanted an order of separation to be made; she wanted an order for maintenance to be paid; and she wanted an order for the custody of her children up to sixteen years of age. The outcome was curious, and suggests that, in this case, the husband, Octavius Dyson, was afraid that the magistrate would deal with him harshly. With his wife's agreement, he wrote the following letter in longhand to avoid appearing before the court:

> Maud Dyson v Octavius Dyson.
>
> In consideration of Mrs Dyson, my wife, withdrawing the summons issued against me for a separation order, I agree to keep away from her, to live separately and apart from me, and that I will not molest her but will contribute what I can for the maintenance of the children.
> Signed: Octavius D. Dyson.
> I hereby withdraw the above complaint.
> Signed: Maud Mary Dyson.

A final example of the activity of the magistrate in the Police Court after 1896 concerns the case of Richard Wells, whose wife, Frances May Wells, made the accusation that she had been treated with such persistent cruelty that she had been obliged to live separately and apart from him. Wells was summoned to appear before the court and the following order was made, according to the law passed in 1896.[396] It was set out formally on a typed sheet, documenting the details of the case and the decision of the magistrate.

Order

Under 10 Victoria 10, Western Australia

> To Wit   Be it remembered that on the 18 October 1898 complaint was made before Edward Shenton, one of Her Majesty's Justices of the Peace in and for the said Colony of Western Australia for that Richard Wells of Malcolm Street Perth in the Colony aforesaid had treated

Frances Mary Wells his wife with persistent cruelty, and by such cruelty had caused her to leave and live...separately and apart from him against the form of the Statute in such case made and provided and now at this day, to wit, on the 20 October 1898 at the Police... Court Perth the parties aforesaid appear before me...Augustus Sanford Roe, Police Magistrate, and now having heard the matter of the said complaint I do order that the said Frances Mary Wells be not bound to co-habit with her husband for six calendar months from the date of... this Order, leave being reserved for either party to...apply to extend or vary this Order and I do further order that the legal custody of the children of the marriage between the said Frances Mary Wells and Richard Wells while under the age of sixteen years be committed to the said Frances Mary Wells , and I do further order the said...Richard Wells to pay to the Clerk of the Court on behalf of the said Frances Mary Wells and for her use the sum of £1 on Monday of every week until this Order shall be varied or discharged, the first payment to be made on Monday the 24th day of October 1898, and to pay the sum of £1.8.0, costs of Court herein.

Given under my Hand and Seal the 20th Day of October in the year of Our Lord 1898 at Perth in this Colony aforesaid.

Signed Aug. S. Roe,

Police Magistrate[397]

In the last three decades of the nineteenth century, the 1863 Divorce Act and the amendments of 1879 and 1896 made it possible for many women to transform their lives without recourse to the Divorce Court. Women were given custody of young children and then, after 1896, of children up to sixteen years of age, while their husbands were bound to support them and the children. After 1892, the Married Women's Property Act allowed women to become the sole custodians of their own earnings and property. These laws gradually removed the necessity to cohabit with a violent husband by removing his control over all the family resources. This last was a tremendous step forward in the establishment of equality and independence for women, although the act involved increased responsibilities for women as well as increased freedom of action.

As the powers of the Magistrate's Court began to be enforced, they influenced women's choice of petitions before the Divorce Court. The first change was the ending of petitions by women for judicial separation, because this degree of freedom could now be obtained by a much cheaper appeal to a magistrate. The other obvious explanation is that, because women could now control their own incomes, they had much greater freedom to leave their marriage partners.

There were three petitions for judicial separation during 1890 and 1891 but, for the rest of the decade after 1892, all but one woman petitioned for dissolution of marriage, claiming adultery, violence and/or desertion. A woman still had to produce evidence of more than adultery in order to argue successfully before the Divorce Court. However, from that time onwards, the court was almost entirely engaged in determining whether a marriage should be dissolved with the possibility of remarriage in the future.

The second great change in the Divorce Court concerned an overall increase in the number of petitions by both men and women for dissolution of marriage. This may have been a response in some way to the social dislocation caused by the gold rush of the 1890s. While there were only fifteen cases overall in the ten years from 1880 to 1889, there were seventy-two cases from 1890 to 1899. The percentage increase in the number of petitions for divorce was greater than the percentage increase in population.

The total number of petitions remained below five per year until 1896. In that year there were eight petitions, in 1897 there were nine, in 1898 there were sixteen, and in 1899 there were twenty-five.

Petitions to the Divorce Court, 1890–99

Gender	Men	Women
Judicial separation	0	4
Divorce	40	28
Total	40	32

There were seventy-four cases listed in the last ten years of the nineteenth century, but this included two (De Souza and Denton) that were postponed and then resumed. The correct number of petitions in these ten years was therefore seventy-two, some of which were heard in the Divorce Court after 1900. The number of petitions by both men and women increased enormously in these ten years, with forty petitions for divorce from men and thirty-two petitions from women, four for judicial separation and twenty-eight for divorce.

The following cases of women's petitions for dissolution of marriage have the characteristics common to many divorce petitions that came before the court in the last ten years of the century. The married couples had lived in several places during their short married lives. The petitions referred to adultery by the husband but the wife was unable to provide a name for the co-respondent. This was coupled with the claim that she had been subjected to various kinds of violence.

Because the decision of the judge was not always recorded, either in the case files or the index of cases, it is not possible to state the number of successful petitions with any accuracy. However, those cases that record the decision are usually in the affirmative. It might be concluded that the lawyers representing the petitioner would refuse to undertake the necessary work if they thought the petition unlikely to succeed.

The first of these two cases reveals the failure of the couple to establish a permanent home. On 1 February 1899, Winifred Evelyn Howe petitioned for dissolution of marriage with Thomas James Howe.[398] They had been married on 18 August 1894, at the Anglican Church in Adelaide and had one child who died. At first they lived in Adelaide, then he went to Coolgardie for a while before returning home. They both moved to Pinjarra in Western Australia for six months and then moved to Perth. They then spent six months in New Zealand before returning to Perth for three months. Their next destination was Sydney before they again returned to Perth.

Winifred Howe accused her husband of adultery with a woman whose name was unknown to her. She claimed that she had been treated with cruelty and violently assaulted. Newspaper reports of the court proceedings provide additional detail about the nature of the extreme violence suffered by Winifred Howe, as well as witness reports confirming her husband's adultery.[399] The judge granted her dissolution of marriage.

This second example reveals the near-impossible task faced by a woman who tried to support herself and her children. On 4 May 1899, Marian Gertrude Noble[400] petitioned for dissolution of marriage from Thomas Noble, a bookkeeper. They were married in Melbourne on 12 November 1890 when she was between fifteen and sixteen years of age, with the consent of her parents. They had two children.

Her husband had treated her with violence and made threats with a knife. As a result, she returned to Melbourne and attempted unsuccessfully to keep herself and the children. She returned to her husband in Perth but discovered that he had committed adultery with a woman, name unknown. She left him but stayed in Perth, but was unable to support her children, who were taken by her husband. She stated that 'I am at present earning my living as a house-keeper and, after payment of my just debts, I am not worth the sum of £25, save except my wearing apparel'.[401] Thomas Noble offered no defence and his wife was granted a dissolution of marriage on the grounds of adultery and cruelty. The custody of the children was to be decided at a later sitting of the court.[402]

There were few cases of bigamy recorded in the nineteenth century but it was not unknown. Since the charges of bigamy at this time usually involved an earlier marriage in England, information had to be obtained from overseas. On 19 April 1899, Jane Elderson, defined as a spinster in the records, petitioned for a declaration of nullity of marriage with John Millabone.[403] According to the records, they were married on 5 December 1882.

She discovered that her husband had already married Anne Hannah Wickens of Middlesex, England, on 30 January 1864. John Millabone was now a ship's steward at Fremantle. The respondent did not appear to defend himself and the judge declared that, since the marriage was illegal, he would declare it instantly dissolved, without the usual wait of six months before a decree nisi could be issued. The respondent was obliged to pay the court costs.

Some general observations can be made about the changes in the last few years of the century after an examination of the evidence presented to the court. The first is that, during this period, many petitioners had been married for relatively short periods before they sought a divorce. Many of the participants in these appearances before the court described how they had married in one of the eastern colonies (or occasionally in England or New Zealand) and had come to Western Australia in search of new opportunities. The lure of the goldfields explained the movements of many people. Their accounts of marital difficulties were often accompanied by reference to frequent changes of address and periods of isolation from one another.

Many divorcing couples in this period had no children. For example, of the twenty-five petitions for dissolution of marriage in 1899, there were ten couples with no children. If there were any children, men seldom petitioned for their custody. Prostitution and venereal disease were now occasionally cited in the evidence brought before the court, and there were also several cases where illegitimate children were reported as evidence of adultery. In some cases the petitioner claimed damages from the co-respondent, who was usually also required to pay the costs of the court case. In many cases, neither respondent nor co-respondent appeared before the court to answer the charges.

The following cases provide examples of some of these general patterns in petitions from men, which were generally comparatively brief. On 18 June 1892, James Millar successfully petitioned for dissolution of marriage on grounds of adultery by his wife, Margaret Ellen Millar.[404] They were married on 24 June 1888 at Fremantle. They had one child three years of age. James Millar claimed that his wife had subsequently given birth to two 'bastard children', the birth certificates of these children being presented to the court. The petitioner was not able to identify the father but he claimed that he had been informed that his wife was living as a prostitute in a brothel in Perth. Two witnesses then gave evidence to support this claim.

On 15 September 1893, Roger Buckingham petitioned for dissolution of marriage on grounds of adultery by his wife, Elizabeth Buckingham.[405] They married at the Congregational Church on 14 May 1882 and had two children, seven and four and a half years of age. Buckingham went to the Murchison goldfields in April 1892, returning in September 1893. His wife resided with her parents during that period of one and a half years. When he returned, he discovered that she had given birth to a 'bastard child', the certificate for which was provided. The judge granted dissolution of marriage on 6 December 1893.[406]

On 17 November 1899, Henry Vandeleur Wrigley petitioned for his marriage with Isabelle Ellen Wrigley to be dissolved, and named the co-respondent as Geoffrey Bird.[407] The petitioner had married on 6 October 1894 at Glenelg in South Australia. He and his wife had lived at Hawker in South Australia before moving to the goldfields in Coolgardie in Western Australia. They had one child who was four years of age. In his evidence, the petitioner claimed that his wife had committed adultery with Geoffrey Bird in September 1899.

After this date, his wife and Bird lived together as man and wife at the Menzies Hotel in Melbourne. Henry Wrigley claimed damages from

Geoffrey Bird of £500. This case was straightforward, both because there were witnesses who supported the petitioner's account, and because neither his wife nor the co-respondent appeared to defend the charges. Wrigley was granted dissolution of marriage, and the co-respondent was to pay the £500 damages as well as the court costs.

In conclusion, it is apparent that the cost of a petition before the Divorce Court made it inaccessible to many poorer men and women in the community, since the lawyers investigated whether a husband or co-respondent could afford the cost of the case. After the passage of the Married Women's Property Act of 1892, women could also be required to pay the costs.

But it is also the case that many men and women who petitioned for dissolution of marriage in the 1890s were comparatively young and had no children. They undoubtedly wished to be legally free to reorder their lives. While women had to prove both adultery and one or more other causes in order to be granted a divorce, the evidence gives the strong impression that most of the petitions of both men and women were treated sympathetically.

Although the 1863 Divorce Act still gave greater power to men than to women, it was instrumental in opening up a more realistic consideration of the position of women in matrimony, both as wives and as responsible parents. These new laws reflected changing attitudes towards men's responsibility within marriage, and their influence went beyond simply legislating for divorce. This was now a field for regular intervention by the magistrates to prevent the possibility of women being placed in a helpless position due to the irresponsible or violent behaviour of their husbands.

After 1880, it was also one of the important tasks of judges in the Supreme Court, sometimes with the assistance of a jury, to determine whether marriage partners should be separated or whether a marriage should be dissolved. Divorce legislation and new laws about the rights of women to own their own property were a powerful impetus towards the transformation of the unequal gender relations of previous centuries.

The evidence available from an examination of the petitions for judicial separation and for dissolution of marriage reveals a great deal about the lives of people in the last three decades of the nineteenth century. While many people could not afford the costs of petitioning, they were finally offered considerable satisfaction because of the increased power given to magistrates.

However, the number of children in institutions between 1870 and 1900 increased gradually, suggesting that these new laws offered little or no help to many women in the community. Why were many women with young children unable to seek help under these new laws? What happened to women whose children were illegitimate? Why were there so many abandoned children? The conclusion will offer some observations about this paradox.

Conclusion

The record of nineteenth-century marriage legislation is not complete without noting the passage of some minor legislation, either passed or contemplated, on very particular subjects. In 1867, a British statute that concerned the processes connected with establishing legitimacy and the validity of marriages, and the right to be deemed a natural-born subject, was incorporated into Western Australian law.[408] This was undoubtedly important for a few people arriving in the colony whose marriage status might need to be investigated or confirmed, especially because of the passage of the new divorce law in 1863.

In the following decade, two other attempts were made to bring in minor changes to marriage law. One was to try to pass a bill allowing a man to marry his deceased wife's sister.[409] This was attempted in 1877 but the bill was deferred. It was finally passed as part of the 1894 marriage law. In 1879, another short act designed as an amendment to the 1856 act clarified some of the issues surrounding the notice required before any marriage could be celebrated.[410]

A law to prevent bigamous marriages was passed with considerable difficulty in 1879. The Honourable G. W. Leake, the Acting Attorney-General, stated in his introduction to the second reading that the existing law presented very little obstacle to bigamous marriage, owing to 'the ready means and facilities afforded the public for entering the holy bonds of matrimony'.[411] He also wanted to discourage thoughtless marriages by young men and women (he called them 'boys and girls') 'fired with romantic visions of the bliss of matrimonial life', who rushed into marriage 'swearing eternal friendship to each other'.

These restraints on bigamy and hasty marriage were to be achieved, according to the bill under discussion, by requiring that a notice of marriage be given to the district registrar for at least seven days before the date fixed for the marriage. This notice would be entered in an official marriage notice book, which could be inspected by anyone, and those wishing to prevent the marriage could write 'Forbidden' alongside the names. After considerable debate, the new act required that no marriage could be celebrated without notice of seven days, 'except under special license for that purpose issued by the Governor, or except after due publication of banns'.

In 1894, all previous acts concerning the Registration of Births, Deaths and Marriages were repealed, having remained virtually unchanged since 1856. The Attorney-General, Septimus Burt, introduced two new bills concerning the Registration and *Celebration* of Marriage. The term 'solemnization' was no longer used. The two bills were discussed together at the second-reading stage. In his second-reading speech, referring to the celebration of marriage, Attorney-General, Burt explained why a change to the law was deemed necessary:

> if you look at the three marriage Acts now in force, it will take you a long time to find who are legally entitled to celebrate marriages, and the time and place where they may be celebrated.[412]

These three acts were the two enacted during the time of Governor Kennedy in 1856, and the 1879 act concerning the notice required before marriage could occur.

As might be expected, both 1894 acts copied much that had gone before. Burt's comments suggest that the government thought that, after nearly forty years, some issues needed clarification rather than any major change. There were clauses in the Registration Bill concerning the appointment of the Registrar-General and district registrars. The fees were listed, the government undertook to provide the necessary books for recording purposes, and the actual wording of various certificates was set out in the bill.

The ministers who wished to be recorded as marriage celebrants had to supply proof of their bona fides and the Registrar-General could remove the name of anyone who was not a minister of a church. Marriage certificates were now to be issued in triplicate: one for the participants, one for the Registrar-General and one for the local registrar.[413] The administrative details were more clearly defined but did not incorporate any radical new instructions.

The bill concerning the celebration of marriage proved more contentious. In his second-reading speech, when both bills were under discussion, the Attorney-General explained the reasons for some of the clauses in the new Celebration of Marriage Bill, although he claimed that 'it was hard to decide what needs to be done'. The first issue to be raised in debate concerned the time and place of marriage. According to the original wording of the bills, people duly registered could perform marriages in a church, in a district registry office or in a place authorised by the government as appropriate. The service had to take place between 8.00 am and 4.00 pm.

The other issue concerned the Church of England requirement to publish banns for three consecutive Sundays in the church where the wedding was to occur, or for one week in a registrar's office. It was claimed that great difficulties might be experienced by a young woman who arrived to join her intended husband and had nowhere to live for the two weeks of waiting. In due course, after discussions in the committee stages of the bill and in the Legislative Council, the time was extended from 8.00 am to 6.00 pm. Other changes were made concerning special licenses and places designated for marriage celebration.

There was, however, one important change in the Celebration of Marriage Act, which passed without substantial opposition. The right of a man to wed his deceased wife's sister was now stated quite clearly, with Clause 32 of the act underlining the legitimacy of such a marriage:

No marriage between any man and the sister of his deceased wife shall within Western Australia be voidable or in anywise impeachable upon the ground only of such affinity between the parties thereto, any law, usage, or custom to the contrary notwithstanding.[414]

The act also stated that Quakers and Jews now had to register their marriages within seven days, so that they would be 'as legal and valid as any other marriage duly celebrated under this Act'.[415] Four years later, in 1898, another short act listed the clauses of the 1894 Marriage Act that did not apply to Quakers and Jews. Presumably to avoid some uneasiness in the Jewish community, Clause 3 stated that

> Marriages between parties both of whom are Jews shall only be celebrated by a Minister of the Jewish religion ordinarily officiating as such, whose name, designation, and usual place of residence have been and continue to be duly registered according to law...[416]

Except for the requirement to register their marriages from 1847, this was the first time that the secular state had passed legislation concerning Jewish marriage.

In 1900, another act amended the 1894 Births, Deaths and Marriages Registration Act. But this concerned the registration of births, with no reference to marriage law.[417]

My examination of the 1863 Divorce Act and its three following amendments seems to suggest that it offered new security for many women, and the possibility for men and women to end their failed marriages. Equally importantly, the introduction of the Married Women's Property Act in 1892 reduced gender inequality in the community. However, in spite of this obvious progress towards a more enlightened society, not everyone had access to these apparent advantages. Towards the end of the century, one of the main problems concerned the high levels of unemployment. This affected the stability of marriages, the possibility of divorce, and the lives of many children.

The most obvious problem was the cost of petitions to the Divorce Court. In many families, neither husband nor wife had any savings and would be unlikely to find a lawyer willing to represent them in court. After 1892, and the passage of the Married Women's Property Act, both husband and wife were responsible for legal costs. Women may have separated from their partners because of adultery, or because of abuse and violence, but been unable to appeal to the Divorce Court. In some cases, women sought help from the Magistrate's Court and were provided with protection from their husbands, and financial support for their families.

However, many married women deserted by their husbands found it almost impossible to support their children. A woman could not petition for divorce unless her husband could be found. In some instances, this was not possible. She could appeal to a magistrate, pleading that her husband had deserted her, but the best she could hope from this procedure was some form of poor relief.

The Anglican, Catholic and Wesleyan marriage services all contained references to the married state as intended to provide care and support for children. It is ironic that many women had to seek judicial separation, divorce or a magistrate's ruling in order to guarantee this support. The difficulties faced by many married couples had disastrous effects on the lives of many children.

Some were sent to orphanages so that their mothers could go out to work to provide the orphanage with the necessary financial support for their keep. The numbers of children in the Roman Catholic and Protestant orphanages increased rapidly after 1870, some paid for by their mothers, but most supported with a weekly payment from the government.

Some of the children in the orphanages had been abandoned by their parents and been found begging or committing minor crimes. In the period from 1870 onwards, these unfortunate children were variously defined as paupers, delinquents and larrikins. At first they were committed to an adult gaol, but after 1881 most of them spent time in the Rottnest Reformatory.[418] The government struggled with problems connected with housing, educating and employing them.[419]

Women with illegitimate children were in the most difficult position. The obligation of men to support their illegitimate children had long been enshrined in colonial law, beginning in 1845.[420] Two new laws dealing with men's responsibility for their illegitimate children were also passed in 1871,[421] and in 1875.[422] According to the first of these acts, a woman could make application to a justice of the peace for a summons to be served on the father of the child. A judge of petty sessions could then make an order on the putative father to pay maintenance and the costs of the case. On the other hand, the mother could be punished for the neglect or desertion of her 'bastard' child. The second act was longer than the first and elaborated on what had to be proved and corroborated before the court.

The laws seem clear enough, yet young women were often unable to secure any assistance. Some preferred to conceal the birth of their child in order to retain their employment. In any case, it was not easy in these cases to establish the identity of the father. Many women with an illegitimate child chose to leave their baby soon after birth with a 'baby-farmer', the name given to those women who cared for other people's babies in return for a deposit and a regular weekly payment.[423] Sometimes, the desperate mother then abandoned the baby. In other cases, she returned regularly to check on the child's welfare while maintaining her employment as a servant. The survival of these children was very uncertain, depending on the honesty and integrity of the baby-farmer.

In 1898, the problem of abandoned and destitute children led to the introduction in parliament of a bill to make provision for the adoption of children.[424] The consent of the parents had to be obtained except where the child had been absolutely deserted, and the adopted child continued to be entitled to inherit property rights from its natural parents. In the committee stages of the bill in the Upper House, the members agreed to change the clause concerning the required age of the adopting father from forty years older to thirty years older than the adopted female child. The debate does not spell out the purpose of this clause but there is the veiled suggestion of the possibility of sexual exploitation by a younger man. However, the majority clearly favoured the younger father.[425]

It was also recognised that abandoned and destitute children were likely to suffer some kind of sexual exploitation. The increasing evidence of prostitution in the colony, as well as a concern about other illegal sexual acts, especially those concerning children, resulted in the introduction in 1892 of a complex act about the keeping of brothels and the prostitution of underage girls.[426] The crimes of procuring a person for prostitution, defilement, carnal knowledge, rape and incest were all defined, and declared to be punishable by various periods of imprisonment.

The marriage laws of 1856 and the divorce law of 1863 laid the legal foundations for the social transformation of the relationships of many people in Western Australia. Governor Kennedy's laws finally removed all cause for religious conflict over the marriage issue. From 1856, people could choose to marry according to the customs of their church, with very little secular intervention. The only requirement was the relatively cheap marriage license. They could also be married by a district registrar for a small sum, without any religious service. The divorce law of 1863 and subsequent changes, including the Married Women's Property Act, were radical initiatives in a very conservative society.

The divorce legislation of the late nineteenth century considered questions of child support and custody. However, the evidence suggests that the most extreme disadvantage was suffered by the illegitimate offspring of single women, and by the children of parents who could not afford a divorce. The issues surrounding divorce, and the fate of children caught up in the cycles of poverty and unhappy marriages, continued to be of major concern in the twentieth century.

NOTES

Abbreviations

acc.	accession
AJCP	Australian Joint Copying Project
AN	Anglican Church Records
c.	(in listings of statutes and acts) chapter
COD	Colonial Office Despatches/Documents
CONS	consignment
CSR	Colonial Secretary's Records
26 Geo. 2	in the twenty-sixth year of the reign of King George II
SROWA	State Records Office of Western Australia
4 Vict.	in the fourth year of the reign of Queen Victoria
vol.	volume

1: The English background

1   H. A. Finlay and R. J. Bailey-Harris, *Family Law in Australia*, fourth edition, Butterworths, Sydney, 1989, chapters 3 and 4.

2   Anthony Dickey, *Family Law*, fifth edition, Law Book Co., Sydney, 2007, pp. 4–5.

3   A reduction of the number to twelve bishops was being considered in 2011.

4   Now usually spelt 'licence' in Australia, this was the spelling of the noun in the nineteenth century. It is the form used in all legislation under consideration in this book.

5   'An Act for the Better Preventing of Clandestine Marriage', Acts of the Parliament of Great Britain, 26 Geo. 2, c. 33, 1753.

6   Lisa O'Connell, 'Marriage acts: stages in the transformation of nuptial culture', *differences: A Journal of Feminist Cultural Studies*, vol. 11, no. 1, 1999, pp. 68–111.

7   Rebecca Probert, 'Control over marriage in England and Wales, 1753–1823: the Clandestine Marriages Act of 1753 in context', *Law and History Review*, vol. 27, no. 2, 2009, pp. 1–26.

8   'An Act to repeal certain Provisions of the 26 George 2, for the Better Preventing of Clandestine Marriage', Acts of the Parliament of the United Kingdom, 4 Geo. 4,

c. 17, 1823; and 'An Act for amending the Laws respecting the Solemnization of Marriages in England', 4 Geo. 4, c. 76, 1823.

9   Joan Perkin, *Women and Marriage in Nineteenth-century England*, Routledge, London, 1989, Chapter 1.

10   Claire Tomalin, *The Life and Death of Mary Wollstonecraft*, Penguin, Harmondsworth, 1985, p. 254.

11   Richard Reeves, *John Stuart Mill: Victorian firebrand*, Atlantic, London, 2007, p. 438.

12   For a discussion of these laws, see Anthony Dickey, *Family Law*, p. 175ff.

13   Albert Labriola, 'Divorce and Matrimonial Causes Act', *Literary Encyclopedia*, 9 February 2004, http://www.litencyc.com/php/stopics.php?rec=true&UID=690, accessed 17 September 2012.

14   Henry Finlay, 'Divorce and the status of women: beginnings in nineteenth century Australia', seminar paper presented at the Institute of Family Studies, Melbourne, 20 September 2001.

15   Common law refers to law and the corresponding legal system developed through decisions by courts and similar tribunals (called case law), rather than through legislative statutes or executive action.

16   'An Act to amend the Law relating to the Custody of Infants', Acts of the Parliament of the United Kingdom, 2 and 3 Vict., c. 54, 1839.

17   Dickey, *Family Law*, pp. 6–7.

18   Lawrence Stone, *Road to Divorce: England 1530–1987*, Oxford University Press, Oxford, 1990, p. 369ff.

19   'Custody of Infants Act, 1873', Acts of the Parliament of the United Kingdom, 36 and 37 Vict., c. 12, 1873.

20   Stone, *Road to Divorce*, p. 390ff.

21   See Joan Perkin, *Women and Marriage in Nineteenth-century England*; and Mary Lyndon Shanley, *Feminism, Marriage and the Law in Victorian England*, Princeton University Press, Princeton, 1993.

2: Church of England dominance

22   Pamela Statham-Drew, *James Stirling: admiral and founding Governor of Western Australia*, UWA Press, Crawley, 2003.

23   Harry Dillon and Peter Butler, *Macquarie: from colony to country*, Random House, Sydney, 2010.

24   F. K. Crowley, 'Stirling, Sir James (1981–1865)', *Australian Dictionary of Biography*, vol. 2, Melbourne University Press, 1967, pp. 484–88.

25   Crowley, 'Stirling, Sir James (1791–1865)'.

26   J. M. R. Cameron, *Ambition's Fire: the agricultural colonisation of pre-convict Western Australia*, UWA Press, Nedlands, 1981, Chapter 3, for an account of the origins of the Colonial Office decision to agree to the settlement, and for the planning of the voyages of the first ships.

27   Malcolm Uren, 'Roe, John Septimus (1797–1878)', *Australian Dictionary of Biography*, vol. 2, Melbourne University Press, 1967. pp. 390–92.

28   Ray Oldham, 'Reveley, Henry Willey (1788–1875)', *Australian Dictionary of Biography*, vol. 2, Melbourne University Press, 1967, pp. 376–77.

29   P. McCarthy, 'The foundations of Catholicism in Western Australia, 1829–1911', *University Studies in History*, vol. 2, no. 4, 1956, pp. 5–76.

30   See *Perth Gazette*, 22 October 1836 to 2 December 1837, for at least twelve articles and letters concerning support for this organisation in the colony and questions concerning people's responses to Reverend Giustianini, the first missionary appointed.

31   Frederick Chidley Irwin, *The State and Position of Western Australia: commonly called the Swan-River Settlement*, Simpkin, Marshall, London, 1835.

32   Ross Border, 'Scott, Thomas Hobbes (1783–1860)', *Australian Dictionary of Biography*, vol. 2, Melbourne University Press, 1967, pp. 431–33.

33   A. E. Williams, *West Anglican Way: the growth of the Anglican Church in Western Australia from its early beginnings*, Province of Western Australia of the Anglican Church of Australia, Perth, 1989, p. 23.

34   See *Australian Dictionary of Biography* for details about the major political figures in the early Colony of Western Australia. See also Percy U. Henn, 'Mainly about [Western Australian] people', manuscript, Battye Library Ephemera Collection, call no. PR 555.

35   Alfred H. Chate, 'Moore, George Fletcher, (1798–1886)', *Australian Dictionary of Biography*, vol. 2, Melbourne University Press, 1967, pp. 252–54.

36   M. Medcalf, 'Leake, George (1786–1949)', *Australian Dictionary of Biography*, vol. 2, Melbourne University Press, 1967, pp. 99–100.

37   David Mossenson, 'Nash, Richard West (1808–1850)', *Australian Dictionary of Biography*, vol. 2, Melbourne University Press, 1967, p. 278.

38   See, for example, Emma Christopher, *A Merciless Place: the lost story of Britain's convict disaster in Africa and how it led to the settlement of Australia*, Allen & Unwin, Sydney, 2010; and Alan Frost, *Botany Bay: the real story*, Black Inc., Melbourne, 2011.

39   See Bevan Carter and Lynda Nutter, *Nyungah Land: records of invasion and theft of Aboriginal land on the Swan River, 1829–1850*, Black History Series, Swan Valley Nyungah Community, Guildford, WA, 2005.

40   See Cameron, *Ambition's Fire*, especially the chapter on the so-called 'Swan River mania'.

41   Sir George Murray to Captain Stirling 1828, despatch no. 1, *Historical Records of Australia*, series 3, vol. 6, p. 601.

42   Sir George Murray to Lieutenant-Governor Stirling, 30 May 1830, *Swan River Papers*, vol. 11.

43   Lord Goderich to Lieutenant-Governor Stirling, 5 March 1831, Clause 14, *Swan River Papers*, vol. 11.

44   Lord Goderich to Lieutenant-Governor Stirling, 5 March and 28 April 1831, *Swan River Papers*, vol. 11.

45   'A Bill for the Adoption of the following Acts of the British Legislation', *Minutes of the Proceedings of the WA Legislative Council*, 22 March 1836, pp. 78–79. See a list of eighteen English acts following this bill. (Note: the WA Legislative Council Minutes are available at http://www.parliament.wa.gov.au/Parliament/Library/Minutes1832to1870.nsf/Main?openview)

46 *Minutes of the Proceedings of the WA Legislative Council*, 22 March 1836, pp. 77–79.

47 To be discussed later in this book.

48 See Jacqueline O'Brien and Pamela Statham-Drew, *On We Go, the Wittenoom Way: the legacy of a colonial chaplain*, Fremantle Press, Fremantle, 2009.

49 *Perth Gazette* and *West Australian*, 19 February 1848.

50 Despatch to Richard Madden from the Secretary of State for the Colonies, WA *Government Gazette*, 14 November 1848.

51 See Brian Kyme and Edward Doncaster, *The Wollaston Legacy*, John Septimus Roe Anglican Community School for the Institute of Anglican Studies, St George's Cathedral, Perth, 2007; Rev. Canon A. Burton, 'Notes on the three archdeacons: Thomas Hobbes Scott, John Ramsden Wollaston, Matthew Blagden Hale', *Early Days: Journal of the Royal Western Australian Historical Society*, vol. 2, part 17, 1935, pp. 20–27.

52 See John Tonkin, *Cathedral and Community: a history of St George's Cathedral, Perth*, UWA Press, Crawley, 2001, p. 6.

53 See C. L. M. Hawtrey, *The Availing Struggle: a record of the planting and development of the Church of England in Western Australia, 1829–1947*, n.p., Perth, 1949, for a map showing that the Anglican Church in Australia was under the control of the Diocese of Calcutta from 1824. All of Western Australia and South Australia was under the Diocese of Adelaide from 1847. The Diocese of Perth was created in 1856.

54 Hawtrey, *The Availing Struggle*, p. 41.

55 Governor Fitzgerald to Bishop Short, SROWA, CSR, acc. 49, vol. 25, folio 1282, 28 November 1848.

56 Bishop Short to Governor Fitzgerald, SROWA, CSR, acc. 36, vol. 188, folio 154, 6 January 1849.

57 Bishop Short to Governor Fitzgerald, SROWA, CSR, acc. 36, vol. 188, folio 198, 14 March 1849.

58 Governor Fitzgerald to Bishop Short, SROWA, CSR, acc. 49, vol. 27, folio 460, 2 May 1849.

59 Bishop Short to Governor Fitzgerald, SROWA, CSR, acc. 36, vol. 175, folio 129, 18 December 1848.

60 Governor Fitzgerald to Bishop Short, SROWA, CSR, acc. 49, vol. 25, folio 1395, 20 December 1848.

61 Governor Fitzgerald to Bishop Short, SROWA, CSR, acc. 49, vol. 27, folio 463, 3 May 1849.

62 WA Government, *Census of Population, and Returns of Stock and Crops*, 1848.

63 See Jenkins, C. A. 'Early years of the Methodist Church in Western Australia', *Early Days: Journal of the Royal Western Australian Historical Society*, vol. 2, part 13, 1933, pp. 1–15; Rev. William McNair, 'A second look at the early years of Methodism in Western Australia, 1830–1855', *Early Days: Journal of the Royal Western Australian Historical Society*, vol. 7, part 1, 1969, pp. 79–87.

64 The early history of Methodism is explained succinctly by William Hague in his biography *William Wilberforce: the life of the great anti-slave trade campaigner*, HarperCollins, London, 2008, pp. 8–16. Hague discusses the distinctions between Methodists and Evangelicals on p. 90ff.

65 Carson, Alfred, 'A farmer of 1832: extract of a letter written by Joseph Hardy... 14 July 1832', *Early Days: Journal of the Royal Western Australian Historical Society*, vol. 3, part 1, 1938, p. 63.

66 See Wesley Lutton, *The Wesley Story: centenary of Wesley Church, Perth, Western Australia, 1870–1970*, Central Methodist Mission, Perth, 1970. Held in the Uniting Church Archives, 91 Edward Street, Perth.

67 See Irwin, *The State and Position of Western Australia*, pp. 52–54, for a contemporary description of the Methodist farming settlements.

68 See Lutton, *The Wesley Story*; Thea Shipley, *Full Circle: A History of Wesley Church*, Uniting Church in Australia, Synod of Western Australia, Perth, 2003; and C. A. Jenkins, *A Century of Methodism in Western Australia, 1830–1930*, Patersons Printing Press, Perth, 1930.

69 WA Government, *Census of Population, and Returns of Stock and Crops*, 1848.

70 See Patrick O'Farrell, *The Catholic Church and Community: an Australian history*, revised edition, UNSW Press, Sydney, 1992 (first published 1985), p. 75ff.

71 Kathleen O'Donohue, 'Brady, John (1800?–1871)', *Australian Dictionary of Biography*, vol. 1, Melbourne University Press, 1966, pp. 146–47. See also the entries about Joseph Serra and Bishop Martin Griver.

72 P. J. Coles, 'Trigg, Henry (1791–1882)', *Australian Dictionary of Biography*, vol. 2, Melbourne University Press, 1967, p. 539.

73 See S. H. Cox, *The Seventy Years History of the Trinity Congregational Church, Perth, 1845 to 1916*, E. S. Wigg & Son, Perth, 1916.

74 See Stuart Bonnington, *Like a Mustard Seed: a history of the Presbyterian Church of Western Australia from 1829 to 1901*, S. Bonnington, Melbourne, 2004; and Bruce Devenish, *Man of Energy and Compassion: the life, letters and times of Henry Trigg, Swan pioneer and church founder*, Wongaburra Enterprises, South Perth, 1996, pp. 53–59.

75 'Pastoral letter to the Scotch and other Presbyterian inhabitants of the Colony of Swan River. On board the ship Portland, King George's Sound, 13 November 1837', WA *Government Gazette*, 27 January 1838.

76 WA Government, *Census of Population, and Returns of Stock and Crops*, 1848.

77 See *British Parliamentary Papers 1800–1900: Colonies Australia*, vol. 13, 'Correspondence and papers relating to the Australian Colonies, 1851–1852', Irish University Press, Dublin, c. 1974, p. 73. There was apparently still some doubt about the precedence of the Church of England, since the Bishop of Sydney requested confirmation that the Church of England clergy would have precedence for grand occasions over Roman Catholic prelates.

78 WA *Government Gazette*, 18 November 1837, p. 130.

79 See Rowan Strong, 'The Reverend John Wollaston and colonial Christianity in Western Australia, 1840–1863', *Journal of Religious History*, vol. 25, no. 3, 2001, pp. 261–85, and 'An Antipodean Establishment: institutional Anglicanism in Australia, 1788–1934', *Journal of Anglican Studies*, vol. 1, no. 1, 2003, p. 61–90.

80 J. S. Battye, *Cyclopedia of Western Australia*, vol. 2, published for the Cyclopedia Co. by Hussey & Gillingham, Adelaide, 1913, p. 85.

81 Hawtrey, *The Availing Struggle*, p. 47.

82 WA *Blue Book*, 1848.

3: Marriage practice, 1829–41

83   Williams, *West Anglican Way*, p. 24; Kyme and Doncaster, *The Wollaston Legacy*, p. 1.

84   J. S. Battye, *The Cyclopedia of Western Australia*, vol. 2, p. 81.

85   John Tonkin, *Cathedral and Community*, p. 6ff.

86   Williams, *West Anglican Way*, p. 23.

87   I have found no evidence of any charge being levied for a special license.

88   SROWA, CSR, acc. 49, vol. 11, folio 814, 6 October 1840.

89   'Marriage records kept by the Anglican Church, 1829–1841', SROWA, AN 9/1, acc. 703/ 1–9.

90   'The form of solemnization of matrimony 1662', in The Anglican Diocese of Perth, *The Year Book for 1897*, Church of England in Australia, Diocese of Perth, Perth, 1897, p. 299.

91   See *Australian Dictionary of Biography* and also Williams, *West Anglican Way*, p. 23.

92   'Marriage records kept by the Anglican Church, 1829–1841'.

93   See *Swan River Guardian*, 12 January 1837 – 14 December 1837. Louis Giustiniani wrote a great many letters and articles of protest in this weekly paper concerning his objections to the policies of the colonial government. See 12 October 1837 for his 'Address to the jury on the late native tribes'. See also Williams, *West Anglican Way*, pp. 53–61.

94   'Marriage records kept by the Anglican Church, 1829–1841'.

95   See also Percy U. Henn, 'Mainly about [Western Australian] people', manuscript, Battye Library Ephemera Collection, call no. PR 555, which includes a seven-page letter by Mrs Mitchell, 'Life of a missionary on the Swan'.

96   Malcolm Queckett 'Stations echo colonial history', *West Australian*, 3 April 2010, p. 8. This article recounts the events at an Easter Church service in the still-surviving building at Henley Brook.

97   See Hal Colebatch, *A Story of One Hundred Years: Western Australia, 1829–1929*, Government Printer, Perth, 1929, pp. 68–77, for the personal history of Sir Richard Spencer.

98   *Perth Gazette*, 28 September 1839, p. 154.

99   'Marriage records kept by the Anglican Church, 1829–1841'.

100   Williams, *West Anglican Way*, p. 37.

101   See J. M. McDermott, 'The Turners at Augusta 1830–1850', *Early Days: Journal of the Royal Western Australian Historical Society*, vol. 1, part 8, 1930, pp. 35–56.

102   Richard Miles to the Colonial Secretary, Peter Brown, SROWA, CSR, acc. 36, vol. 80, folio 41, 15 December 1841.

103   SROWA, CSR, acc. 49, vol. 13, folio 1084, 16 December 1840.

104   'Marriage records kept by the Anglican Church, 1829–1841'. The marriage entry is number 44, in Perth, on 19 December 1840.

105   According to *The Westminster Dictionary of Church History*, edited by Jerald C. Brauer (The Westminster Press, Philadelphia, 1971) a dispensation was 'an official relaxation of canon law in particular so that acts normally contrary to the law are allowed. The practice of granting dispensations is a recognition of the fact that the letter of the law is not applicable in all cases. Of the various kinds of dispensations, some are reserved for the Pope, whereas others may be granted by bishops or priests'.

106 'Marriage: Ritual of', in *Catholic Encyclopedia*, vol. 10, Robert Appleton, New York, 1911.

107 These acts are discussed later in this book.

108 'Marriage records kept by the Anglican Church, 1829–1841'. See the lists for the Wellington and Sussex districts. See also *Perth Gazette*, 23 March 1839.

109 'An Act for Marriages in England', Acts of the Parliament of the United Kingdom, 6 and 7 Will. 4, c. 85, 1836; 'An Act to explain and amend Two Acts passed in the last Session of Parliament, for Marriages, and for Registering Births, Deaths, and Marriages, in England', 7 Will. 4 and 1 Vict., c. 22, 1837.

110 'An Act to provide for the Solemnization of Marriages in the Districts in or near which the Parties reside', Acts of the Parliament of the United Kingdom, 3 and 4 Vict., c. 72, 1840.

111 SROWA, CSR, acc. 36, vol. 79, folio 188, 27 November 1840.

112 SROWA, CSR, acc. 49, vol. 13, folio 1084, 16 December 1840.

113 Editorial, *The Inquirer*, 16 December 1840.

114 Letters to the editor, *The Inquirer*, 16 December 1840.

4: The Church Buildings Act, 1840

115 A. C. Staples, 'Hutt, John (1795–1880)', *Australian Dictionary of Biography*, vol. 1, Melbourne University Press, 1967, pp. 575–77.

116 See Royal Western Australian Historical Society, 'Collection of papers on Western Australian history, 1829–1966', manuscript, Battye Library, MN 1388, Western Australian Historical Society papers, acc. 4308A.

117 'Clapham sect', *The New Encyclopaedia Britannica*, Encyclopaedia Britannica Inc., Chicago, vol. 3, p. 344, col. 2.

118 'An Act to promote the Building of Churches and Chapels, and to contribute towards the maintenance of Ministers of Religion in Western Australia', passed on 6 July 1840, WA Statutes, 4 Vict., no. 6, 1840. (Note: WA Statutes are available at http://www.slp.wa.gov.au/legislation/statutes.nsf/default.html)

119 Hawtrey, *The Availing Struggle*, p. 23.

120 'An Act to explain and amend certain Acts now in force relating to the Building of Churches, Chapels and Ministers' Dwellings', WA Statutes, 6 Vict., no. 7, 1842.

121 'Governor's correspondence with the Wesleyans concerning a building allotment at Fremantle', SROWA, CSR, acc. 49, vol. 11, folios 685, 20 August 1840, and folio 794, 25 September 1840; 'Wesleyan responses to the Governor', SROWA, CSR, acc. 36, vol. 79, folio 16, 5 October 1840, folio 61, 20 October 1840, and folio 200, 30 November 1840.

122 See *The Inquirer*, 6 January 1841, concerning the laying of a stone for the Wesleyan Church. See also *Perth Gazette*, 2 January 1841.

123 Tonkin, *Cathedral and Community*, p. 11.

124 Speech of Governor Hutt at the laying of the foundation stone for the Church of England in Perth, *The Inquirer*, 6 January 1841. See also *Perth Gazette*, 2 January 1841.

125 WA *Blue Books*. The 'Quarterly returns of government revenue and expenditure' were also published regularly in the *Government Gazette*.

126 The Wesleyan interests to the Colonial Secretary, Peter Brown, SROWA, CSR, acc. 36, vol. 97, 1841, folios 93–95, 103, 115, 116, 119–121 and 136, 12 January – 5 November 1841.

127 The Colonial Secretary to the Wesleyan interests, SROWA, CSR, acc. 49, vol. 15, folio 754, 28 July 1841.

128 A report of the Governor's speech to the Legislative Council, WA *Government Gazette*, 7 May 1841.

129 Tonkin, *Cathedral and Community*, pp. 12–15.

130 See T. G. Heydon, 'The early church in Western Australia', *Early Days: Journal of the Royal Western Australian Historical Society*, vol. 2, part 11, 1932, pp. 1–15.

131 Report by Reverend King, *Perth Gazette*, 12 August 1843.

132 See D. F. Bourke, *The History of the Catholic Church in Western Australia*, Archdiocese of Perth, Perth, 1979.

133 Report of the ceremony of laying the foundation stone, *Perth Gazette*, 20 January 1844.

134 'Religious instructions', Colonial Secretary's Office, WA *Government Gazette*, 22 August 1840. Also published in *The Inquirer*, 26 August 1840.

135 WA *Blue Books*. Between 1844 and 1851 only the Church of England chaplain received £250 per year and some other chaplains £100 per year.

136 'An Act to promote the Building of Churches and Chapels, and to contribute towards the maintenance of Ministers of Religion in Western Australia', Clause 5.

137 The Wesleyan interests to the Colonial Secretary, Peter Brown, SROWA, CSR, acc. 36, vol. 79, folio 200, 30 November 1840; vol. 80, folios 63 and 76–77, 22–29 December 1840; vol. 97, folios 98–100, 19 January 1841.

138 The Colonial Secretary to the Wesleyan committee, SROWA, CSR, acc. 49, vol. 13, folio 1087, 18 December 1840.

139 The Colonial Secretary to George Johnson, SROWA, CSR, acc. 49, vol. 13, folio 16, 6 January 1841.

140 The Colonial Secretary to the Wesleyan Committee, SROWA, CSR, acc. 49, vol. 13, folio 24, 23 January 1841.

141 The Colonial Secretary to George Johnson, manager of the Wesleyan interests, SROWA, CSR, acc. 49, vol. 13, folio 63, 15 January 1841, and folio 80, 20 January 1841.

142 Three letters to the editor from 'a Wesleyan' and two from 'an old settler', *Perth Gazette*, 20 February 1841, 6 March 1841, 13 March 1841, 27 March 1841 and 17 April 1841.

143 Letters from the Colonial Secretary concerning a stipend for a minister at Fremantle, SROWA, CSR, acc. 49, vol. 13, folio 132, 4 February 1841; vol. 13, folio 220, 3 March 1841, and folio 242, 9 March 1841.

144 The Colonial Secretary to the Church of England committee at Fremantle, SROWA, CSR, acc. 49, vol. 15, folio 475, 12 May 1842.

145 The Colonial Secretary to Captain Irwin and Reverend Wittenoom, SROWA, CSR, acc. 49, vol. 13, folio 174, 19 February 1841, and vol. 13, folio 234, 6 March 1841.

146 The Colonial Secretary to Captain Irwin, SROWA, CSR, acc. 49, vol. 16, folio 1072, 11 October 1842.

147 Colonial Secretary's reply concerning Reverend Mitchell, SROWA, CSR, acc. 49, vol. 15, folio 1152, 4 November 1842.

148 Letters to the editor, *Perth Gazette*, 26 August 1843, 16 September 1843 and 14 October 1843.

149 See Pamela Statham (compiler), *The Tanner Letters: a pioneer saga of Swan River and Tasmania, 1831—1845*, UWA Press, Nedlands, 1981.

150 William Tanner to Governor Hutt, *Perth Gazette*, 29 July 1843.

151 Wesleyan Society's letters to the Governor and his reply, *Perth Gazette*, 14 October 1843.

152 The Colonial Secretary to the Wesleyan Committee, SROWA, CSR, acc. 49, vol. 17, folio 1224, 14 November 1843.

153 The Colonial Secretary to the Catholic committee, SROWA, CSR, acc. 49, vol. 17, folio 104, 12 February 1844.

154 The Colonial Secretary to particular Church of England representatives, SROWA, CSR, acc. 49, vol. 17, folio 244, 21 March 1844, and folio 245, 22 March 1844.

155 An appeal from the Church of England in Fremantle, n.d., SROWA, CSR, acc. 36, vol. 128, folio 154, 1844.

156 The Colonial Secretary to Bishop Brady, SROWA, CSR, acc. 49, vol. 17, folio 437, 31 May 1844.

157 Notice, WA *Government Gazette*, 22 and 29 December 1843.

158 'An Act to repeal so much of an Act passed in the fourth year of the reign of Her present Majesty Queen Victoria, intituled "An Act to promote the Building of Churches and Chapels, and to contribute towards the Maintenance of Ministers of Religion in Western Australia," as authorises the issue of money from the Colonial Treasury for such purposes', WA Statutes, 7 Vict., no. 16, 1844.

159 See G. C. Bolton, 'Wollaston, John Ramsden (1791–1856)', *Australian Dictionary of Biography*, vol. 2, Melbourne University Press, 1967, pp. 619–20.

160 The Colonial Secretary to Reverend Wollaston, SROWA, CSR, acc. 49, vol. 15, folios 128, 9 February 1842, and folio 140, 11 February 1842.

161 The Colonial Secretary to Reverend Wollaston, SROWA, CSR, acc. 49, vol. 22, folio 201, 20 March 1846, and folio 234, 28 March 1846.

162 Reverend Wollaston to Governor Clarke, SROWA, CSR, acc. 36, vol. 147, folio 181, 6 April 1846.

163 Letter from Reverend Wollaston to the Colonial Secretary accepting his appointment, SROWA, CSR, acc. 36, vol. 175, folio 64, 19 February 1848.

5: First marriage laws, 1841

164 Editorial, *The Inquirer*, 16 December 1840.

165 See *The Inquirer*, 7 April 1841, for this report of the Governor's speech.

166 *Minutes of the Proceedings of the WA Legislative Council*, 1 April (pp. 157–58), 3 May (pp. 166–67) and 13 May (pp. 168–70) 1841.

167 WA *Government Gazette*, 10 September 1841.

168 'An Act to provide for the Registration of Births, Deaths, and Marriages, in the Colony of Western Australia' (this was not an adoption of an English act), passed 27 May 1841, WA Statutes, 4 and 5 Vict., no. 9, 1841.

169 This book does not discuss those aspects of the Registration Act concerning the registration of births and deaths.

170 See *The Inquirer*, 6 October 1841, for this report of the Governor's speech.

171 'An Act to regulate the Solemnization of Matrimony in the Colony of Western Australia', passed 27 May 1841, WA Statutes, 4 and 5 Vict., no. 10, 1841, Clause 9.

172 Some of these clergy records are held in the Battye Library and are available to the researcher on request. A few are available online.

173 'An Act to regulate the Solemnization of Matrimony in the Colony of Western Australia', clauses 1 and 5.

174 See J. M. Lely, *The Statutes of Practical Utility: arranged in alphabetical and chronological order, with notes and indexes [Chitty's Statutes]*, vol. 7, Sweet & Maxwell, London, 1895; 'An Act for Marriages in England', Acts of the Parliament of the United Kingdom, 6 and 7 Will. 4, c. 85.

175 It proved difficult to determine the cost of banns for the early period but was confirmed as three pounds by later contemporary discussion over changes to the marriage acts.

176 'An Act to regulate the Solemnization of Matrimony in the Colony of Western Australia', passed 27 May 1841, WA Statutes, 4 and 5 Vict., no. 10, 1841, Clause 9.

177 See WA *Government Gazette*, 10 September 1841, for the announcement of this appointment.

178 See Table 5, showing the costs involved in the schedule at the end of the Solemnization of Marriage Act passed in 1841.

179 'Native marriage at Perth', *Perth Gazette*, 27 November 1841. Names have been omitted from my account.

180 'Western Australian Register of Marriages 1841– '.

181 'Native marriage in Perth', *Perth Gazette*, 13 January 1844.

182 *Perth Gazette*, 8 March 1845. Reference to this marriage can be found in William McNair and Hilary Rumley, *Pioneer Aboriginal Mission: the work of Wesleyan Missionary John Smithies in the Swan River colony*, UWA Press, Nedlands, 1987, pp. 104–105.

183 'Western Australian Register of Marriages 1841– '.

184 Details are provided in the table later in this chapter.

185 This building, completed in 1844 and now called the pro-cathedral, is still standing in Victoria Street, behind the Catholic Cathedral.

186 *Rituale Romanum: Pauli V Pontificis Maximi, Jussu Editum*, Typis S. Congregationis de Propaganda Fide, Rome, 1847.

187 'Marriage: Ritual of', *Catholic Encyclopedia*, vol. 10.

188 Editorial, *The Inquirer*, 23 September 1840.

189 Letter to the editor by Reverend Smithies, *The Inquirer*, 30 September 1840.

190 *The Inquirer*, 7 September 1842.

191 Letter to the editor from Reverend George King, *The Inquirer*, 7 September 1842.

192 Letter to the editor from Reverend Wollaston, *The Inquirer*, 28 September 1842.

193 An abstract of the Act for Births, Deaths and Marriages, *Perth Gazette*, 2 July 1842.

194 A two-column letter by 'an Observer', *Perth Gazette*, 10 December 1842.

195 An editorial by Francis Lochee castigating the author of three letters in the *Perth Gazette*, *The Inquirer*, 21 December 1842.

196 Editorial regarding the letters of 'an Observer', 'a Wesleyan' and 'a subscriber', *The Inquirer*, 28 December 1842.

197 Letter from 'an Observer', *Perth Gazette*, 31 December 1842.

198 Report of the Registrar of Births, Deaths and Marriages for the year 1841–42, *The Inquirer*, 12 October 1842.

199 Editorial, *The Inquirer*, 12 October 1842.

200 Letter from Henry Trigg, *The Inquirer*, 4 January 1843.

201 Letter to the editor by 'a Wesleyan', *Perth Gazette*, 14 January 1843.

202 Letter by 'a Wesleyan', *Perth Gazette*, 21 January 1843.

203 Letter by 'a Hermit of Western Australia', *Perth Gazette*, 21 January 1843.

204 Letter from 'an Observer', *Perth Gazette*, 28 January 1843.

205 Governor Hutt to the Registrar of Births, Marriages and Deaths, SROWA, CSR, acc. 49, vol. 15, folio 1094, 18 October 1842.

206 *WA Government Gazette,* 13 October 1843. Report of the Registrar of Births, Deaths and Marriages.

207 *WA Government Gazette,* 18 October 1843. Report of the Registrar of Births, Deaths and Marriages.

208 Report of the Registrar of Births, Deaths and Marriages, 1845, WA *Government Gazette*, 17 October 1845.

209 'The Seventh Annual Report of Births, Deaths and Marriages, 1848', WA *Government Gazette*, 26 September 1848.

210 Governor Hutt to Reverend George King, SROWA, CSR, acc. 49, vol. 16, folio 495, 28 April 1843.

6: Changes to marriage laws, 1847

211 See Cyril Bryan and F. I. Bray, 'Peter Nicholas Brown, 1797–1846, first Colonial Secretary of Western Australia (1829–1846)', *Early Days: Journal of the Royal Western Australian Historical Society*, vol. 2, part 18, 1935, pp. 1–33.

212 *Minutes of the Proceedings of the WA Legislative Council*, 23 March 1848, p. 515. The despatch confirming Madden's appointment as Colonial Secretary was laid on the table at this first Council meeting in 1848.

213 David R. Murray, 'Richard Robert Madden: his career as a slavery abolitionist', *Studies: An Irish Quarterly Review*, vol. 61, no. 241, 1972, pp. 41–53.

214 See Thomas Madden (ed.), *The Memoirs (chiefly autobiographical) from 1798 to 1886 of Richard Robert Madden*, Ward & Downey, London, 1891.

215 See Madden, *The Memoirs*, p. 232, for a copy of the letter from the Secretary of State for the Colonies approving Madden's decision to remain in Ireland.

216 Reported in *Perth Gazette*, 6 January 1849 and 'Supplement', *The Inquirer*, 10 January 1849.

217 Letter to the editor, *The Inquirer*, 10 January 1849.

218 Letter from Richard Madden to the Vicar-General of the Diocese of Dublin, 27 September 1853, cited in Bourke, *History of the Catholic Church in Western Australia*, pp. 28–29.

219 Reverend George King to Governor Clarke, SROWA, CSR, acc. 36, vol. 147, folios 172–73, 10 March 1846.

220 Governor Clarke to Reverend George King, SROWA, CSR, acc. 49, vol. 22, folio 357, 24 April 1846.

221 A letter and petition from Reverend George King to Governor Clarke, SROWA, CSR, acc. 36, vol. 147, folios 191–92, 2 June 1846.

222 Governor Clarke to Reverend George King, SROWA, CSR, acc. 49, vol. 22, folio 531, 6 July 1846.

223 Reverend George King to Governor Clarke, SROWA, CSR, acc. 36, vol. 147, folio 196, 13 July 1846.

224 Colonial Secretary to Reverend Wittenoom, concerning a pauper family, SROWA, CSR, acc. 49, vol. 22, folio 574, 20 July 1846. He refers to Governor Clarke's illness.

225 Report of the Legislative Council Proceedings of 10 June 1847, *The Inquirer*, 16 June 1847.

226 Report of the Legislative Council Proceedings of 24 June 1847, *The Inquirer*, 30 June 1847.

227 Reports on the Legislative Council Proceedings, *The Inquirer*, 16 June, 30 June and 21 July; a letter of protest, *The Inquirer*, 28 July 1847.

228 *WA Executive Council Records*, AJCP, vol. 1120, p. 86.

229 Editorial, *The Inquirer*, 10 November 1847.

230 *Minutes of the Proceedings of the WA Legislative Council* did not provide verbatim reports of debates before 1876. References to the 1847 Marriage Bill can be found in the 1847 *Minutes*, pp. 462 (3 June), 491ff (24 July), 498 (12 August) and 501 (3 September).

231 See the explanatory note in the 19 December 1846 edition of the *Perth Gazette*. When the editor of the *Perth Gazette*, Charles Macfaull, died in 1846, the paper was edited by his wife, Elizabeth Macfaull, from 16 December 1846 to 25 December 1847.

232 Editorial, *Perth Gazette*, 10 July 1847.

233 Bishop Brady or Father Joostens to the Colonial Secretary, Richard Madden, SROWA, CSR, acc. 36, vol. 160, folio 209, 10 July 1847, folio 211, 27 July 1847, and folio 215, 5 August 1847.

234 Report of Legislative Council Proceedings of 24 July 1847, *The Inquirer*, 28 July 1847.

235 Report of Legislative Council Proceedings of 24 July 1847, *The Inquirer*, 28 July 1847.

236 *Minutes of the Proceedings of the WA Legislative Council*, 29 July 1847, pp. 494.

237 *Minutes of the Proceedings of the WA Legislative Council*, 5 and 12 August 1847, pp. 496–98.

238 Letter from 'a Liberal', *Perth Gazette*, 14 August 1847.

239 *The Inquirer*, 25 August 1847. There is no author's name attached to this article, which the editor stated he had been persuaded to print for the consideration of members of the Church of England. It has been conjectured that the author was Reverend Wollaston.

240 Report of Legislative Council Proceedings of 5 August 1847, *The Inquirer*, 11 August 1847, which makes reference to a petition from the Roman Catholic community against the bill.

241 'An Ordinance to repeal the existing Laws respecting the Solemnization of Matrimony; and to make other regulations respecting the same', WA Statutes, 10 Vict., no. 18, 1847.

242 Ibid., Clause 24.

243 'An Ordinance to amend an Act entitled "an Act to provide for the Registration of Births, Deaths, and Marriages, in the Colony of Western Australia" ', WA Statutes, 10 Vict., no. 17, 1847.

244 Report of Legislative Council Proceedings of 5 August 1847, *The Inquirer*, 11 August 1847.

245 *Minutes of the Proceedings of the WA Legislative Council*, 9 September 1847, pp. 503–504.

246 Bishop Brady to the Colonial Secretary, SROWA, CSR, acc. 36, vol. 160, folio 222, 9 September 1847.

247 Report of Legislative Council Proceedings of 9 September 1847, *The Inquirer*, 15 September 1847.

248 Letter from Reverend Wollaston, *The Inquirer*, 29 September 1847.

249 'An Ordinance to amend an Act entitled "an Act to provide for the Registration of Births, Deaths, and Marriages, in the Colony of Western Australia" ', WA Statutes, 10 Vict., no. 17, 1847.

250 'An Ordinance to repeal the existing Laws respecting the Solemnization of Matrimony: and to make the regulations respecting the same', WA Statutes, 10 Vict., no. 18, 1847.

251 WA *Government Gazette*, 26 November 1847.

252 Colonial Registrar George Stone to the Colonial Secretary, SROWA, CSR, acc. 36, vol. 165, folio 13, 2 November 1847.

253 Marriages by Bishop Brady on 12 May 1849 and 22 May 1849, 'Western Australian Register of Marriages 1841– '.

254 Registrar-General's report on births, deaths and marriages, WA *Government Gazette*, 26 September 1848.

7: Towards a solution, 1849

255 These colonial secretaries were Revett Bland, acting, January 1849 – March 1850; Thomas Yule, acting, March 1850 – October 1850; Charles Piesse, October 1850 – March 1851; Thomas Yule, acting, March 1851 – December 1851; Thomas Falconer, appointed in 1851 but never arrived in the colony; and William Sandford, January 1852 – July 1855.

256 WA *Government Gazette*, 5, 12 and 26 September 1848.

257 'Address to Governor Fitzgerald by Bishop Brady on behalf of the Roman Catholic Clergy and community', WA *Government Gazette*, 12 September 1848.

258 For Bishop Brady's correspondence with Governor Fitzgerald in 1848, see SROWA, CSR, acc. 36, vol. 175, folio 129, 18 December 1848, and folio 132, 29 December 1848. For correspondence in the first half of 1849, see SROWA, CSR, acc. 36, vol. 188, folios 162, 164, 168, 185, 190, 192, 208, 212, 217, 219, 227 and 228. For Governor Fitzgerald's replies to Bishop Brady in the first half of 1849, see SROWA, CSR, acc. 49, vol. 28, folios 84, 85, 100, 102–103, 105, 153, 155, 172 and 184–85.

259 Report of the Proceedings of the Legislative Council, *Perth Gazette*, 21 April 1849.

260 'Return of ships and emigrants despatched by public funds to Western Australia from 1851–1854', SROWA, COD, acc. 41, 1856, p. 32.

261 Secretary of State for the Colonies, Henry Labouchere, to Governor Kennedy, SROWA, COD, acc. 41, 1856, p. 12, 25 January 1856.

262   'An emigration marriage', *The Inquirer*, 13 June 1849.

263   Earl Grey to Governor Fitzgerald, SROWA. *Minutes of the Proceedings of the WA Legislative Council*, 18 April 1849, p. 551. This part of the despatch is mentioned as no. 18 in papers laid on the table in the Legislative Council in April 1849.

264   See *Perth Gazette*, 17 June 1848, p. 3, for a discussion about the bill and the comments of the editor.

265   Despatches. Earl Grey, Secretary of State for the Colonies, to Governor Fitzgerald, 8 June 1848, AJCP, microform reel no. 775, CO 18, piece no. 9, 1848–51.

266   'Western Australian Register of Marriages 1841– ', 6 May 1850.

267   Governor Fitzgerald to Earl Grey, 1 November 1848, AJCP, microform reel no. 442, CO 18, piece no. 48, part 2.

268   Governor Fitzgerald to Bishop Brady, SROWA, CSR, acc. 49, vol. 25, folio 950, 26 September 1848.

269   Bishop Brady to Governor Fitzgerald, SROWA, CSR, acc. 36, vol. 175, folios 111–13, 30 September 1848.

270   The Registrar issued two certificates instead of a marriage license when the couple marrying attended different churches.

271   Governor Fitzgerald to Bishop Brady, SROWA, CSR, acc. 49, vol. 25, folio 1016, 11 October 1848.

272   Bishop Brady to Governor Fitzgerald, SROWA, CSR, acc. 36, vol. 175, folios 118–19, 21 October 1848.

273   *The Inquirer*, generally critical of the government, was owned by William Tanner, who returned to England in 1844. Edmund Stirling became the proprietor between 6 January 1847 and 27 June 1855, and did the editing in 1847. He was followed by Arthur Shenton.

274   Editorial by Arthur Shenton, *The Inquirer*, 7 March 1849.

275   Report of Proceedings of the Legislative Council of 26 April 1849, *Perth Gazette*, 4 May 1849.

276   Report of Proceedings of the Legislative Council of 27 April 1849, *Perth Gazette*, 4 May 1849.

277   'An Ordinance to provide for the Solemnization and Registration of Marriages of persons belonging to certain Denominations of Christians, not being Members of the Church of England', WA Statutes, 12 Vict., no. 11, 1849, Clause 1.

278   'An Ordinance to provide for the Solemnization and Registration of Marriages of persons belonging to certain Denominations of Christians, not being Members of the Church of England', Clause 5.

279   Despatches. Earl Grey, Secretary of State for the Colonies, to Governor Fitzgerald, 5 January 1850, AJCP, microform reel no. 775, piece no. 9, 1848–51.

280   'An Ordinance to amend the existing Laws concerning the Solemnization of Matrimony', WA Statutes, 12 Vict., no. 12, 1849, Clause 2.

281   Report of the proceedings of the Legislative Council of 26 April 1849, *Perth Gazette*, 27 April 1849.

282   'An Ordinance to amend an Ordinance intituled "An Act to provide for the Registration of Births, Deaths and Marriages, in the Colony of Western Australia"', WA Statutes, 12 Vict., no. 13, 1849.

283 See Catholic Church, 'Records 1844–1976', manuscript, Battye Library, acc. 2747A/1, Marriages, New Norcia, Toodyay, for a note recording six Aboriginal marriages in 1862–63.

284 See WA *Government Gazette*, 18 June 1850, for the proclamation of acts 12 Vict., nos 11–13.

285 Bishop Brady to Governor Fitzgerald, SROWA, CSR, acc. 36, vol. 188, folio 208, 24 April 1849.

286 Bishop Brady to Governor Fitzgerald, SROWA, CSR, acc. 36, vol. 188, folio 212, 27 April 1849.

287 Bishop Brady to Governor Fitzgerald, SROWA, CSR, acc. 36, vol. 188, folio 213, 27 April 1849.

288 Governor Fitzgerald to Bishop Brady, SROWA, CSR, acc. 49, vol. 26, folio 155, 27 April 1849.

289 Bishop Brady to Governor Fitzgerald, SROWA, CSR, acc. 36, vol. 188, folio 217, 8 May 1849.

290 Governor Fitzgerald to Bishop Brady, SROWA, CSR, acc. 49, vol. 26, folio 172, 10 May 1849.

291 'An Ordinance to regulate the temporal affairs of Churches and Chapels of the United Church of England and Ireland, in Western Australia', WA Statutes, 16 Vict., no. 22, 1853.

292 Bolton, 'Wollaston, John Ramsden, (1791–1856)'.

293 WA *Blue Book*, 1851, p. 137.

294 Letter from 'an Independent', *The Inquirer*, 4 July 1849.

295 'An Act for Marriages in England', Acts of the Parliament of the United Kingdom, 6 and 7 Will. 4, c. 85, 1836.

296 Editorial comment, *The Inquirer*, 5 December 1849.

297 These laws are listed in the 1856 acts as the ones repealed.

298 Governor Fitzgerald's reply to farewell memorials, *Perth Gazette*, 27 July 1855.

8: Marriage problems settled, 1856

299 Report of the arrival of Governor Kennedy on the *Avalanche*, *Perth Gazette*, 27 July 1855.

300 Report of preparations for Governor Kennedy's arrival, *Perth Gazette*, 6 July 1855.

301 Farewell memorials to Governor Fitzgerald, *Perth Gazette*, 20 July and 3 August 1855.

302 WA Government, *Census of Population, and Returns of Stock and Crops*, Perth, 1848, and *Western Australia: report on the general statistics of the colony for the year*, Perth, 1859.

303 See Rica Erickson, *Dictionary of Western Australians 1829–1914*, vol. 3, UWA Press, Nedlands, 1979.

304 Kyme and Doncaster, *The Wollaston Legacy*, p. 20.

305 Letter to Governor Kennedy sending a copy of the Queen's Letters Patent, dated 11 June 1856, commanding the erecting and constituting of a bishop's see to be held by Mathew B. Hale, Archdeacon of Adelaide, SROWA, COD, acc. 41, p. 107, 23 May 1856.

306 Report of the Proceedings in the Legislative Council of 3 June 1856, *Perth Gazette*, 6 June 1856.

307 Editorial, *Perth Gazette*, 23 May 1856.

308 Editorial, *The Inquirer*, 21 May 1856.

309 This included WA Statutes, 4 and 5 Vict., no. 9, 1841, and 10 Vict., no. 17, 1847. The latter dealt only with matters concerning the reporting of deaths.

310 'An Ordinance for the better Registration of Births, Deaths, and Marriages in the Colony of Western Australia', WA Statutes, 19 Vict., no. 12, 1856.

311 'An Ordinance to amend and consolidate the Laws affecting the Solemnization of Marriage in the Colony of Western Australia', repealing 10 Vict., no. 18; 12 Vict., no. 11; and 12 Vict., no. 12, WA Statutes, 19 Vict., no. 11, 1856.

312 'An Ordinance for the better Registration of Births, Deaths, and Marriages in the Colony of Western Australia', 1856.

313 Governor Kennedy to the Secretary of State for the Colonies concerning Mr Yule, a magistrate, and the licensing of public houses, despatch no. 13, 26 January 1856, despatches to the Colonial Office from January 1855 to December 1859, SROWA, Despatch Book.

314 Governor Kennedy to the Secretary of State for the Colonies concerning calls for a more representative system of government, despatch no. 99, 6 October 1856, despatches to the Colonial Office from January 1855 to December 1859, SROWA, Despatch Book.

315 *Perth Gazette*, 4, 11, 18 and 25 July and 8 August 1856; and *Inquirer and Commercial News*, 11 June, 18 June and 2 July 1856.

316 Letter from Secretary of State for the Colonies, Henry Labouchere, to Governor Kennedy, SROWA, COD, acc. 41, 14 April 1856.

317 J. M. H. Honniball, 'The country tours of a colonial secretary', *Early Days: Journal of the Royal Western Australian Historical Society*, vol. 7, part 3, 1971, pp. 83–115.

318 See *Early Days: Journal of the Royal West Australian Historical Society* for many accounts of family settlement, frequently based on contemporary private journals.

319 'An Ordinance to provide for the Maintenance and Relief of Deserted Wives and Children, and other Destitute Persons, and to make the property of Husbands and near Relatives, to whose assistance they have a natural claim, in certain circumstances, available for support', WA Statutes, 9 Vict., no. 2, 1845.

320 See Penelope Hetherington, *Paupers, Poor Relief and Poor Houses in Western Australia, 1829–1910*, especially chapters 3 and 6.

321 List of criminal charges from 1832 to 1887, no. 55, 18 December 1832, SROWA, Criminal Court Records, 3422/1. For Dent's appearance in court, see Supreme Court Indictment Files, SROWA, CONS 3472/11, case 55, January 1833.

322 List of criminal charges from 1832 to 1887, no. 776, 5 January 1859, SROWA, Criminal Court Records, 3422/1. For Allison's appearance in court, see Supreme Court Indictment Files, SROWA, CONS 3472/11, case 776, January 1859.

323 List of criminal charges from 1832 to 1887, no. 503, 6 June 1872, SROWA, Criminal Court Records, 3422/1. For Drabble's appearance in court, see Supreme Court Indictment Files, SROWA, CONS 3473, case 503, 3 July 1872.

324 Supreme Court Indictment Files, SROWA, CONS 3473/36, case 250, July 1867.

325 SROWA, *Swan River Papers*, vol. 11. Lord Goderich to Lieutenant-Governor Stirling, 5 March and 28 April 1831, part of Clause 14. The *Swan River Papers vols 1–16* contain copies of selected documents from the Public Record Office in London. They cover the period 1827–1833.

9: Divorce law, 1863

326   Peter Boyce, 'Hampton, John Stephen, (1810?–1869)', *Australian Dictionary of Biography*, vol. 1, pp. 508–509.

327   T. S. Louch, 'Weld, Sir Frederick Aloysius (1823–1891)', *Australian Dictionary of Biography*, vol. 6, 1976, pp. 377–79.

328   'An Ordinance to provide for the establishment of a Legislative Council, the division of the Colony into Electoral Districts, and the election of Members to serve in such Council', WA Statutes, 33 Vict., no. 13, 1870.

329   'Custody of Infants Act, 1839', Acts of the Parliament of the United Kingdom, 2 and 3 Vict., c. 54, 1839.

330   An act for adopting and applying certain imperial acts including an act as to voidable marriages and an act concerning custody of children, WA Statutes, 7 Vict., no. 13, 1844.

331   'An Ordinance to provide for the Maintenance and Relief of Deserted Wives and Children, and other Destitute Persons, and to make the property of Husbands and near Relatives, to whose assistance they have a natural claim, in certain circumstances, available for support', WA Statutes, 9 Vict., no. 2, 1845.

332   Copy of an article from the *Hampshire Advertiser*, *The Inquirer*, 13 June 1849.

333   'An Ordinance to regulate Divorce and Matrimonial Causes', WA Statutes, 27 Vict., no. 19, 1863.

334   *Minutes of the Proceedings of the WA Legislative Council*, 8 July 1863, p. 1043.

335   See the notice of the impending meeting of the Legislative Council and the list of legislation to be considered in WA *Government Gazette*, 12 May 1863.

336   *Minutes of the Proceedings of the WA Legislative Council*, 8 July 1863, p. 1044.

337   See *Perth Gazette*, 10 July 1863, and *The Inquirer*, 15 July 1863.

338   The English acts copied here were 'An Act to amend the Law relating to Divorce and Matrimonial Causes in England', passed 28 August 1857, 20 and 21 Vict., c. 85, 1857.

339   See the preamble to 'An Ordinance to regulate Divorce and Matrimonial Causes', WA Statutes, 27 Vict., no. 19, 1863.

340   'An Act to make provision for the better Administration of Justice in the Supreme Court of Western Australia', WA Statutes, 44 Vict., no. 10, 1880.

341   See *WA Parliamentary Debates*, 1880, pp. 144–48. Second reading of the Supreme Court Bill, 13 August 1880.

342   See clauses 13–15 of 'An Ordinance to regulate Divorce and Matrimonial Causes', WA Statutes, 27 Vict., no. 19, 1863.

343   WA *Blue Book*, 1869, pp. 85–99.

344   'An Ordinance to regulate Divorce and Matrimonial Causes', WA Statutes, 27 Vict., no. 19, 1863, Clause 21.

345   Ibid., Clause 11.

346   Ibid., Clause 29.

347   'An Act to amend the procedure and powers of the Court for Divorce and Matrimonial Causes', WA Statutes, 34 Vict., no. 7, 1871.

348   The first two petitions of Sarah Duffield and Adelaide Isaacs can be found in Records of Her Majesty's Court for Divorce and Matrimonial Causes, SROWA,

CONS 3409/1–5, nos 1–41, 1864–94. Details of the Duffield case appear in Record Book No. 2, SROWA, WAS 40. Details of the Isaacs case appear in Record Book Nos 1 and 2, SROWA, WAS 40.

349   Divorce Files, SROWA, CONS 3404, 3/1865–6/1890; CONS 3404, 2/1890–6/1898 and CONS 3404, 7/1898–1899.

350   See the next chapter for more details about incomes.

10: Divorce law and the courts, 1863–79

351   Divorce Files, SROWA, CONS 3404, 3/1865–6/1890, box 1, Robson, packet 4A/1865, item 3. The decision of the court can be found in Records of Her Majesty's Court for Divorce and Matrimonial Causes, SROWA, CONS 3409/1–5.

352   See *Order in the Court: a guide to the records of the Supreme Court of Western Australia*, pp. 5–6.

353   Court Charges, 1873–89, Records of the Perth Police Court, SROWA, AN 17, CONS 3308, item 2.

354   Records of the Perth Police Court, April 1868 – December 1868, SROWA, CONS 1386, item 141.

355   Records of the Perth Police Court, January–December 1875, SROWA, CONS 1386, item 143.

356   'An Ordinance to regulate Divorce and Matrimonial Causes', WA Statutes, 27 Vict., no. 19, 1863, Clause 13.

357   Details about the case of Emma Collins appear later in this chapter.

358   Divorce Files, SROWA, CONS 3404, box 1, Thompson, packet 16/1879, item 22.

359   *Inquirer and Commercial News*, 16 June 1880, p. 3.

360   There are historically several ways to select a jury. A common jury consists of people selected at random.

361   *Perth Gazette*, 31 December 1842.

362   Divorce Files, SROWA, CONS 3404, box 1, Vincent, packet 5/1868, item 4.

363   *Inquirer and Commercial News*, 10 August 1870, p. 3.

364   Divorce Files, SROWA, CONS 3404, box 1, Collins, packet 11/1872, item 13.

365   I have been unable to find any report of this case in the local newspapers.

11: Divorce law and the courts, 1880–89

366   'An Act to amend the Ordinance to regulate Divorce and Matrimonial Causes', WA Statutes, 43 Vict., no. 9, 1879, Clause 3.

367   Charge Book, 1879–80, Perth Magistrate's Court, SROWA, CONS 1386, item 144.

368   See Hetherington, *Paupers, Poor Relief and Poor Houses*, chapters 3 and 6.

369   Divorce Files, SROWA, CONS 3404, box 2, Taaffe, packet 1/1886, item 30.

370   *Inquirer and Commercial News*, 17 March 1886, p. 5.

371   Divorce Files, SROWA, CONS 3404, box 2, Taaffe, packet 1/1886, item 30.

372   *Inquirer and Commercial News*, 24 March 1886, p. 5.

373   Divorce Files, SROWA, CONS 3404, box 2, Laurence, packet 3/1886, item 32.

374   Divorce Files, SROWA, CONS 3404, box 2, Harper, packet 6/1886, item 35.

375   *Inquirer and Commercial News*, 14 September 1887, p. 6.

376   Divorce Files, SROWA, CONS 3404, box 2, Thomas, packet 4/1886, item 33.

377 'Marriage Regulations', Anglican Diocese of Perth, *The Year Book* for 1897, Church of England in Australia, Diocese of Perth, Perth, 1897, p. 59.

378 WA Government, *Seventh census of Western Australia taken for the night of 31st March, 1901*, compiled under the direction of Malcolm A. C. Fraser, Registrar-General, Government Statistician and Superintendent of Census, WA Government Printer, Perth, 1901. This volume also includes details of earlier censuses.

379 A variety of websites explains all these complexities and provide information about the church canons on which they are based.

380 See 'Divorce', in *Catholic Encyclopedia*, vol. 5, 1909.

381 Divorce Files, SROWA, CONS 3404, box 2, Lakeman, packet 1/1880, item 23, and Harper, packet 6/1886, item 35.

382 'An Act to amend the Law relating to the Property of Married Women', WA Statutes, 55 Vict., no. 20, 1892.

12: Divorce law and the courts 1890–99

383 WA Government, *Seventh census of Western Australia*, 1901.

384 *WA Parliamentary Debates*, 1892, pp. 369–79. Second reading of the Married Women's Property Bill, 27–28 January 1892.

385 'An Act to amend the Law relating to the Property of Married Women', WA Statutes, 55 Vict., no. 20, 1892.

386 'An Act to amend "The Married Women's Property Act, 1892" ', WA Statutes, 59 Vict., no. 22, 1895; and 'An Act to amend the Sixteenth Section of the Married Women's Property Act, 1892', 60 Vict., no. 8, 1896.

387 Information and Summonses for 1890, Records of the Perth Police Station, SROWA, CONS 3287, items 108–11; and Charge Books for 1890, Records of the Perth Police Station, SROWA, CONS 1386, item 159.

388 A surety was an arrangement whereby one person undertook to accept responsibility for another's debt, in this case to pay the stated sum if Jeffcott reoffended.

389 Summons and Execution Books, Perth Police Court, SROWA, CONS 1386, item 162, 3 February 1893 – 8 May 1893.

390 See *WA Parliamentary Debates*, 1896, pp. 155–56. Second reading of the Summary Jurisdiction (Married Women) Bill, 22 July 1896.

391 This point is discussed in greater detail later in this chapter.

392 'An Act to amend the Law relating to the Summary Jurisdiction of Magistrates in reference to Married Women', cited as the Summary Jurisdiction (Married Women) Act, WA Statutes, 60 Vict., no. 10. 1896, Clause 4.

393 See Hetherington, *Paupers, Poor Relief and Poor Houses*, p. 66.

394 Information and Summonses, Perth Police Court, SROWA, CONS 3287, item 158, and CONS 3287, item 159.

395 Information and Summonses, Perth Police Court, SROWA, CONS 3287, item 179, October 1898, 1 of 2.

396 Information and Summonses, Perth Police Court, SROWA, CONS 3287, item 179, October 1898, 2 of 2.

397 This is an exact copy of the document.

398 Divorce Files, SROWA, CONS 3404, box 4, Howe, packet 1/1899, item 11.

399 See *West Australian*, 18 October 1899, p. 2.

400 Divorce Files, SROWA, CONS 3404, box 5, Noble, p, 8/1899, item 18.

401 Divorce Files, SROWA, CONS 3404, box 4, Howe, packet 1/1899, item 11.

402 See *Daily News*, 4 August 1899, p. 2; *West Australian*, 4 August 1899, p. 2; *Western Mail*, 11 August 1899, p. 55.

403 Divorce Files, SROWA, CONS 3404, box 5, Elderson, packet 6/1899, item 16.

404 Divorce Files, SROWA, CONS 3404, box 2, Millar, packet 2/1892, item 7.

405 Divorce Files, SROWA, CONS 3404, box 2, Buckingham, packet 1/1893, item 9.

406 See *Inquirer and Commercial News*, 17 November 1893, p. 23, and 8 December 1893, p. 22.

407 Divorce Files, SROWA, CONS 3404, Wrigley, packet 32/1899, item 22.

Conclusion

408 'An Ordinance for adopting certain Acts of the Imperial Parliament', according to Clause 1, 'to enable persons to establish Legitimacy, and the validity of Marriages, and the right to be deemed Natural-born Subjects', WA Statutes, 31 Vict., no. 8, 1867.

409 'An Act to legalize the marriage of a Man with the Sister of his Deceased Wife', WA Statutes, 41 Vict., no. 21, 1877.

410 'An Act further to regulate the Celebration of Marriage in the Colony of Western Australia', WA Statutes, 43 Vict., no. 28, 1879.

411 *WA Parliamentary Debates*, 1879. P. 106, pp. 118–19, 99. 128–31. Second reading of the Celebration of Marriage Bill, 25–27 August and 2 September, 1879.

412 *WA Parliamentary Debates*, 1894, pp. 264–59. Second reading of the Registration of Births, Deaths and Marriages Bill, 16 August 1894.

413 'An Act to consolidate and amend the Law relating to the Registration of Births, Deaths, and Marriages', WA Statutes, 58 Vict., no. 16, 1894

414 'An Act to consolidate and amend the Law relating to the Celebration of Marriage', repealing 43 Vict., no. 2, 1879, WA Statutes, 58 Vict., no. 11, 1894.

415 Ibid., Clause 35.

416 'An Act to amend the Marriage Act, 1894', concerning the celebration of marriages between Jewish couples, WA Statutes, 62 Vict., no. 23, 1898.

417 'An Act to amend the Registration of Births, Deaths, and Marriages Act, 1894', WA Statutes, 64 Vict., no. 31, 1900.

418 The first major act concerning pauper and delinquent children was the Industrial Schools' Act, passed in 1874, which was followed by an Act to amend "The Police Ordinance, 1861" (also known as the Larrikin Act), 44 Vict., no. 3, 1880; the Rottnest Reformatory and Industrial Schools Amendment Act of 1882; and the Industrial and Reformatory Schools Act of 1893. In 1898, there was a Commission of Inquiry into the reformatory system and, in 1902, the laws were finally consolidated in the criminal code.

419 See Penelope Hetherington, *Settlers, Servants and Slaves: Aboriginal and European children in nineteenth-century Western Australia*, UWA Press, Nedlands, 2002, Chapter 4.

420 See Hetherington, *Paupers, Poor Relief and Poor Houses*, pp. 14–15, for reference to 'An Ordinance to provide for the Maintenance and Relief of Deserted Wives

and Children, and other Destitute Persons, and to make the property of Husbands and near Relatives, to whose assistance they have a natural claim, in certain circumstances, available for support', WA Statutes, 9 Vict., no. 2, 1845.

421   'An Act to make further provision for the Maintenance of Bastard Children by their Putative Fathers', WA Statutes, 35 Vict., no. 4, 1871.

422   'An Act to amend the Bastardy Laws', WA Statutes, 39 Vict., no. 8, 1875.

423   See Penelope Hetherington, 'Baby-farming in Western Australia: the case against Alice Mitchell, 1907', *Studies in Western Australian History*, issue 25, 2007, pp. 75–97.

424   'An Act to make Provision for the Adoption of Children', WA Statutes, 60 Vict., no. 6, 1896.

425   See *WA Parliamentary Debates*, 1896, p. 153. Second reading of the Adoption of Children Bill, 22 July 1896.

426   'An Act to make better Provision for the Protection of Women and Girls, and for other Purposes', WA Statutes, 55 Vict., no. 24, 1892.

BIBLIOGRAPHY

Anglican Diocese of Perth, *The Year Book for 1897*, Church of England in Australia, Diocese of Perth, Perth, 1897.

Battye, J. S., *Cyclopedia of Western Australia*, vol. 2, published for the Cyclopedia Co. by Hussey & Gillingham, Adelaide, 1913.

Bonnington, Stuart, *Like a Mustard Seed: a history of the Presbyterian Church of Western Australia from 1829 to 1901*, S. Bonnington, Melbourne, 2004.

Border, Ross, 'Scott, Thomas Hobbes (1783–1860)', *Australian Dictionary of Biography*, vol. 2, Melbourne University Press, 1967, pp. 431–33.

Brauer, Jerald C. (ed.), *The Westminster Dictionary of Church History*, The Westminster Press, Philadelphia, 1971.

Bryan, Cyril and F. I. Bray, 'Peter Nicholas Brown (1797–1846), first Colonial Secretary of Western Australia (1829–1846)', *Early Days: Journal of the Royal Western Australian Historical Society*, vol. 2, part 18, 1935, pp. 1–33.

Bourke, D. F., *The History of the Catholic Church in Western Australia*, Archdiocese of Perth, Perth, 1979.

Boyce, Peter, 'Kennedy, Sir Arthur Edward (1810–1883)', *Australian Dictionary of Biography*, vol. 5, Melbourne University Press, 1974, p. 15.

——, 'Hampton, John Stephen, (1810?–1869)', *Australian Dictionary of Biography*, vol. 1, Melbourne University Press, 1966, pp. 508–509.

Burton, Rev. Canon A., 'Notes on the three archdeacons: Thomas Hobbes Scott, John Ramsden Wollaston, Matthew Blagden Hale', *Early Days: Journal of the Royal Western Australian Historical Society*, vol. 2, part 17, 1935, pp. 20–27.

Cameron, J. M. R., *Ambition's Fire: the agricultural colonisation of pre-convict Western Australia*, UWA Press, Nedlands, 1981.

Carson, Alfred, 'A farmer of 1832: extract of a letter written by Joseph Hardy... 14 July 1832', *Early Days: Journal of the Royal Western Australian Historical Society*, vol. 3, part 1, 1938, p. 63.

Carter, Bevan and Lynda Nutter, *Nyungah Land: records of invasion and theft of Aboriginal land on the Swan River, 1829–1850*, Black History Series, Swan Valley Nyungah Community, Guildford, WA, 2005.

Catholic Encyclopedia, vols. 4 and 10, Robert Appleton, New York, 1909 and 1911.

Chate, Alfred H., 'Moore, George Fletcher (1798–1886)', *Australian Dictionary of Biography*, vol. 2, Melbourne University Press, 1967, pp. 252–54.

Christopher, Emma, *A Merciless Place: the lost story of Britain's convict disaster in Africa and how it led to the settlement of Australia*, Allen & Unwin, Sydney, 2010.

Colebatch, Hal, *A Story of One Hundred Years: Western Australia, 1829–1929*, Government Printer, Perth, 1929.

Coles, P. J., 'Trigg, Henry (1791–1882)', *Australian Dictionary of Biography*, vol. 2, Melbourne University Press, 1967, p. 539.

Cox, S. H., *The Seventy Years History of the Trinity Congregational Church, Perth, Western Australia, 1845 to 1916*, E. S. Wigg & Son, Perth, 1916.

Crowley, F. K., 'Stirling, Sir James (1791–1865)', *Australian Dictionary of Biography*, vol. 2, Melbourne University Press, 1967, pp. 484–88.

Devenish, Bruce, *Man of Energy and Compassion: the life, letters and times of Henry Trigg, Swan pioneer and church founder*, Wongaburra Enterprises, South Perth, 1996.

Dickey, Anthony, *Family Law*, fifth edition, Law Book Co., Sydney, 2007.

Dillon, Harry and Peter Butler, *Macquarie: from colony to country*, Random House, Sydney, 2010.

Erickson, Rica, *Dictionary of Western Australians 1829–1914*, vol. 3, UWA Press, Nedlands, 1979.

Finlay, Henry, 'Divorce and the status of women: beginnings in nineteenth century Australia', seminar paper presented at the Institute of Family Studies, Melbourne, 20 September 2001.

—— and R. J. Bailey-Harris, *Family Law in Australia*, fourth edition, Butterworths, Sydney, 1989.

Frost, Alan, *Botany Bay: the real story*, Black Inc., Melbourne, 2011.

Hawtrey, C. L. M., *The Availing Struggle: a record of the planting and development of the Church of England in Western Australia, 1829–1947*, n.p., Perth, 1949.

Hetherington, Penelope, 'Baby-farming in Western Australia: the case against Alice Mitchell, 1907', *Studies in Western Australian History*, issue 25, 2007, pp. 75–97.

——, *Settlers, Servants and Slaves: Aboriginal and European children in nineteenth-century Western Australia*, UWA Press, Nedlands, 2002.

——, *Paupers, Poor Relief and Poor Houses in Western Australia, 1829–1910*, UWA Publishing, Crawley, 2009.

Heydon, T. G., 'The early church in Western Australia', *Early Days: Journal of the Royal Western Australian Historical Society*, vol. 2, part 11, 1932, pp. 1–15.

Honniball, J. M. H., 'The country tours of a colonial secretary', *Early Days: Journal of the Royal Western Australian Historical Society*, vol. 7, part 3, 1971, pp. 83–115.

Irwin, Frederick Chidley, *The State and Position of Western Australia: commonly called the Swan-River Settlement*, Simpkin, Marshall, London, 1835.

Jenkins, C. A., *A Century of Methodism in Western Australia, 1830–1930*, Patersons Printing Press, Perth, 1930.

——, 'Early years of the Methodist Church in Western Australia', *Early Days: Journal of the Royal Western Australian Historical Society*, vol. 2, part 13, 1933, pp. 1–15.

Kyme, Brian and Edward Doncaster, *The Wollaston Legacy*, John Septimus Roe Anglican Community School for the Institute of Anglican Studies, St George's Cathedral, Perth, 2007.

Labriola, Albert, 'Divorce and Matrimonial Causes Act, *Literary Encyclopedia*, 9 February 2004, http://www.litencyc.com/php/stopics.php?rec=true& UID=690, accessed 17 September 2012.

Lely, J. M., *The Statutes of Practical Utility: arranged in alphabetical and chronological order, with notes and indexes [Chitty's Statutes]*, vol. 7, Sweet and Maxwell, London, 1895.

Louch, T. S., 'Weld, Sir Frederick Aloysius (1823–1891)', *Australian Dictionary of Biography*, vol. 6, Melbourne University Press, 1976, pp. 377–79.

Lutton, Wesley, *The Wesley Story: centenary of Wesley Church, Perth, Western Australia, 1870–1970*, Central Methodist Mission, Perth, 1970.

McCarthy, P., 'The foundations of Catholicism in Western Australia, 1829–1911', *University Studies in History*, vol. 2, no. 4, 1956, pp. 5–76.

McDermott, J. M., 'The Turners at Augusta 1830–1850', *Early Days: Journal of the Royal Western Australian Historical Society*, vol. 1, part 8, 1930, pp. 35–56.

McNair, Rev. William, 'A second look at the early years of Methodism in Western Australia, 1830–1855', *Early Days: Journal of the Royal Western Australian Historical Society*, vol. 7, part 1, 1969, pp. 79–87.

—— and Hilary Rumley, *Pioneer Aboriginal Mission: the work of Wesleyan missionary John Smithies in the Swan River Colony, 1840–1855*, UWA Press, Nedlands, 1987.

Madden, Thomas Moore (ed.), *The Memoirs (chiefly autobiographical) from 1798 to 1886 of Richard Robert Madden*, Ward & Downey, London, 1891.

Medcalf, M., 'Leake, George (1786–1949)', *Australian Dictionary of Biography*, vol. 2, Melbourne University Press, 1967, pp. 99–100.

Mossenson, David, 'Nash, Richard West (1808–1850)', *Australian Dictionary of Biography*, vol. 2, Melbourne University Press, 1967, p. 278.

O'Brien, Jacqueline and Pamela Statham-Drew, *On We Go, the Wittenoom Way: the legacy of a colonial chaplain*, Fremantle Press, Fremantle, 2009.

O'Connell, Lisa, 'Marriage acts: stages in the transformation of nuptial culture', *differences: A Journal of Feminist Cultural Studies*, vol. 11, no. 1, 1999, pp. 68–111.

O'Donohue, Kathleen, 'Brady, John (1800?–1871)', *Australian Dictionary of Biography*, vol. 1, Melbourne University Press, 1966, pp. 146–47.

O'Farrell, Patrick, *The Catholic Church and Community: an Australian history*, revised edition, UNSW Press, Sydney, 1992 (first published 1985).

Oldham, Ray, 'Reveley, Henry Willey (1788–1875)', *Australian Dictionary of Biography*, vol. 2, Melbourne University Press, 1967, pp. 376–77.

Perkin, Joan, *Women and Marriage in Nineteenth-century England*, Routledge, London, 1989.

Probert, Rebecca, 'Control over marriage in England and Wales, 1753–1823: the Clandestine Marriages Act of 1753 in context', *Law and History Review*, vol. 27, no. 2, 2009, pp. 1– 26.

Reeves, Richard, *John Stuart Mill: Victorian firebrand*, Atlantic, London, 2007.

Rituale Romanum: Pauli V Pontificis Maximi, Jussu Editum, Typis S. Congregationis de Propaganda Fide, Rome, 1847.

Shanley, Mary Lyndon, *Feminism, Marriage, and the Law in Victorian England*, Princeton University Press, Princeton, 1993.

Shipley, Thea, *Full Circle: a history of Wesley Church*, Uniting Church in Australia, Synod of Western Australia, Perth, 2003.

The Small Ritual: being extracts from the Rituale Romanum in Latin and in English authorized by the Hierarchy of Australia, Burns & Oates, London, 1964.

Staples, A. C., 'Hutt, John (1795–1880)', *Australian Dictionary of Biography*, vol. 1, Melbourne University Press, 1966, pp. 575–77.

Statham, Pamela (compiler), *The Tanner Letters: a pioneer saga of Swan River and Tasmania, 1831–1845*, UWA Press, Nedlands, 1981.

Statham-Drew, Pamela, *James Stirling: admiral and founding Governor of Western Australia*, UWA Press, Crawley, 2003.

Stone, Lawrence, *Road to Divorce: England 1530–1987*, Oxford University Press, Oxford, 1990.

Strong, Rowan, 'The Reverend John Wollaston and colonial Christianity in Western Australia, 1840–1863', *Journal of Religious History*, vol. 25, no. 3, 2001, pp. 261–85.

——, 'An Antipodean establishment: institutional Anglicanism in Australia, 1788–c. 1934,' *Journal of Anglican Studies*, vol. 1, no. 1, 2003, pp. 61–90.

Tomalin, Claire, *The Life and Death of Mary Wollstonecraft*, Penguin, Harmondsworth, 1985 (first published 1974).

Tonkin, John, *Cathedral and Community: a history of St George's Cathedral, Perth*, UWA Press, Crawley, 2001.

Uren, Malcolm, 'Roe, John Septimus (1797–1878)', *Australian Dictionary of Biography*, vol. 2, Melbourne University Press, 1967, pp. 390–92.

Williams, A. E., *West Anglican Way: the growth of the Anglican Church in Western Australia from its early beginnings*, Province of Western Australia of the Anglican Church of Australia, Perth, 1989.

www.ingramcontent.com/pod-product-compliance
Lightning Source LLC
Chambersburg PA
CBHW020611270326
41927CB00005B/273